THE SOCIAL HISTORY

OF LABOR IN

THE MIDDLE EAST

The Social History of the Modern Middle East

SERIES EDITOR: EDMUND BURKE III

This series seeks to provide a forum for historically grounded studies on the Middle East in a broad, interdisciplinary context. New research has challenged tacit acceptance about how the Middle East came to modernity and has enlarged our understanding of the complex changes in the region over time and their impact on people and popular culture. By focusing on the nuances of everyday life and the experiences of nonelites—women, workers, peasants, and minorities—stereotypes about what it means to be Arab and Islamic can be challenged and broken down. Far from being a "history with the politics left out," a social history of the Middle East provides a way of reinterpreting the political history of the region, including the development of nationalism and the so-called Islamic revival.

The Social History of Labor in the Middle East
edited by Ellis Jay Goldberg

FORTHCOMING

The Social History of Cities in the Middle East
edited by Peter Sluglett

A Social History of Women and the Family in the Middle East
edited by Margaret Lee Meriwether and Judith Tucker

The Social History
of Labor in
the Middle East

edited by
Ellis Jay Goldberg

UNIVERSITY OF WASHINGTON

WestviewPress
A Division of HarperCollins*Publishers*

The Social History of the Modern Middle East

Copyright © 1996 by Westview Press, Inc., A Division of HarperCollins Publishers, Inc., except Chapter 4, © the United Nations University on behalf of UNU/WIDER.

Published in 1996 in the United States of America by Westview Press, Inc., 5500 Central Avenue,
Boulder, Colorado 80301-2877, and in the United Kingdom by Westview Press, 12 Hid's Copse Road,
Cumnor Hill, Oxford OX2 9JJ

Library of Congress Cataloging-in-Publication Data
The social history of labor in the Middle East / edited by Ellis Jay
  Goldberg.
    p.   cm. — (The social history of the modern Middle East)
  Includes index.
  ISBN 0-8133-8495-8 (hc). — ISBN 0-8133-8498-2 (pb)
    1. Working class—Middle East—History.   I. Goldberg, Ellis.
II. Series.
HD8656.S63   1996
305.5'5'0956—dc20   95-45132
                                                                                          CIP

The paper used in this publication meets the requirements of the American National Standard for
Permanence of Paper for Printed Library Materials Z39.48-1984.

10   9   8   7   6   5   4   3   2   1

Contents

Series Editor's Preface

It is crucially important for Americans to get beyond the essentialist stereotypes about Islam and Middle Easterners that have tended to obscure our understanding of the region and its peoples. Over the past decades, important new perspectives have become available on the modern Middle East. The old paradigms, rooted in modernization theory and the emergence of nationalism in the region, are giving way to more complex understandings grounded in social and cultural history.

The field of Middle Eastern studies has formerly been preoccupied with the state and elite groups and has utilized official documents and literary sources. More recently, researchers have increasingly focused upon the experiences of nonelites—women, workers, peasants, and ethnic minorities—and drawn upon new sources or have devised new strategies for rereading the old ones. This process is still continuing, but already the outlines of a new social history are visible. In this moment of intellectual transition, a series devoted to the social history of the Middle East has much to contribute.

In an effort to provide a measure of coherence to the mainstreaming of social history across the disciplines, The Social History of the Middle East series focuses on historically grounded social science research on the Middle East. History is seen as a broad interdisciplinary space within the social sciences, a zone of convergence between anthropology, politics, sociology, and history rather than as a particular academic discipline. The purpose of the series is to stimulate and focus methodological reflection and scholarship on topics of importance to the Middle Eastern field and to make more widely available the research of a new generation of scholars.

Often new scholarly debates take place in hard-to-find specialized journals, and their findings are slow to make their way into the mainstream. Scholars tend to address one another, using specialized languages that are not widely understood by a general audience. Within the field, research has proceeded unevenly across the region, and scholarship has tended to develop within the confines of national literatures. As a result, scholars working on similar topics but in different countries are often unaware of one another's work. Research on Middle Eastern workers, women, and the family, or urbanism, has thus been slow to find its way into textbooks.

By providing a convenient summary of up-to-date research together with useful bibliographies on important topics, the series facilitates the wider dissemination of new work on Middle Eastern culture and society. The volumes in the series are designed to supplement courses at the upper division and graduate levels not only in modern Middle Eastern history but in anthropology, politics, and sociology. Whereas the coverage will vary, each volume will survey the region broadly, from the Maghreb to the Hindu Kush. All volumes will contain chapters on Turkey, Egypt, and Iran, the three most populous countries in the region.

Edmund Burke III

Acknowledgments

An edited book acquires many debts. I am grateful to Professor David Olson, who as the Harry Bridges Professor of Labor Studies helped to make it possible for Valentine Moghadam and Michael Shalev to come to the University of Washington. I also wish to extend my warmest thanks to Professor Joel Migdal of the Institute for International Studies, who provided additional funds for Moghadam's and Shalev's visits as well as helped Donald Quataert come to the University of Washington. The Jewish Studies Center and Middle East Center also provided support for Shalev's trip.

I cannot express fully enough my thanks to the colleagues who contributed to this book. There was neither a conference nor the promise of financial reward. They all undertook the obligation of writing lengthy, original articles with a wonderful spirit of scholarly generosity and dedication. Then, in response to questions and comments, they wrote them again.

Terry Burke first suggested this project to me several years ago, and it has been a truly rewarding undertaking. I have benefited from discussions with him about this and other projects and from his engaging responses to the essays as they came in. In the course of editing this book, other projects have intervened that helped me to broaden my thinking. In 1992 the Department of Near Eastern Studies at Princeton invited me to give a talk on the history and historiography of Egyptian labor, which helped to clarify my own thinking on many relevant issues. For numerous discussions that have deeply enriched my understanding, I would like to thank Ahmad Abdulla, Mai Ghoussoub, Resat Kasaba, Kanan Makiya, Chibli Mallat, Joel Migdal, Hazem Saghiyah, and Bob Vitalis. Jere Bacharach, Margaret Levi, Joel Migdal, and Robert Tignor were kind enough to read and comment on portions of the book.

My wife has borne patiently this book's demands on our family despite constant and unbearable pain from an automobile accident four years ago. Colleagues who came to Seattle enchanted our children, who have decided to visit all the countries discussed in the book. They have even agreed to let us come along.

Ellis Jay Goldberg

Note on Translations and Transliterations

The essays by Professors Liauzu and Longuenesse were originally written in French. The translations are mine. Transliterations from Turkish include relevant accents available for typesetting. A single quotation mark has been employed for the Arabic letter 'ayn and for initial or final hamza where appropriate. Specialists will recognize relevant references.

E.J.G.

1

Introduction

Ellis Goldberg

Since the early 1970s there has been a vast outpouring of research and writing in English, French, Arabic, Persian, and Turkish on social history and labor to which historians, political scientists, economists, and sociologists have contributed. Social history has an intimate yet adversarial relation to modern market economies. The widespread literacy, rich numerical data, and self-conscious political choices that allow social history to be written occurred during the social transformations called modernity and capitalism.[1] The irony is that social historians usually seek resistance to capitalism and a human agency capable of building a more just society.[2] In so doing they often suggest that human consciousness is a unique instrument for transforming an unjust world into a better one.[3]

Social historians' focus on the ethical and political content of human actions vigorously contrasts with the more abstractly structural approaches of sociology and economics.[4] The world of social history is a remarkably talky one.[5] If the modern social sciences place an undue burden on the cognitive capacities of human beings, social history often places an unrealistically great burden on their moral faculties. Having recognized that human society results from human action, the constructivists who now dominate social history too often suggest we can make new worlds simply by thinking new thoughts. Alas, in a nice phrase adopted by Nasr Hamid Abu Zayd, "the effectivity of the word resides not in its creation but in its consumption."[6]

This book addresses a larger conversation about social history and the writing of social history through Middle East history. We share with social historians a wish that the world could be a better place. We also believe that improving the lives of those whose income derives from labor must be part of making the world better. These chapters betray a somewhat

greater skepticism about the role of changes in consciousness affecting society than many labor historians may share. As Valentine Moghadam's description of conversations with an Iranian militant suggests, the desires,
intentions, and beliefs of workers are not necessarily progressive. Even
when workers do have the appropriately progressive consciousness, it may
not, as Michael Shalev's chapter on Israel suggests, matter very much.

It is appropriate to have this conversation now because we know so
much more about the creation of industrial workforces in the Middle East
than we did even a decade ago. We have also learned much about their formal and informal organizations and the urban social and political movements that accompanied them.[7] A large descriptive literature exists that
suggests connections among social and political structures (classes, nations, and states), institutions (unions, parties, and bureaucracies), and
consciousness (Marxism, nationalism, and Islam) in the late nineteenth
and early twentieth centuries. This book focuses attention primarily on
works in English and French because they are the most readily available
for readers who wish to pursue its topics.

The Recent Historiographical Tradition

The wealth of empirical detail alone tempts us to make comparative judg-
ments about labor and labor movements in the Middle East and North
Africa. Empirical richness is not all that distinguishes the wealth of new
material. Since the early 1980s, scholars of Middle Eastern social history
have developed increasing methodological sophistication. As recently as
1975, studies of the Middle East focused not only on elite behavior but
more specifically on the emergence of a so-called new middle class and its
relation to army coups.[8]

Two books that appeared toward the end of the 1970s decisively
changed the nature of the English-language scholarship on labor. The first
was the publication in English of Mahmoud Hussein's *Class Conflict in
Egypt*, which appeared much earlier in French. In 1977 its schematic
Marxism was a novel way to look at Egyptian history in the context of the
existing American academic milieu. A year later Hanna Batatu published
The Old Social Classes and the Revolutionary Movements in Iraq, which
employed the concept of class to examine an extremely complex social reality. Batatu's book must be counted, along with E. P. Thompson's *The
Making of the English Working Class*, as one of the most deeply detailed accounts of labor social history ever written.[9] The core of Batatu's book is a

description of the origins and outcomes of the July 1958 revolutionary crisis. For Batatu this crisis had its roots in the class relations of the old regime but was not reducible to them. The revolutionary regime supported by the communists and laboring poor and the bloody destruction of this regime in 1963 by the Arab nationalist Ba'th Party were fruits of the crisis. In retrospect, of course, we can no longer share Batatu's optimism about the appearance of the Ba'thi regime in 1968 and the emergence of Saddam Hussein.[10]

Among the books that appeared in English in the following decade were Ervand Abrahamian's *Iran Between Two Revolutions* (1982), Donald Quataert's *Social Disintegration and Popular Resistance in the Ottoman Empire* (1983), Robert Bianchi's *Interest Groups and Political Development in Turkey* (1984), my own *Tinker, Tailor and Textile Worker*, and Joel Beinin and Zachary Lockman's *Workers on the Nile* (1987). The analytic methods employed ranged from Bianchi's manipulation of aggregate statistical data to study interest groups through my orientation toward rational choice to Beinin and Lockman's Marxism. This diversity opened up an implicit debate about class formation, global markets, individual identity, and social structure in modern Middle Eastern history that echoed similar debates about Latin America, Europe, and East Asia.

Unfortunately, this debate was framed by scholars trying to explain the absence of socialist projects among emerging industrial workforces as the effect of competing consciousnesses of nation and class. Middle East social history thus moved in the opposite direction of equivalent studies in Europe and the United States that have dispensed with explaining the absence of socialism.[11]

Thematic Dimensions of the Studies

Several common themes unite the chapters here. First, there has been a secular trend in the twentieth century throughout the Middle East toward the creation of larger urban working classes as modern manufacturing, commercial, and service sectors grow. The pace of this trend varies considerably from country to country and has not been either as rapid or as complete as any earlier observers believed it would be. Such changes recapitulate a common theme in European history of class formation and industrial investment setting society on a path to modernity. As Donald Quataert shows in his chapter, the specific roots of this process in much of the Middle East lie in the Ottoman political economy.

Second, there is the equally common theme of socialist or communist movements as way stations on that long and winding path. The association of labor and the left has been ended at least partly through various combinations of coercion, the satisfaction of material want, and the failure of the vision of socialism embodied in communist parties and the Soviet Union. Nowhere in the Middle East is the interplay of class, socialism, and revolution more apparent than in Iran; Moghadam's chapter reveals the prolonged and complex passage to the Islamic revolution, which transformed Iran and accepted theories of revolution.

Third, to say that a path to modernity is long and winding is also to say that older forms of production, investment, and labor discipline retain their vitality in most countries of the Middle East. Small workshops remain common in the Middle East. Large factories are not the efficient engines of mass production that popular and academic imaginations envision when the available markets for their outputs remain small. Elisabeth Longuenesse and I, in our respective chapters on Syria and Egypt, pay close attention to this problem. Causal relations between gender, industrialization, and state policies are dim, but the descriptive elements of the historical process are far more clear. State-initiated industries in the Middle East generally preferred to hire adult men in formal production, often excluding women altogether in the process; recent policies of privatization are often linked to the feminization of work.

Fourth, although workers figure strategically in social outcomes, they do not seem to be able to intentionally employ collective action to affect government policy. Quite the reverse: Labor movements appear to be remarkably sensitive to decisions by political authorities. Even if workers were only the rational owners of labor power divided into numerous economic sectors, society would be a complicated affair. Workers are men and women who pass from youth to old age with distinctively different religious, linguistic, and cultural experiences. They do not, therefore, form a single homogenous group liable to make effective and coherent political decisions. Shalev's chapter on Israeli labor is especially revealing of such processes, which are also directly discussed by Günseli Berik and Cihan Bilginsoy.

Because the working class is increasingly important in all societies, there is often intensely partisan competition to explain and appropriate its history. Claude Liauzu provides an especially detailed picture of this process in North Africa. Only some of the partisan competition is between nationalism and socialism; academic and (increasingly) policy conflicts over explanation emerge. Small workshops, for example, may be the sites where backward traditions flourish or where the remnants of unalienated human labor are still to be found or where entrepreneurial growth awaits a state that finally guarantees property rights and efficient markets.

Narrative Dimensions of the Studies

The social history of labor in the Middle East is based, broadly speaking, on a narrative about the division of labor. This story was initially received from studies of modernization and can be told rather briefly.[12] Although it is not an economic narrative, it incorporates crucial microeconomic and macroeconomic themes.

Over the past century and a half throughout the Middle East a relatively undeveloped and poorly capitalized division of labor has been replaced by one that is significantly more clearly articulated. New means of production and increased capitalization have led to the creation of a group of workers who own nothing but their labor power. Artisans are turned into workers, workshops become factories, and workers lose control of their labor, their leisure, and ultimately their lives.[13]

Until 1980 it was possible to believe that the crucial period of transition from the traditional to the modern (or capitalist) mode of production was the late colonial era. It was also widely thought that the transformation progressed relatively smoothly and quickly as modern forms of work organization and collective action displaced older ones. This displacement was supposed to be due in part to the inherently greater efficiency of large industrial factories. Modernization and socialist stories alike portrayed the modern factory as the crucible of a new, rational culture and as the paragon of economic efficiency.[14]

Most of the chapters in this collection suggest that such stories are debatable and probably contain much wishful thinking. As an emerging debate between Donald Quataert and Sevket Pamuk about Ottoman industrialization attests, we are still far from certain exactly how rapidly hand weaving in the Ottoman Empire declined.[15] Craft and industrial undertakings have coexisted in most of the Middle East, sharing territory and economic sectors well into the present.[16] Artisanal production (and its associate, the small-scale provision of services) and industrial firms segment existing markets for prolonged periods of time. Only when the market share of industrially produced goods has become very large are artisans forced from a particular market.

The artisanal world of family enterprises, small-scale production, and informal arrangements for marketing and finance bears a striking resemblance to what was called, a generation ago, the traditional urban world. At one end it shades imperceptibly into a truly marginal world in which a vendor may sell a package of cigarettes one by one. At the other end it connects with tiny but remarkably efficient and often well-financed enterprises. The contemporary relevance of the debate about artisanal production is twofold. First, it provides the empirical base for institutional and cultural arguments that the social outlook of artisans remains alive in the moral economy of the urban industrial workforce. Second, it provides empirical material and a subtext for the arguments about whether economic development, efficient use of factor resources, and political equality can thrive among relatively small enterprises.[17]

On recognizing that artisanal and craft production were not destroyed quickly and thoroughly by colonialism, we might easily draw the conclusion that the historical trajectory of the Middle East toward capitalism differed greatly from that in Europe. This presents far too simple a picture of how capitalism or industrialization triumphed in modern Europe. Throughout most of the Middle East, the coming of industrial capitalism—to the extent that it has arrived—looks somewhat like the coming of industrial capitalism in Europe. It was filled with protoindustrialization, vigorous nonindustrial urbanism, and a vital and ambitious peasant world even before capitalists.[18] Stories about the sudden exogenous imposition of markets may, as William Reddy and William Sewell suggest in another context, have hastened the growth of market cultures, but they can no longer be taken at face value.[19]

Even if we do away with industrialization as an exogenous and catastrophic event, we are left with colonialism. Early competition with European production dramatically affected domestic artisanal and craft producers. Direct colonial control in North Africa and Syria and indirect control in countries such as Egypt provided property rights and the government policies European capitalists needed to introduce cheaper goods from outside the Middle East into local markets. It is undeniably true, as Jacques Couland has argued, that colonialism formed the crucial background to the emergence of capitalism in the Middle East.[20] Classical colonialism was characterized by the presence of foreign officials in government ministries that made crucial fiscal, military, and judicial decisions. Implicitly or explicitly, nationalist historiography argues not just that these officials made the European trajectory impossible but also that the structure of conflict is between the foreign bourgeoisie and an emergent national community.[21]

The relationships between workers and entrepreneurs are far too complex to be reduced to the relationship between whole societies, although nationalist historians throughout the region would like it to be so. Some illumination of the complexity may be achieved by taking the linguistic turn, but society comprises more than linguistic and ideological structures. As Michael Shalev argues in his chapter, the Zionist labor federation Histadrut attracted Jewish workers in Palestine for reasons that seem far more practical than ideological.

Inside (and outside) the Middle East labor unions sought bargaining strength through alliances with powerful politicians. They also sought commitments to legal reforms that would recognize union power directly, enhance it, or direct investment funds to do so. As Berik and Bilginsoy point out in their discussion of Turkey, workers have rarely been able to force politicians to deliver any of the institutional reforms they sought. These extend from the liberty to form unions to the maintenance of protected, high-wage, state-owned enterprises.[22] If the dissociation between labor discourse and labor organization is as great in Europe as in the Middle East, this suggests that the discursive turn focuses on issues of marginal explanatory power.

During the colonial period, entrepreneurs able to mobilize funds abroad used their access to political power to control local labor, raw material, and access to markets. Neither the chapters in this volume nor other studies indicate that colonial states always created efficient markets in labor, capital, or goods. More and more capital was invested in port facilities, railroads, utilities, mining, and raw material transformation everywhere in the Middle East. Claude Liauzu's comments on the miserable conditions under which miners worked reveal the degree to which physical compulsion (better described as slavery than market clearing) could be the organizing principle of colonial labor relations. Labor markets were highly segmented, often along ethnic lines, and state-licensed monopolies often controlled the sale and production of goods.

The presence of highly remunerated European labor at the highest levels of production—to the exclusion of native-born workers—was common in Egypt, North Africa, and even Ottoman Anatolia. As Moghadam's chapter shows, non-European migrants also sought and won such positions until local political power made such hiring impossible. After independence, new ruling coalitions ensured that noncitizens were quickly replaced. The idea, current in nationalist and some Marxist historiography, that the political coalitions that made these replacements possible also made for more efficient capitalism (or constituted a move toward efficient socialism) is far-fetched.

Communists and socialists played key roles in creating some of the earliest labor unions and other similar institutions throughout the Middle East beginning shortly after the Russian Revolution. In the Middle East, Marxists sought out labor as a constituency. Here as elsewhere, they believed that the industrial working class would necessarily create new social and economic structures through revolutionary political action. The early historiography of labor movements is also due largely to communist and socialist intellectuals, for whom it provided the foundations of partisan policymaking and a way to attract a desired audience.

The influence of Marxism in the working class arose through the fusion of two distinct processes. On the one hand Marxist intellectuals from outside the working class (and not infrequently from ethnic or national minorities) sought workers in order to bring them ideas of class struggle and scientific socialism. They also recruited workers into socialist (and later communist) parties. On the other hand, militant workers hostile to the domination of their movements by liberal professionals attempted to create their own independent unions. Shorn of expectations of the historical inevitability of socialism, this relationship had important implications because it provided socialists with a social base. It was (and remains) a game that activists from other ideological currents including Islamism can play.

Communist and socialist parties had their greatest influence during the rapid industrialization and import-substitution policies during and just after World War II. During the war, local industries often expanded in order to supply goods that could no longer be imported but for which significant domestic (or military) demand existed. After the war, some colonial and semicolonial governments and the emerging nationalist governments were often willing to undertake social welfare expenditures in excess of anything previously known.[23] The dramatic growth in industrial employment, the prominence of leftists in union leaderships, and the emergence of the Soviet Union as a global power provided communists with a period of unparalleled influence and prestige.

The role of the left among workers was never unchallenged, and by the early 1950s it was to be severely tested. Communists themselves were never very numerous. Even where they supplied significant leadership to trade unions or political parties rooted in the urban workforce, their followers never understood the intricacies of Marxist theory, let alone strongly agreed with it. Communist militants were willing to provide scarce organizational and political skills for the creation of larger organizations because they saw these as desirable for the achievement of various political goals. Insofar as communists played these roles, they were lightning rods for repression. Governments exacted an often ferocious toll on communists and trade union organizations for reasons that usually had to do with international alliances or fears of domestic unrest and only rarely with any economic calculation. That the social history of labor and especially the struggle for power in the factory is intimately entwined with productivity, gender roles, and development seems inescapable today.[24] Local capitalists are disadvantaged when labor, through politics, maintains employment and wage levels, but artificially depressing wages or income does not seem to promote industrialization or economic efficiency.[25]

World War II and the acquisition of independence by most states by 1956 ended one era and began another. Seen from the viewpoint of Middle East labor, the postcolonial era might best be called a period of new mercantilism. During these years most states took control of the export-oriented sectors of the economy in order to buy guns, safeguard national boundaries, and guarantee employment. The timing and rhythm with which governments entered the economies of the Middle East as investors and employers varied throughout the century, but not long after mid-century, state-owned enterprises were prominent everywhere. Although political scientists and development economists refer to these policies as import substitution, mercantilism seems a more apt description for these ventures in statism.[26] These state-owned enterprises often provided the base for the expansion of centralized and state-dominated labor movements. Wages were made by state fiat in these experiments in nationalist socialism, and unions were stripped of the capacity to act independently, whether through strikes, bargaining, or shifting political allies.[27] As unions became instruments of state policies, however, workers often became disenchanted with the formal institutional structures that ostensibly existed to defend their rights. Seen in this light, the tightly connected development of state bureaucracies, trade unions, and working classes has greater similarities in Turkey, Israel, and the Arab states than appears to the casual observer.

Institutional and Ideological Commonalities

The extension of the power of the state over firms was believed to be a partial and tentative victory over capitalist production, which nationalist and communist intellectuals claimed was really a form of external domination. It is fair enough to ask which of these large enterprises were efficient, but behind the question of efficiency looms another issue: the substitution of public power for private. The common view in European and U.S. labor studies has been similar to that championed in the standard account of colonial industrialization: Capitalists use the power of the state to destroy the richer, more democratic, and more cooperative world of the craftsperson and artisan.[28] The working class, like the Ottoman Empire, seems to have been on a downward spiral since its inception and for almost as long a time. My own studies of working-class memoirs have led me to disbelieve this story.[29] It seems to me that at least some Egyptian workers wanted to replace the arbitrary power of the employer, even in small shops, with the more bureaucratic and routinized power of the state. A somewhat similar argument has been made about the United States. What Karen Orren has called "the legislative turn" implies that unions benefited from and helped expand legislative sovereignty over the workplace to the detriment of the largely judicial proceedings in civil or equitable law that governed the relations between employer and employee until the early twentieth century.[30] A closer look at the huge body of Middle East labor law produced in the 1950s and 1960s would be richly rewarded if the terms of reference were changed. The dramatic increase in the sheer quantity of labor legislation in the 1940s and 1950s has, until now, largely been viewed teleologically, that is, as promoting either socialism or capitalism. It is more fruitful to imagine this lawmaking as a joint effort to bring the private activity of entrepreneurs into the public arena, where both the state and labor attempted to mold it.

Important as the study of Middle Eastern labor law might be, Middle Eastern societies lack capital even more than authority.[31] It is a bitter irony that the decades since the dramatic rise in oil prices have not been particularly kind to most of the Middle Eastern states or economies. The 1973 oil embargo and the subsequent manyfold rise in prices forced the advanced capitalist countries to achieve massive efficiencies in the use of energy and petroleum-based raw materials and drove a global search for new sources of oil. No economies (and especially none in the Middle East) entered the mid-1980s with the capacity to subsidize consumption at the levels that had been possible a decade earlier. Everywhere states found that the ownership of large, unprofitable enterprises was a burden to be shed rather than a source of prestige, wealth, or political power. The era of returning large sections of the economy to private hands (liberalization) and integrating to achieve a vastly more competitive international market (structural adjustment) had begun. Its effects are largely uncertain and differ greatly from country to country. Structural adjustment and liberalization can be carried out without introducing much (if any) democracy.[32]

It is equally clear that the left no longer exists to echo the cries of anger and pain of the urban working class as it is made to pay much of the cost of putting the new economic policies in place.

Renewed Labor Radicalism and Religion

The growth of Islamic movements since the early 1980s has followed a trajectory similar to the search for allies that brought the communists (and following Michael Shalev, the Zionists) to lead working-class movements in the 1930s and 1940s. Such movements, if they assume power, may wreak havoc on their own societies, but their size tells us little about the depth of commitment or emotional life of the followers they attract by providing valuable material payoffs. No one knows if Islamic movements will take power; in the 1970s few believed that the traditional Islamic Shi'i establishment could ride the wave of revolution in Iran. Islamic philosophy and history retain a considerable fund of images and concepts to bring to a utopian politics. Only a portion of these have been employed within radical movements that seek to employ the state to dominate society.[33] Among the few certainties we have are that Islamic revolutionaries can no more reshape the unruly and recalcitrant world of human beings to full conformity with their projects than could insurgent Jacobins or Bolsheviks. It does seem, however, that if Islamists wish to reverse the legalization of the working class that occurred in the 1950s and 1960s and reintroduce more personal power and greater reliance on the judiciary, they will not find continued support within the working class.[34] As Moghadam points out, some sections of the working class in Iran were especially reserved even as the revolution against the shah was in full swing.[35]

Islamist movements have affected general social mores in the Middle East and especially women, but we have relatively little knowledge of how such movements shape life among the working classes. This is all the more surprising because it is apparent from the gross data that some very important changes in the lives of all women, but especially urban women, have occurred.[36] Fertility and family size have been declining since 1970. As family sizes decrease and the age of marriage advances, there must be some very important changes inside families as they confront the dramatic changes in the world economy. Women's participation in the formal workforce is generally under 10 percent in the Arab countries and Iran, and yet with growing numbers of young women receiving an education, there must be a growing desire on the part of many women to work. One obvious shortcoming of the study of Middle East history, sociology, and politics is how little we know of the lives of urban women and especially employed urban women.[37]

For the authors of this collection the concept of class as defined through the ownership of labor retains analytic utility. None of the authors believe that class is the only theoretical entity worth discussing or even that the behavior of all the members of a class are described solely by that membership. The political and economic structure of the modern world—not only in Europe but in Asia, Africa, Latin America, and the Middle East—results from the intervention of the working classes in the creation of uniquely modern institutions: trade unions, mass political parties, and comprehensive social service regimes including public education. Obviously none of these institutions existed before the coming of capitalism, and yet none of them arose because capitalists made them. If we can explain them at all, it seems to me it must be because class based on unequal ownership of productive assets is a social fact. A variety of remarkably similar institutions have been created across the world to integrate the working class into contemporary capitalist societies. Any reconstruction—including the ones in this volume—of the processes by which these institutions were created must be subject to a formal or rhetorical logic and to the instrumental professional concerns of those doing the reconstructing. Institutions are not reducible, however, either to the formal rhetoric of explanation or to the professional interests of explainers. It is cautionary to recall that not very long ago we were told that markets in labor and capital were superfluous: epiphenomena rather than institutions that corresponded to any social reality. Workers have shaped capitalism far more profoundly than slaves shaped slavery, and there is every reason to believe they will continue to do so.[38]

Notes

1. Extraordinary social histories of the late medieval and early modern periods have been written, but not until the nineteenth century is it possible to get the rich texture and dense argument accompanying books such as Jacques Ranciére's *La nuit des prolétaires* (Paris: Fayard, 1981), which provides us with the vivid imaginings of nineteenth-century French artisans.

2. William Reddy, for example, concludes a study of French social history saying, "Conscious reflection on the limitations of market language can provide the starting point for a new, genuinely free, social order" (*The Rise of Market Culture*

[Cambridge: Cambridge University Press, 1984], 336). "Placing labor at the center of modern history," in the words of Charles Bergquist, "works to empower not modern capitalists and their world system, but the working people who have struggled most consistently to democratize that system" (*Labor in Latin America* [Stanford: Stanford University Press, 1986], 386). Or in the vastly influential words of E. P. Thompson, "The greater part of the world is still undergoing problems of industrialization, and of the formation of democratic institutions. . . . Causes which were lost in England might, in Asia or Africa, yet be won" (*The Making of the English Working Class* [New York: Vintage Books, 1966], 13). Theda Skocpol ended her comparative historical account of revolutions with similar sentiments; see *States and Social Revolutions* (Cambridge: Cambridge University Press, 1979), 293.

3. See, for example, William Sewell, whose *Work and Revolution in France* (Cambridge: Cambridge University Press, 1980) marked a giant step in the study of meanings and consciousness.

4. "Labor historians," as Charles Bergquist puts it, "have always empathized with the democratic struggles of working people." See "Labor History and Its Challenges: Confessions of a Latin Americanist," *American Historical Review* (June 1993):758.

5. It has already been nearly two decades since Ernest Gellner pointed out that because words have no price, talk is indeed cheap. See Ernest Gellner, "What Is structuralisme?" in *Relativism and the Social Sciences* (Cambridge: Cambridge University Press, 1985), 149. Sewell is aware of this problem, and Elizabeth Perry has recently addressed it by arguing that class activity can occur without arising from class (or any other larger) consciousness. See Elizabeth J. Perry, *Shanghai on Strike* (Stanford: Stanford University Press, 1993), 8–9.

6. Nasr Hamid Abu Zayd, "Isyan al-din am isyan al-dawlah?" *Al-Naqid* (July 1994): 9–15, 13, citing Faisal Darraj.

7. When René Gallisot collected a somewhat similar set of essays twenty-five years ago the empirical and conceptual range was far more limited than in this book. Most of the essays dealt with regional communist parties, nationalists, and the gross structural characteristics of the economy. See René Gallisot, *Mouvement ouvrier, communisme et nationalismes dans le monde arabe* (Paris: Les Éditions Ouvrières, 1978). The writing of Middle Eastern social history, as Judith Tucker has pointed out, still has much room to unfold. See her "Taming the West: Trends in the Writing of Modern Social History in Anglophone Academia," in Hisham Sharabi (ed.), *Theory, Politics and the Arab World* (London: Routledge, 1990).

8. The classic study is Manfred Halpern, *The Politics of Social Change in the Middle East and North Africa* (Princeton: Princeton University Press, 1963), one of whose chapters is titled "The New Middle Class as the Principal Revolutionary and Stabilizing Force." Other contributors to the debate about army rule and social structure included Anouar Abdel Malek, *Egypt: Military Society* (New York: Random House, 1968); and Amos Perlmutter, *Egypt: The Praetorian State* (East

Brunswick, N.J.: Transaction Books, 1974). For a cogent critique of the larger "military-as-modernizer" discourse in which these arguments were embedded, see Nicole Ball, *Security and Economy in the Third World* (Princeton: Princeton University Press, 1988), 5–15.

9. Viewed as a study of revolutions, Batatu's book (Princeton: Princeton University Press, 1978) is a fruitful comparison to employ with Skocpol's *States and Social Revolutions*.

10. Any account of the development of the Ba'th regime after 1978 must take into account the work of Kanan Makiya, especially *Republic of Fear* (Berkeley: University of California Press, 1987).

11. See Ira Katznelson and Aristide Zolberg, *Working Class Formation: Nineteenth-Century Patterns in Western Europe and the United States* (Princeton: Princeton University Press, 1986) and the influential review essays by Michael Kazin, "Struggling with the Class Struggle: Marxism and the Search for a Synthesis of U.S. Labor History," in *Labor History* 28 (Fall 1987):497–514; and Margaret Ramsay Somers, "Workers of the World, Compare!" *Contemporary Sociology* 18, 3 (May 1989).

12. Most unfortunately, the Middle East narrative has been interpreted in the light of an equally widely received version of European economic history, which has been under significant revision in recent years in ways to which I can only briefly allude here.

13. This is the master narrative of labor studies as received from Marx and Weber, and it has rightly permeated all the social science disciplines. Among the influential and compelling accounts in this vein, see David Gordon et al., *Segmented Work, Divided Labor* (Cambridge: Cambridge University Press, 1982); David Montgomery, *The Fall of the House of Labor* (Cambridge: Cambridge University Press, 1987); and Sean Wilentz, *Chants Democratic: New York City and The Rise of the Working Class 1788–1850* (New York: Oxford University Press, 1984). Some convenient sources to consult for the revisionist accounts are Raphael Samuels, "Workshop of the World: Steam Power and Hand Technology in Mid-Victorian Britain," in *History Workshop*, no. 3 (Spring 1977); Ronald Aminzade, "Reinterpreting Capitalist Industrialization: A Study of Nineteenth Century France," in Steven Laurence Knapp and Cynthia J. Koepp (eds.), *Work in France* (Ithaca: Cornell University Press, 1986), 393–417; and most recently, Geoffrey Timmins, *The Last Shift: The Decline of Handloom Weaving in Nineteenth Century Lancashire* (Manchester: Manchester University Press, 1993), for exceptionally clear accounts of the economic and historiographical debates.

14. Gregory Clark argues that the efficiency of the modern factory is probably linked, as the older socialist literature suggested, to its oppression of the workforce. He also argues that workers benefited materially from the efficiency gains. It is not necessary to accept Clark's further argument that workers hired capitalists to discipline them through oppression, although understanding the complex evolution of the factory system may be furthered by briefly doing so. See Gregory

Clark, "Factory Discipline," *Journal of Economic History* 54, 1 (March 1994): 128–164.

15. Basing his conclusion on a careful examination of trade statistics, Pamuk argues that hand weaving declined rather rapidly in the Ottoman Empire; Quataert, using descriptions of loom capacities, argues in the opposite direction. Compare Sevket Pamuk, *The Ottoman Empire and European Capitalism, 1820–1913* (Cambridge: Cambridge University Press, 1987), 108–123; and Donald Quataert, *Ottoman Manufacturing in the Age of the Industrial Revolution* (Cambridge: Cambridge University Press, 1993), 12–19.

16. For an extensive look at medieval labor see Maya Shatzmiller, *Labour in the Medieval Islamic World* (Leiden: E. J. Brill, 1994). In addition to discussing wage labor, Shatzmiller addresses some of the issues of the size and composition of the servant and slave population.

17. A good survey of the arguments about small firms in terms of innovation, efficiency, and employment is Ian M.D. Little, Dipak Mazumdar, and John M. Page Jr., *Small Manufacturing Enterprises* (New York: Oxford University Press, 1987), 8–21. Patrick O'Brien and Caglar Keyder provide an argument suggesting that French small-firm labor-intensive industrial production was profoundly shaped by market segmentation and consumer preferences. See *Economic Growth in Britain and France* (London: Allen and Unwin, 1978). An influential argument about such enterprises as alternatives to mass production is made by Charles Sabel and Jonathan Zeitlin, "Historical Alternatives to Mass Production: Politics, Markets, and Technology in Nineteenth Century Industrialization," *Past and Present* 108 (August 1985): 133–176.

18. For a good overview of the debate and current conclusions on the Industrial Revolution in Europe see Jan De Vries, "The Industrial Revolution and the Industrious Revolution," *Journal of Economic History* 54, 2 (June 1994):249–267. Most intriguing is DeVries's observation that growing levels of material culture are linked to declining real incomes (254). This issue is different from that of technological innovation and diffusion, discussed by Joel Mokyr in *The Lever of Riches* (London: Oxford University Press, 1990).

19. See William Reddy, *The Rise of Market Culture* (Cambridge: Cambridge University Press, 1984); and Sewell, *Work and Revolution in France*.

20. Jacques Couland, *Le mouvement syndical au Liban 1919–1946* (Paris: Éditions Anthropos, 1969), 18.

21. For an explication of the ways in which Marxist revolutionary thought became transformed into a socialist nationalism in which oppressed nations came to play the role previously assigned oppressed classes, see Zeev Sternhell, *The Birth of Fascist Ideology* (Princeton: Princeton University Press, 1992), 46–47 and 180–186.

22. This aspect of the narratives that is sketched here suggests some profound limits to interpreting state policies as the outcomes of coalitions. Coalition partners are usually too weak and diffuse to impact policymaking. Stretching the

metaphor of coalitions, coupled with the absence of a significant body of studies on economic policymaking in the region, limits, for example, Chaudhry's otherwise lively attempt to sum up postcolonial political economies; see Kiren Aziz Chaudhry, "The Myths of the Market and the Common History of Late Developers," *Politics and Society* 21, 3 (September 1993).

23. The complex relationship between colonial officials (at home and abroad), investors, industrialization, and social welfare has been best examined by Jacques Marseille, *Empire colonial et capitalisme français* (Paris: Albin Michel, 1984).

24. The literature on wages, labor productivity, and the often very different capacity for collective action by men and women workers for power in the workplace is growing. See Gregory Clark's provocative article "Why Isn't the Whole World Developed? Lessons from the Cotton Mills," in *Journal of Economic History* 47 (March 1987):141–173; Susan Wolcott, "The Perils of Lifetime Employment Systems: Productivity Advance the Indian and Japanese Textile Industries, 1920–1938," in *Journal of Economic History* 54 (June 1994):307–323; Andrew Gordon, "The Disappearance of the Japanese Working Class Movement," Comparative Labor History Series working paper no. 5, Center for Labor Studies, University of Washington, 1994.

25. Stephan Haggard has advanced such claims in *Pathways from the Periphery* (Ithaca: Cornell University Press, 1990), which are strikingly at variance with the ways in which social historians usually view labor movements (247). Haggard's argument does connect with the concerns of social historians in that some evidence exists to link income equality and growth rates (see, for example, World Bank, *World Development Report 1991* [London: Oxford University Press, 1992], 137). It appears unlikely that dictatorship alone causally contributes to income equality or growth.

26. For a review of the massive literature and experiences regarding import substitution from Turkish, Egyptian, Indian, and Mexican history, see John Waterbury, *Exposed to Innumerable Delusions* (Cambridge: Cambridge University Press, 1994). The most recent review of the mercantilism debate is Lars Magnusson, *Mercantilism: The Shaping of an Economic Language* (London: Routledge, 1994), but his analysis is too largely historiographic. Eli Hecksher's classic study concluded with the too quickly forgotten admonition that socialism and protectionism had much in common and that under Soviet-style planning "it may be said that the idea of mercantilism has been given a new lease of life." See Eli Hecksher, *Mercantilism*, 2 vols., trans. Mendel Shapiro (London: George Allen and Unwin, 1935) vol. 2, 339.

27. It is regrettable that Maxime Rodinson's expression "nationalitarian" never caught on, for it expresses better than anything else the highly fragile and ideologically narrow nature of nationalism in the region in the 1950s and 1960s. See, for example, Rodinson's "Mythes dans les mouvements socio-politiques," in *Marxisme et monde musulmane* (Paris: Éditions du Seuil, 1972), 248.

28. Wilentz's *Chants Democratic* is an example, although the locus classicus is Thompson, *The Making of the English Working Class.*

29. See Ellis Goldberg, "Worker's Voice and Labor Productivity in Egypt," in Zachary Lockman (ed.), *Workers and Working Classes in the Middle East* (Albany: State University of New York Press, 1994).

30. See Karen Orren, *Belated Feudalism* (Cambridge: Cambridge University Press, 1991), 222–223. For an account that focuses more strongly on judicial intentions and the autonomy of judicial ideology but that also links the factory with an older private law of the family, see Bernard Edelman, *La légalisation de la classe ouvrière*, vol. 1 (Paris: Christian Bourgeois, 1978), 41. Alain Cottereau develops this theme, among many others, in an essay that deserves more readers among scholars of the Middle East; see his "Working-Class Cultures, 1848–1900," in Katznelson and Zolberg, *Working Class Formation*.

31. See Alan Richards, "Economic Imperatives and Political Systems," *Middle East Journal* 47, 2 (Spring 1993): 217–228, on capital shortage. For a specific discussion of why lenders choose not to invest see Stephen Wippel, "Réforme économique et investissements directs en Egypte," *Egypte/Monde Arabe* 12–13(1992–1993):49–71.

32. Steven Heydemann, "Taxation Without Representation: Authoritarianism and Economic Liberalization in Syria," in Ellis Goldberg, Resat Kasaba, and Joel Migdal (eds.), *Rules andRights in the Middle East* (Seattle: University of Washington Press, 1993).

33. For an insight into the highly contested nature of what Islamic law and history mean for contemporary politics, see Abdullahi Ahmed An-Na'im, *Toward an Islamic Reformation* (Syracuse: Syracuse University Press, 1990).

34. Any historically accurate "return" to the shari'ah could entail dismantling much of the legislative, positive law enacted since the 1950s. See Zayd, "Isyan al-din," for a review of some relevant theoretical issues.

35. A sensible view of Islamic movements that disentangles some of the threads is Ibrahim Karawan, "Monarchs, Mullahs and Marshalls: Islamic Regimes," *Annals of the American Academy* (November 1992):103–119.

36. The theme of the sacrifice of daughters for the survival of the working class family as an irreducible aspect of economic change is sounded in Tessie Liu's study of French artisanal weavers in western France and suggests fruitful research strategies in Middle East labor studies. See Liu, *The Weaver's Knot: The Contradictions of Class Struggle and Family Solidarity in Western France: 1750–1914* (Ithaca: Cornell University Press, 1994), 234–249. For the classic introduction to this set of themes see Louise A. Tilly and Joan W. Scott, *Women, Work and Family* (New York: Holt, Rinehart and Winston, 1978).

37. A recent introduction to the practice methodology and theories of doing the history of women and work is Ava Baron, "Gender and Labor History: Learning from the Past, Looking to the Future," in Ava Baron (ed.), *Work Engendered* (Ithaca: Cornell University Press, 1991).

38. Even describing contemporary economic systems as capitalist appears to have occurred in response to the popularity of socialist thought within the working class. Both the *Oxford English Dictionary* and *Robert* indicate that the first appearance of

"capitalism" and "capitalisme," respectively (in the mid- to late 1840s) postdates the initial appearances of "socialism" and "communism." The first edition of Grimm's philological dictionary of German (1860) has no entry for "capitalism"; neither do equivalent early dictionaries in Spanish or Italian. That we live in a system called capitalism is a concept developed rather late in the day.

2

The Social History Of Labor in the Ottoman Empire: 1800–1914

Donald Quataert

An artificial barrier imposed by politicians, nationalists, and historians alike separates the nation-states of the contemporary Middle East from their Ottoman past. In the aftermath of World War I, the 600-year-old Ottoman Empire vanished after profoundly altering the history of its former subjects in the Balkan, Anatolian, and Arabian provinces.

The Ottoman state had come into existence during the turmoil of the late medieval period as Turkish nomadic migrations brought a new people into the Middle East. Brilliantly flexible in this chaotic environment, Ottoman sultans and administrators rapidly expanded from a foothold in western Asia Minor. Within three and a half centuries of its origins in the late thirteenth century, the Ottoman Empire had captured Constantinople and extended its dominion to Hungary in the north, Baghdad and Mecca in the east and south, and the North African lands in the west. At its peak, it fought on the Italian peninsula, in the suburbs of Vienna, and on the waters of the western Mediterranean and the Indian Ocean. Until the mid-seventeenth century, it was a world-class military and political power.

The explosive dynamism of the West, however, was not to be denied, and for its final 250 years of existence, the Ottoman Empire mainly was on the defensive, suffering increasingly frequent military and political defeats. To save the state, Ottoman officialdom increasingly turned to Western models. Restructuring accelerated with some real successes during the nineteenth century, but by then nationalism had joined with imperialism to chew off most of the Ottoman lands.[1] In 1914, the Ottoman Empire contained only its Anatolian and Arab provinces, with a tiny European toehold in the land behind its capital of Istanbul.

The disintegrative impact of nationalism was more important in the European and Anatolian provinces, where revolutionary cadres (among them Macedonians, Albanians, and Armenians) sought to break away from their Ottoman overlords. Most in the Arab provinces had remained quiescent, even content with Ottoman rule. But when the British and French forcibly substituted their own domination for the Ottoman, local Arab elites began adapting to these new realities. Seeking to justify their own rule and build a new and viable identity, both the occupiers and occupied found reason to denounce and trivialize the Ottoman legacy. Over the decades, as a result, Arab intellectuals and popular classes alike have come to view the Ottoman experience both with considerable hostility and as irrelevant.[2] More generally, historical writing in the post-Ottoman world has scarcely dared to cross the new nation-state boundaries that were erected after World War I, even when that writing is about the Ottoman Empire itself. Thus, Turkish authors write about the Anatolian provinces of the empire, Arab writers about the Arab provinces, and the Bulgarian, Hungarian, and Romanian historians about their respective territories as if each had existed in isolation from the rest—as a separate entity rather than part of an imperial one. The result has been bad history—a fragmented, scattered historical record of a once-interconnected imperial system.

There probably is greater continuity between the Ottoman and contemporary worlds in the Arab lands than elsewhere in the former empire. It is true that most former Ottoman officers and bureaucrats served the republican Turkish state; but many were found in the Arab states as well. The demographic base of the Arab world was *comparatively* less disrupted, even after the dislocations of World War I are taken into account. In the European provinces that became independent states over the course of the nineteenth century, the Muslim populations routinely were expelled in order to accommodate the new forms of state identity formation. In the Anatolian world, the emerging Turkish nationalist cadres largely eradicated the substantial Armenian and Greek presences through deportation, massacre, and population exchange. By contrast, the pre- and postwar populations of the Arab world, with the notable exception of the Zionist Jewish settlers in Palestine, were more or less the same. All this agrees with the memories of workers living in the 1920s and 1930s. In their encounters with the French and British occupiers, they carried with them their Ottoman experiences of labor organization and mobilization, expectation and disappointment. These experiences and memories must have had a powerful impact on the post-Ottoman evolution of labor in the Arab world, an influence widely, if unwisely, ignored today.

Why We Know So Little About Ottoman Labor

For most of the Ottoman period, 1300–1922, there is relatively little information about the industrial labor force and even less about the social history of labor. There are two basic reasons: the historiography and the sources. First, Middle East history was dominated by an elite perspective that focused on the interests and concerns of the upper, literate classes. The concern of historians was with modernizers, who were changing society from the top down. In this narrative, there was scarcely room for anyone but the elites.[3] Therefore, workers and peasants were ignored except in their roles as supporters (or opponents) of elite programs.

The second reason is that until the latter part of the nineteenth century, most of the evidence comes in the form of government documents that are fiscally oriented. Only after about 1850 do increasingly rich sets of alternative sources become available. The reliance on state documents means dependence on materials that are only secondarily concerned with workers and primarily interested in issues regarding taxation or the supply of goods for Ottoman administrative or military personnel.

We seek to overcome the bias of these sources and ask questions that they never were intended to answer. Documents dealing with workers, however indirectly, were innately biased toward those producers who were more easily countable and taxable. Such workers generally were town dwellers, organized into guilds and producing in worksites that were readily identifiable. Government bean counters were not so able to tax manufacturers whom they could not identify or find. These were producers working at home with looms, spindles, and other implements. They might have argued to the authorities that they toiled only for autoconsumption, but in fact they also worked for commercial purposes. Home-based producers located in the rural countryside were still more difficult to find, enumerate, and write documents about that later historians might find and use.

There is a relatively enormous amount of state-generated material about workers in the larger enterprises that were directly under the governmental thumb. There are mountains of documents about the arsenal and the shipyards in the Istanbul capital that, for many centuries, provisioned the Ottoman army and navy. Such manufactories were important and employed several thousands of workers whose stories should be told, but their significance pales before the hundreds of thousands of other Ottoman workers whose lives never have been documented or recounted. When dealing in time periods for which government sources are the only viable ones, historians need to be more aggressive in teasing from the documents tales that their authors did not seek or intend to pass down.[4]

The enforced reliance on state documents is doubly dangerous because of the nature of the Ottoman workforce. Historically, the vast majority of Ottoman workers labored in small-scale enterprises. Large-scale workshops and factories remained the great exception, and even in the final century of Ottoman existence, most workplaces employed few workers. Ottoman factories, in the sense of inanimately powered establishments that employed numbers of workers ranging from dozens to hundreds, remained anomalous in the industrial landscape, even at the very end of the period. A significant proportion of the workers were located in the countryside, where they were virtually invisible to outside observers.

The presence of rural workers often can only be guessed at, and their numbers and importance will remain unquantifiable. But evidence shows clearly both that major rural production networks existed and that some of the industrial production taxed in a particular town actually was made, in whole or in part, in an adjacent or distant rural district. Goods were sometimes taxed at the point of sale rather than the point of production. In these cases it is very difficult to track and discuss the rural producers and to construct an authentic social history of labor.

Two final problems with the sources must be noted. First, these sources tend to be gender neutral, since the Ottoman language employed is undifferentiated in this regard. Second, the documents are often (but not always) ethnically mute. So even when documentation is comparatively abundant, we often learn nothing about the gender or ethnic identity of the workers. For the period before 1800, a few alternatives to these sources exist. Certainly information can be gleaned from the accounts of European diplomats and travelers, and these can be invaluable.

In the nineteenth century, Western sources become abundant, and at the end of the period, extraordinarily so; Ottoman alternatives to the archives also emerge. These materials include European consular reports, which often offer more data than do the Ottoman state documents, and Ottoman-language materials in the form of special reports, newspaper accounts, and, occasionally, writings by members of the labor force itself.[5] The reports of European and American consuls form an indispensable source. Their greatest value, moreover, is for the study of nonorganized labor, a group that rose in importance during the nineteenth century. These foreign government agents wrote about workers because they sought to imitate the products being made or because of the social unrest in their own European homelands. Thus, they paid attention to Ottoman workers, and sometimes there are reports solely on workers. Very late in the century, both the German and the American materials became fantastically rich; for example, there are published *daily* consular reports by U.S. officials. In using the foreign sources, historians must take care to account for these officials' class biases as well as their often-prejudiced views of Ottoman society. For the nineteenth century, there also are the published Ottoman materials in the form of both newspapers and provincial yearbooks (*vilayet salnameleri*) that, even in periods of censorship, have much of value.[6]

A Chronology of Nineteenth-Century Labor History

Ottoman labor history during the nineteenth century is demarcated by a number of dates and events. The first is 1826, when Sultan Mahmud II annihilated the Janissary Corps. In a stroke, he eliminated the armed foes of his reform policies. This story is well known among Ottoman specialists, but these Janissaries have another quality less remarked on. Drawn from the lower ranks of the working classes, usually unskilled, they repeatedly fought against and often terrorized the state. Thus, the effects of their actions served to protect the interests of Ottoman workers as a whole (whether these effects were intended is not clear). Once the Janissaries were gone, the state could act with relative disregard for the interests of labor.

In 1831, the government officially forbade the formation of any new *gedik*. The government had established *gedik*s in the early eighteenth century as a means of solidifying guild masters' control over the workplace. The master obtained a certification from the courts that effectively gave him monopoly control over the particular workplace.[7] The military action of 1826 had removed Janissary protection for many workers and paved the way for erasure of labor privileges. The 1831 prohibition against the formation of new *gedik*s eroded the monopoly powers of the guild masters.[8] This series of military and legislative initiatives against labor power and privilege took on a more mature form in 1838 and 1839 with the signing of the Anglo-Turkish Trade Convention and the promulgation of the Hatt-i Sherif of Gulhane reform decree, twin enactments that inaugurated the free trade era and officially abolished monopolies.

The state reaffirmed its commitment to free trade in an 1856 decree but partially reversed the direction of the tariff legislation of 1861–1862. This change of heart reflects a certain inconsistency in state relations with labor. On the one hand, the overall tendency of the post-1826 era was toward a dismantling of the privileges of organized labor in favor of free market forces. When confronted with the day-to-day business of making decisions about workers, however, the state sometimes supported and sometimes denied guilds' petitions for special treatment for the maintenance of restrictive practices and for exclusive control of certain sectors of production. The path from protected to free labor was not a straight one, but it was clear.

Whether this situation in any way suggests the power or influence of labor is unclear. The language that guilds used in their negotiations with the state is not very helpful in this regard. Sometimes they wrote in self-assured terms, asserting their rights. But at other times, they appealed timidly to an apparently all-powerful state apparatus. After 1826 and the decisive shift in military power in favor of Mahmud II's version of the state, we only infrequently find the kinds of demands or ultimatums that suggest a workforce in *open* opposition to the government.[9]

In 1881, the Ottoman Public Debt Administration was formed. This was an international oversight body of foreign holders of Ottoman obligations, but it was also important from the perspective of labor and marks another milestone in its history. The Debt Administration resulted from the near bankruptcy of the Ottoman state in the 1870s, when interest payments on a ballooning debt were suspended. In the 1850s, Ottoman statesmen abandoned their policy of avoiding international loans, quickly becoming overcommitted. Spent to finance wars and governmental modernization, as well as court extravagance, the borrowed monies soon overwhelmed the treasury's repayment capabilities. Hence the 1881 inauguration of Debt Administration operations signaled a new, semicolonial status for the Ottoman Empire. The Debt Administration controlled substantial chunks of the Ottoman economy and forwarded the tax proceeds to foreign bondholders of the Ottoman debt. Ultimately, it administered upward of one-third of all Ottoman revenues. The consequent foreign influence and interference seems obvious enough.

The foreign corporations that proliferated in the final decades of Ottoman existence displayed a stratified workforce: Foreigners were always at the top, Ottoman Muslims were always at the bottom, and Ottoman Christians usually held the intermediate ground. Because the Ottomans were only a semicolony, the government anxiously sought to impede foreign encroachment. Hence, a battery of Ottoman laws and regulations sought to restrict the employment of foreigners and demanded that when filling positions, the companies first seek qualified Ottoman subjects. The founding charter of every foreign corporation specified that such preference be given in all hirings. Nonetheless, we find the foreign-minority-Muslim labor stratification pattern just indicated. The presence of foreign workers certainly did reflect international influence. But it also often was a function of the technological sophistication required for tasks involved in running railroads, tramways, and modern mining operations, as well as of the fundamentals of the accounting procedures in Western corporations. Ottomans would lack such skills until a generation of indigenous apprentices matured.[10]

An important landmark in the history of late Ottoman labor is the great wave of labor strikes and unrest that erupted in the months following the July 1908 Young Turk Revolution.[11] The revolutionaries—military officers and intellectuals—who caused the change of government were moved to action by continuing Ottoman territorial losses and the absolutism of the reigning sultan. Hoping to reverse the tide, they seized power and restored a long-ignored constitution that had been promulgated in 1876. Workers, frustrated by stagnating or declining real wages and taking advantage of the political uncertainty that developed with this challenge to the state of Sultan Abdul Hamid II, launched scores of usually successful strikes for higher wages. The nature of the strikes also makes clear the limits of worker power. Whenever the strikers seemed to challenge the prerogatives of state or capital, as in their demands for a role in company management, they were rebuffed decisively and, if persistent, crushed militarily.

The Geographical Distribution of Labor

The vast majority, more than 80 percent, of Ottoman subjects lived in the countryside, where they grew crops, raised animals, extracted minerals, and manufactured goods both for their own subsistence and for sale to others. During the sixteenth century, there had been a division of manufacturing labor between certain Ottoman towns and the countryside. In textile making, cultivators and animal raisers spun and sometimes wove while urban dwellers dyed, finished, and marketed the textiles. In many cases, this pattern continued into the nineteenth century.

There were also profound changes affecting the division of tasks. For example, the urban labor pool grew as many hundreds of thousands of Muslim refugees, fleeing the newly independent states in the former Ottoman Balkans as well as czarist Russian expansion, passed through or settled in Istanbul. There, many of them and other members of the urban poor became available for sweatshop labor, often in the textile trades, which seems to have become increasingly common in more modern times. Thus, Istanbul was an anomaly in an otherwise labor-scarce economy.

From the 1830s, increasingly vast quantities of machine-spun yarn and cloth were imported from abroad, replacing the handmade Ottoman goods and threatening to render their makers redundant. Similarly, the expanding use of artificial and synthetic dyes encroached upon the livelihoods of many professional dyers. Such changes certainly disrupted, to some extent, the division of tasks between town and country. And yet hand spinning of yarn and hand weaving of cloth continued at significant levels. Hand-spun yarn in 1900 accounted for about 25 percent of all yarn—from both domestic and foreign sources—being used at the time. Also, in some areas during the nineteenth century, villagers made coarser cloths of cotton or wool and nearby urban workers made the finer silk or silk-cotton fabrics. Clearly, a division of labor between town and country persisted even through periods of extraordinary change. These nineteenth-century patterns could represent continuities with previous centuries, but they may well have been new ones that emerged in response to the changes triggered by massive European imports.[12]

Sectoral Distribution of Labor

Overall, there were very few workers employed in what we would consider factories—places with many workers and inanimately powered equipment. The enumerations of factory labor available are quite incomplete and defective from a number of perspectives. One estimate suggests that in 1914, only 35,000 persons worked in "large industrial establishments." Whatever that may have meant, it is clear that modern factories numbered in the scores and not the hundreds. It is further certain that the persons employed by such factories numbered in the tens of thousands and not the hundreds of thousands. When we consider that the total Ottoman populace was about 26 million persons, these are very small numbers indeed. This should not be cause for surprise, since the Ottoman pattern parallels developments elsewhere. Scholarship on eighteenth- and nineteenth-century England, France, and the Saxon Oberlausitz shows that very large numbers of workers in industrializing areas labored in small-scale workshops and homes. Indeed, some scholarship argues that large-scale industry is not a historical norm but rather an aberration from the norm of small-scale production.[13]

Child labor was common, and young girls formed an important proportion of all factory workers, particularly in the textile and tobacco industries. In one of the state yarn factories in Istanbul, Christian orphans from central Anatolia were obtained to work for wages. In the silk-spinning mills of Bursa, an important industrial center, many young girls were recruited from villages of the surrounding districts and housed in dormitories near the factories (like their sisters in New England and Japan at about the same time). Girls and women who worked in the Hereke textile factory near Istanbul lived in a similar fashion, there segregated by ethnicity. In cotton-spinning mills of both southeastern Anatolia and the Ottoman Balkans, employers provided benefits that included soup kitchens to recruit and retain workers in the generally labor-scarce Ottoman economy.

In addition to factory labor, the 10,000 coal miners of the Black Sea coastal areas around Eregli and Zonguldak offer another example of massed Ottoman workers. Properly speaking, these men were not miners but cultivator-miners who, since the 1860s, engaged in rotational labor in the mines, regularly returning to their villages in fourteen administrative districts near the coal fields. They were Muslim and worked in the mines for two to three weeks at a stint. For the workers, the part-time labor meant total reliance on neither mining nor agriculture. Shortfalls in the one could be made up by additional efforts in the other. Or to put it another way, opportunities in one sector meant less work in the other, as in times of bumper crops that pulled men out of the mines into the fields to the detriment of coal production.[14]

The comparative absence of mechanized, large-scale factories and massed labor forces hardly implies that the world of Ottoman labor was moribund. To the contrary, it bustled with activity and employed many hundreds of thousands of workers who provided Ottoman subjects with most of the goods that they consumed. The Ottoman workforce overwhelmingly was located in the home and the workshop despite all the changes that took place in the nineteenth century. Household production of goods remained very important both for subsistence and for sale. In many regions, women and men regularly worked at home, making goods either on their own account or on behalf of merchants who picked up and marketed the goods. For example, the famed linens in the town of Rize on the eastern Black Sea coast often were homemade, and women who lived near the village of Erzurum also wove at home. Most workshops were in urban areas, in towns as dissimilar as Van, in eastern Anatolia, and Aleppo. Some of these could be large with several hundreds of workers. More generally, however, workshops were small, employing three or four persons.

Institutional Patterns of Collective Action and Labor History

In Ottoman labor history, much has been written about the guildlike organizations (*esnaf*). They existed in many Ottoman cities from Cairo, Damascus, and Aleppo to Ankara, Istanbul, and Salonica. These *esnaf* were important to the government bureaucracy and military, for they provided goods and services in peace and war. They helped ensure the flow of commodities—ranging from leather for shoes to flour for bread—to the Ottoman capital of Istanbul. These production and supply aspects of guild activities are well documented in state sources, but we know scarcely anything about their social structure, hierarchy, or internal dynamics.

In a few cases, however, we do know more about workers' *esnaf*.[15] Among these are the porters' guilds of Istanbul. Large numbers of porters worked in the politically sensitive capital city, and their jobs—handling goods on the streets, in the port area, and in the customs houses—made them a very visible group. Most porters were workers who, thanks to chain migration along well-established routes, came to work from villages hundreds of miles away from the capital. These workers belonged to guilds according to the area of the city in which they worked. Generally, they seem to have been organized along ethnic lines; Kurds, for example, belonged to one guild and Armenians to another. Living as bachelors in groups of about six, they paid an old man to clean and cook. A guild steward organized the work, controlled entry into the guild, and paid fees to the city for the right to work. Porters paid a large entry fee to the steward, who also received the wages members earned and apportioned these wages among them. He also managed the guild's sickness and disability fund and distributed money to members for the trips back home, which took place every several years.

Thanks to interviews conducted in the 1960s with an ageing population of emigrants to Israel, we have an unusually detailed picture of Jewish porters in Salonica.[16] In its richness, this picture may fill in some of the gaps in our knowledge of Istanbul porters and, perhaps, of Ottoman guilds in general. The Salonica porters belonged to a group that kept account books but, significantly, did not have a formal hierarchical structure. Members met daily for sunset prayer, then changed clothes and gathered for a drink at a pub. On payday the employer paid the money owed to a member who set aside a small sum in a communal chest and distributed the balance among the members. Sick members received their normal share less wages paid to a temporary replacement. Sons automatically could replace their deceased fathers. A widow without male children could hire a permanent substitute and keep the difference between his salary and the average wages of her deceased husband. She could also sell the right to her husband's position and pocket the entire amount. As in Istanbul, the porters of Salonica were divided by location of the work or the kind of commodity carried, and they were both well disciplined and tightly organized (in an informal fashion, as we have seen). Family ties in Salonica fulfilled the functional task that ethnicity played in Istanbul. That is, certain families of these exclusively Jewish porter groups controlled certain worksites just as, in Istanbul, particular ethnic groups monopolized particular job tasks and places.

We have only a handful of examples of Ottoman guild regulations, a few handbooks of the same type that exist by the hundreds in European archival collections.[17] In a rare exception, members of the grocers guild of an Ottoman Balkan town (Moskhpolis) in 1779 agreed on a number of provisions that restricted trade. For example, members could not procure goods outside the town but had to wait until these were brought into the central square; further, they would submit all merchandise for group approval. The appointment of apprentices similarly needed group approval, as did the length of apprenticeships. The general absence of handbooks, which spell out the relationships among members and the duties and responsibilities of the body, might mean that many guilds were not formally organized, but we cannot be sure. The Salonica example, and by association that from Istanbul, suggests that there is no necessary incompatibility between lack of formal structure and tight organization.

We do not really understand, however, the nature and functions of most Ottoman guilds. They were not the mere willing agents of the state, as has been argued in the past, nor were they necessarily monopolistic forces tightly controlling the economy.[18] Rather their nature and functions varied quite considerably not only over time but also contemporaneously by place. In some areas they may have been monopolistic; in others they were only loose associations of persons engaged in the same activity.

Guilds, whatever their actual importance and economic role, were part of the Ottoman scene for many centuries. Unions and syndicates, by contrast, came late in Ottoman history and were a foreign implant rather than an indigenous growth. They date from the final years of the nineteenth century and are part of the rising tide of European capital penetration. Unlike guilds, the unions and syndicates were illegitimate in the eyes of the Ottoman state and appear infrequently in the official sources. These few organizations largely were associated with the foreign corporations being established in the Ottoman lands. Hence, for example, we find unions of railroad workers and of tramway workers. During the strike wave of 1908, many unions were created in the act of striking and often died when the strike was over. The brief legal existence of most unions came to an end within months of the Young Turk Revolution, with legislation forbidding such organizations in the public-service sector. We actually know little about the structure and membership of labor unions.[19]

Unions were most often connected to foreign-capitalized firms and to the "modern" sector, but there are important exceptions to this rule. Recall, for example, the porters and other workers who were employed in the Istanbul port zones that were modernized in the 1890s. These facilities were among the most modern in the Ottoman transport sector, yet the labor force, to the consternation of the corporations, remained dominated by the *esnaf*.

Whatever their actual natures and the differences between them, guilds and unions have a common quality—together they have received the lion's share of the attention devoted to Ottoman labor in general. In part, this is a function of their very nature as organized, identifiable bodies. There are several other reasons. In a mutually useful relationship, the state maintained ties with many guilds; so we have the numerous documents generated by guilds or focused on them in the government archives, and these have come to the attention of historians. Unions also attracted the attention of many scholars because they are part of a progressive model of a modern world. In this vision, unionized labor is in the vanguard of the working class and ultimately will lead nonunionized workers to a better, more egalitarian, socialist society. Since the late 1980s and the fall of the Soviet Union, this model has lost favor.

The focus of much labor history on protesting and striking workers is a part of this same emphasis on the progressive aspects of labor history. Protesting workers, of course, are aware of themselves as workers and of the rights for which they are agitating or striking. In a sense, striking workers proved themselves worthy of scholarly attention because of their self-conscious and progressive actions. Workers in action, moreover, attracted the worry and attention of state and capital, which often recorded their concerns for later historians. The strike wave of 1908, for example, received considerable attention from the contemporary press and foreign observers. Similarly, when guilds caused difficulties for the state or made demands upon it, these actions were written down in reports or petitions. For example, mid-century disputes between Istanbul clothmakers fill dozens of pages of documents, allowing a fairly good understanding of craft-state relations at this critical time.[20]

Most of the literature in labor history has focused on certain kinds of groups. These mainly have been (1) workers massed in relatively large numbers in factories or in mining operations, (2) workers organized either in guilds or in unions, and (3) labor in militant stances, striking and protesting. These have been the favored objects of the labor historians' attentions, and without question, such groups and actions are important. As I argued previously, however, large numbers of Ottoman workers labored in small-scale enterprises located in a home or workshop, not a factory. Very many workers were not organized in guilds or unions, and most of the hours of most workers' lives were spent not in striking or agitating or remonstrating but in working, producing goods, and earning a livelihood. We know of the existence of many scores of thousands of such unorganized workers in homes and small-scale workshops across the empire. For example, most of the estimated 60,000 persons working in the carpet industry around 1914 were neither guild nor union members, and the majority of them did not work in factories.

Ethnic and Religious Composition of the Workforce

Until its demise following World War I, the Ottoman Empire possessed a richly variegated labor force. Ottoman workers belonged to several dozens of ethnicities—Arab, Kurdish, Turkish, Armenian, Albanian, and so on—and a host of faiths ranging, for example, from the various persuasions of Islam (Sunni and Shi'i) to the sects of Christianity (Orthodox and Catholic as well as Chaldean and Maronite). Given the multiethnic, multireligious nature of the centuries-old Ottoman system itself, the heterogeneous character of the labor force seems self-evident. But it was not always so. On some occasions, authors trotted out the hoary notion that Muslims were peasants, soldiers, and administrators (but not very good ones) and, as a corollary, that Christians dominated the nonagricultural labor force and formed the vast majority of the artisans. On other occasions, a more refined version of this division-of-labor argument was employed. More subtly, Christians were seen as the skilled workers—for example, of fine jewelry—and Muslims often worked in the coarser trades such as leather tanning.[21]

There is truth to the assertion that ethnic groups dominated crafts. In Ottoman Salonica, for example, Jews formed the vast majority of the porters and of the labor force in general, and Turkish Muslims prevailed at Usak generally and in its rug industry in particular. If Turkish Muslims were the majority of the rugmakers in Usak, Christians made most of the rugs in Konya. Making statements about such Jewish or Muslim or Christian control in such specific places is one thing; but it is quite another to incorrectly surmise from such facts the presence of a general ethnoreligious division of labor. There simply was not a widespread ethnoreligious division of labor: Particular groups generally did not control or dominate particular activities in the Ottoman Empire as a whole. The nineteenth-century Ottoman labor force was neither largely Turkish, Armenian, nor Greek, and it was not primarily Muslim, Christian, or Jewish. An ethnic or religious group that dominated an economic activity in one particular region did not necessarily do so in another.

To explore the general question of Ottoman worker identity a bit further, I assert that the workers consisted of men and male children *and* very many girls and women. Female labor predominated in some industries at some locales. Here I offer two examples of groups of workers who overwhelmingly were female: the Christian carpet knotters in Sivas and the Jewish tobacco sorters in Balkan Salonica. Whatever forces operated at the local level to create such patterns simply were not identically reproduced at the level of the empire as a whole.

Nimble fingers had little to do with such patterns of employment, since we find men performing identical tasks in other regions. Using the same occupational examples during the same era, we see men knotting rugs at Kula and sorting tobacco in the Balkan district of Xanthi. A few industries were exclusively female: The only example (besides mechanized silk reeling, see further on) about which we are certain is embroidering for both commercial and subsistence purposes. All embroiderers, apparently, were female.

The gender division of labor reflected societal rather than physical requisites. An important example about which we have some information is the textile industry, which, after food processing, was the most significant industrial activity. In textile making, men probably formed the majority of the commercial weavers and women were the subsistence workers, a pattern for which, obviously, there is no compelling physical reason. Thus, men worked the commercial looms in early-twentieth-century Baghdad and Aleppo. This is no Arab peculiarity: Men also dominated in the textile industries of mid-nineteenth-century Diyarbakir and Ankara; workers in Ankara wove the famed mohair cloth.

Even this alleged pattern of male dominance in commercial weaving has exceptions that have their own patterns. Muslim women in the 1830s worked in a home-industry nexus in east Anatolia, weaving linen and cotton cloth for sale; in early-twentieth-century Trabzon, women at home were commercially weaving certain kinds of silk and cotton cloths. In the available examples that attest to women weaving cloth for the market, they tend to be working in the home. There, they balanced the family's need for cash with housekeeping and child-care chores, not to mention, in many cases, gardening tasks that provided food.[22]

Since societal demands varied enormously, males and females of all age groups made various textile products for subsistence and for sale. In some areas, it seems that mostly men or mostly women wove cloth. But in other areas, participation was not based on gender. Similarly, both men and women made shoes in Istanbul workshops. More examples of the rich ethnic, religious, and gender diversity of the Ottoman labor force could be provided, but the details show how cautious we must be when addressing the ethnic, religious, and gender makeup of the labor force in the later Ottoman Empire.

The International Economy and the Division of Labor

During the nineteenth century, international capital began to modify the previously mentioned patterns of labor in important ways, both indirectly and directly. Under its impact, significant numbers of women began working outside their homes. Three leading examples come to mind. The first is that of mechanized silk reeling, the production of a threadlike fiber later woven into cloth. From the 1830s, thanks to European demand, reeled silk became a machine-made good produced in a factory. For the purpose, silk mills sprang up in many Ottoman regions ranging from the Lebanon in the Arab lands to Bursa in Anatolia to the Balkan towns of Salonica and Edirne. West Europeans supplied the initial capital for these factories but shortly were replaced by Ottomans, often but not always Christians. Everywhere, without exception, girls and women entered the factories and became the exclusive labor source for reeling. To the best of my knowledge, this is the earliest Ottoman example of an extensive use of female labor outside the home.

We find a more complex pattern in the second case, also directly tied to international demand for Ottoman products. As early as 1825, the already keen Western appetite for "Oriental" rugs became voracious. Consequently, the agents of merchants in Izmir (and later Istanbul) began founding workshops in towns and cities of Anatolia where the rug-making craft either had been forgotten or had never existed. Once again, the workers in these newly founded ateliers were girls and women laboring outside their homes for wages, probably for the first time in their lives. This case has an additional interest that impinges on the ethnicity issue. These new workers, almost without exception, were Ottoman Christians recruited by the foreign and Ottoman Christian merchants and their agents. By contrast, knotters in the great carpet-making center of Usak, with continuous production for many centuries, were Turkish and Muslim. In these companies and the rug ateliers, we see the promotion of non-Muslim at the expense of Muslim labor. This, like the labor segmentation patterns in the Debt Administration or the foreign-owned firms surely had negative consequences for intercommunal relations.

A third example of women leaving home to enter the workforce is that of the mechanized cotton-spinning mills founded in numerous Ottoman locations. About one-fifth of the mill owners were Muslims; the majority were European residents of the empire or Ottoman Christians. Information is sparse but shows girls and women workers—in these cases Christian, Jewish, and Muslim—as the operators of the spinning equipment.

There can be no doubt that during the period of foreign capital penetration, the subdivision of tasks in some cases became increasingly refined. In the rug industry, many women gradually spent more of their time knotting and less in yarn spinning and other rug-related tasks. But this is true of the rug industry in several, not all, Ottoman areas. An increasingly refined division of tasks under the impact of Western capital also appeared in the shoe and the ready-made clothing industries in Istanbul.

There was not necessarily an overall causal connection between the presence of Western capital and an increasingly refined division of labor. Forms of a refined division of tasks had long existed in the Ottoman world, for example, in the sixteenth and seventeenth centuries. In some cities, there were separate guilds for different kinds of shoes as well as for different colors of the same textile. To give another kind of example, in the mohair cloth industry in Ankara, guildsmen carefully apportioned the different stages of work among different individuals in both country and town, including female workers, who were not counted as members.

As the carpet, shoe, and ready-made clothing examples show, Western capital could prompt refinements in the division of labor in some sectors of the economy, but mounting European capital penetration meant an increasing *un*differentiation of labor elsewhere. Many formerly separate guilds that had made different kinds of textiles merged with one another during the nineteenth century in an effort to cope with Western competition.

In sum, it seems clear that production had moved away from craft guilds and toward unorganized home and workshop labor and that some industries displayed an increasing refinement in the division of labor. Thus, it is likely that multiple-income households were becoming more common over the course of the nineteenth century. Whether undifferentiation and proletarianization increased as a result of growing Western capital penetration, however, seems uncertain, and at this stage of the research, it seems best to withhold judgment.

Notes

1. There is no satisfactory textbook account of late Ottoman history. The most influential accounts are by Bernard Lewis and Stanford J. Shaw. Lewis's account, *The Emergence of Modern Turkey*, 2d ed. (London: Oxford University Press, 1968) is well written and powerfully argued. Throughout the narrative, Lewis implies that the Republic of Turkey was the Ottoman successor state instead of one among many, and he focuses too much on the westernization process and on the elites. The two-volume study by S. J. Shaw, *History of the Ottoman Empire and Modern Turkey* (vol. 2 is co-authored by Ezel Kural Shaw) (Cambridge: Cambridge University, Press, 1976, 1977) is deeply flawed by errors and a hagiographic approach to the Ottoman state and also overemphasizes westernizing elite groups. Roderic Davison, *Turkey* (Englewood Cliffs, N.J.: Prentice-Hall, 1968), is the most accessible general study but also focuses on westernizers during the later period.

2. See William L. Cleveland, *A History of the Modern Middle East* (Boulder: Westview Press, 1994), for arguments about Arab support for the Ottoman state at this time.

3. See the works by Lewis, Shaw, and Davison cited in note 1.

4. Donald Quataert, *Workers, Peasants and Economic Change in the Ottoman Empire, 1730–1914* (Istanbul: Isis Press, 1933), ix–xv.

5. Donald Quataert, "Labor and Working Class History in the Late Ottoman Period, c. 1800–1914," Turkish Studies Association *Bulletin* (September 1991): 357–369.

6. Ibid.

7. Engin Akarli, "Gedik: Implements, Mastership, Shop Usufruct and Monopoly Among Istanbul Artisans, 1750–1850," *Wissenschaftskolleg Jahrbuch* (1986): 225–231.

8. *Gediks* were not suppressed until 1913 (ibid.); the delay between the 1831 and 1913 actions requires further analysis.

9. Donald Quataert, "Ottoman Workers and the State, 1826–1914," in Zachary Lockman (ed.), *Workers and Working Classes in the Middle East* (Albany: State University of New York Press, 1994), 21–40.

10. Donald Quataert, *Social Disintegration and Popular Resistance in the Ottoman Empire, 1891–1908* (New York: New York University Press, 1983), 41–69.

11. Yavuz Selim Karakisla, "The 1908 Strike Wave in the Ottoman Empire," Turkish Studies Association *Bulletin* (September 1992):153–177.

12. Donald Quataert, *Ottoman Manufacturing in the Age of Industrial Revolution* (Cambridge: Cambridge University Press, 1993).

13. For a further development of these examples and ideas, see Quataert, *Ottoman Manufacturing*, 15–19, 161–177, and sources cited therein.

14. See Quataert, *Social Disintegration*.

15. Gabriel Baer is an important early Ottoman labor historian who has written extensively on Egyptian guilds. See, for example, his collected articles in *Fellah and Townsman in the Middle East: Studies in Social History* (London: Frank Cass, 1982). A later and more important study is by André Raymond, *Artisans et commerçants au Caire au XVIIIe siècle*, 2 vols. (Damascus: Institut Français de Damas, 1973 and 1974). For guilds in the Syrian provinces see the work of Abdul Karim Rafeq, especially "Craft Organizations, Work Ethics and the Strains of Change in Ottoman Syria," *Journal of the American Oriental Society* 111 (1991):495–511. For an innovative recent study see Sherry Vatter, "Militant Journeymen in Nineteenth Century Damascus: Implications for the Middle Eastern Labor History Agenda," in Zachary Lockman (ed.), *Workers and Working Classes in the Middle East* (Albany: State University of New York Press, 1994), 1–19.

16. Centre de recherches sur le Judaisme de Salonique Jerusalem-Tel Aviv, *Salonique, Ville-Mère en Israel*, in Hebrew with French summary, 242–243. My thanks to Mr. Izhar Eliaz, Binghamton University, for his translation from the Hebrew. The fragmentary data available provide no reason to doubt the presence of similiar organizational patterns among Muslim and Christian workers.

17. Given the scarcity of research, it is premature to draw any conclusions from the apparent absence of handbooks. There might be scores of them in archival or private collections, or guilds often may not have been constituted so formally.

18. For a fuller discussion of guilds and state-guild relations, see Donald Quataert, "The Age of Reforms, 1812–1914," in Halil Inalcik (ed. with Donald Quataert), *An Economic and Social History of the Ottoman Empire, 1300–1914* (Cambridge: Cambridge University Press, 1994), 890–898.

19. See Quataert, *Social Disintegration*, 72–93, and "Ottoman Workers"; and Karakisla, "Strike Wave," for railroad union petitions and notices that unions sent to newspapers reporting their formation and times and places of meetings.

20. See Quataert, *Ottoman Manufacturing*, 54–55.

21. See Quataert, *Workers and Peasants*.

22. See Quataert, *Ottoman Manufacturing*, 80–89, and sources cited therein.

3

The Labor Movement in Turkey: Labor Pains, Maturity, Metamorphosis

Günseli Berik
Cihan Bilginsoy

Between 1923 and 1990, Turkey evolved from a predominantly agrarian economy into one of the most industrialized economies in the Third World. The political system became more inclusive as it moved from one-party rule to the multiparty system. Democratic and labor rights were broadened, albeit with periodic interruptions and reversals. During the process of industrialization and the development of political institutions, the working class grew and the labor movement emerged. These developments, however, diverge from the "classical" model of proletarianization and labor activism, which is often associated with Western Europe. In this model a wage-earning class separated from the means of production is created. This leads to the growth of class consciousness, which in turn guides the working class in its struggle to acquire political and economic rights.[1] In this chapter we examine these divergences and their underpinnings.

Our main argument is that the labor movement in Turkey did not play an active role in the political and economic transformations of the country. Labor rights came from political-legal changes that were independent from worker struggles. Although workers waged battles in defense of already-acquired rights and indeed became a force to reckon with by the 1970s, neither they nor unions sought to broaden the long-term economic and political rights of workers. Even at the peak of its militancy in the 1970s, labor was on the defensive, not pushing for new rights. At crucial turning points such as the 1971 and 1980 military coups, which reversed labor's political and economic gains, working-class resistance was weak at best.

We argue that the characteristics of industrialization strategies pursued by Turkey in combination with the particulars of Turkish history explain the divergence from the classical model of the creation of the working class and labor activism. An inward-oriented, import-substitution industrialization (ISI) strategy created limited demand for an industrial wage-labor force. Given the persistence of smallholder agriculture, there was also limited impetus for proletarianization and the growth of working-class unity and consciousness. Paternalistic state traditions combined with ISI to deliver high wages to the relatively small industrial working class in the 1960s and 1970s. This context shaped workers' demands around narrow economic concerns, circumscribed the Turkish labor movement, and diminished its effectiveness.

To such a background, the labor movement of the late 1980s and 1990s provides a counterpoint. In reaction to the deteriorating economic conditions and widespread labor repression ushered in by the outward orientation of the economy in 1980, an active grassroots labor movement emerged in the late 1980s. This was a significant turning point in the Turkish labor movement, but it is difficult to ascertain its future. In 1994, Feroz Ahmad anticipated that this new wave of militancy, rising class consciousness, and self-confidence would advance labor's political rights and economic interests, provided that the movement spawned its own leadership and political party.[2] In our opinion he overlooked the expansion of the informal sector, emphasized by Çaglar Keyder, which neither is disposed to unionization nor necessarily shares the objectives of the formal-sector workers.[3] In this changing structure, we argue that worker discontent may assume a reactionary, anticapitalist nature, turning to individualistic solutions and abetting either ultranationalist or Islamic fundamentalist authoritarianism.

We structure our discussion chronologically in four periods: 1923–1945, 1946–1960, 1960–1980, and 1980 to the early 1990s. These constitute distinct episodes in the political, legal, and economic development of Turkey, as well as the creation of the Turkish working class.

1923–1945: State-Led Industrialization and Enforced National Unity

The Turkish Republic was formed in 1923, following the breakup of the Ottoman Empire at the end of World War I and the subsequent victory of Turkish nationalists against the Allied forces that occupied Anatolia. The agenda of the first leaders of the republic was premised on the harmony of interests of all citizens regardless of class, ethnicity, or religion. The political corollary of this ideology was single-party rule and suppression of all political opposition, including from labor organizations. Economically, the period marked the beginnings of a state-led industrialization drive in a predominantly agricultural, subsistence economy.

The Turkish Republic inherited a very small industrial sector from the Ottoman Empire. In the first years of the republic, the government was committed to liberal economic principles. State officials expected the private sector to spearhead economic growth but were disappointed. The existing private enterprises were predominantly engaged in commercial activities, and industrial enterprises were too small and unable to initiate an industrialization drive.[4]

The liberal period lasted until the Great Depression, which provided the opportunity to launch ISI. The establishment in the 1930s of the first State Economic Enterprises (SEEs) to manufacture basic consumer goods created demand for industrial labor. These years were marked by a chronic industrial labor shortage. Throughout this period no less than 75 percent of the population was in the rural areas and engaged in agriculture characterized by small farms, simple technology, and low productivity. The land-tenure system was relatively egalitarian; most households owned small plots of land. Most of the landless were engaged in sharecropping, only a small proportion was agricultural workers. The rural standard of living was poor, and it worsened during World War II as the state followed a squeeze-the-farmer policy to generate an agricultural surplus.[5] In spite of this, there was little incentive for permanent migration to urban areas. Peasants were willing to take urban industrial jobs only seasonally and thus labor turnover was high, hindering the growth of a regular and disciplined urban labor force.

The state used various incentives in order to create an industrial labor force, including subsidized housing, paid vacations, social insurance, relocation of the population to areas where there was high demand for labor, free clothing, and free meals at the workplace. Punitive actions were also taken against those who left employment without notice.[6] Nonetheless, the industrial labor shortage continued until the 1950s, becoming more acute due to conscription during World War II. The chronic labor shortage may be explained by the lack of improvement in the standard of living of workers. Between 1914 and 1945, urban real wages fell by 30 percent, albeit with significant short-term variations.[7] Given dubious data quality and the strong likelihood that workers had widespread access to nonwage incomes, however, it is difficult to reach definitive conclusions about changes in the standard of living. Nonetheless, especially in light of the improvement in real wages after 1950, the earlier trend suggests that the 1923–1945 period was a difficult one for the industrial working class—indeed for all laboring classes.

During this period the state enacted laws and policies to prevent the emergence of a labor movement. After World War I, the economically dominant classes were divided over whether to support the nationalists or the Allied forces that occupied the Ottoman Empire. Various labor organizations were formed to organize workers politically and to start a union movement.[8] In the early 1920s, there were strikes, protests, and demonstrations in Istanbul that supported the war for independence in Anatolia.[9] Given the small size of the working class, however, these forms of action never gained enough momentum to turn into a mass movement. After the creation of the Turkish Republic, some of these organizations continued their activities, and others, including political parties, were formed. Some labor organizations took part in the 1923 Izmir Economic Conference (which was the first forum to discuss the economic policies of the new republic) and demanded the right to form unions and to strike. The final conference document acknowledged the right to unionize and determined the necessity of revising the labor laws inherited from the Ottoman Empire.[10]

In spite of the conciliatory atmosphere of the Izmir conference, however, state policies were hostile to the labor movement in subsequent years. Labor action was rare in the latter half of the 1920s. It included strikes at the Soma-Bandirma and Adana Railroad Companies, the Istanbul Dock Company, the Istanbul Trolley Company, and the Tobacco Company. The passage of a comprehensive public-order law in 1925 (Establishment of Public Order Law), after religious-ethnic rebellions in eastern Turkey were quelled, put an end to union activity along with all political opposition. The 1935 penal code imposed punitive sanctions on strikes. The 1936 labor law made strikes illegal. Finally, in 1938, the revised law of associations abolished unions totally by banning all forms of "organizations based on social class."[11]

1946–1960: Economic Growth, Labor Rights, and Unions Under State Tutelage

After World War II, there were major changes in the political landscape, signaling the beginning of democracy in Turkey. In 1946 the single-party regime was abandoned and several opposition parties were immediately formed. The period, especially after 1950, witnessed growing numbers of industrial wage workers and limited union activity under state tutelage.

The ruling Republican People's Party (RPP) was forced to revise labor laws under international and domestic pressure. Externally, there were demands from the International Labor Organization (ILO) and the UN, of which Turkey became a member. Domestically, the RPP's main contender, the newly formed Democrat Party (DP), recognized the right to form unions and to strike.[12] The working class did not play a significant role in either the transition to the multiparty system or the prolabor legislative changes. With only two strikes between 1936 and 1946, albeit they were illegal, the labor movement was hardly an active one. [13]

In June 1946, the legal obstacle to unionization was removed when the associations law was amended to eliminate the ban against forming class-based organizations. Yet the RPP still imposed tight controls on the right to unionize and permitted only compliant labor organizations to operate. In December, shortly after they were formed, most of the unions and two socialist parties were accused of promoting class warfare and were closed down by the government. The 1947 unions law banned all political activity by unions, including supporting a political party or engaging in political propaganda.

The DP was in tacit agreement with the RPP on this issue. Both parties wanted labor organizations that could be controlled and manipulated for their own agendas. Neither was willing to tolerate an independent labor movement or party. Indeed, one enduring aspect of state policy toward labor organizations in both the single- and the multiparty period was the repression of independent labor organizations under allegations of being either the vanguard or a cover for subversive communist activities. Otherwise, both parties courted labor organizations to win the labor vote.[14]

Whereas the RPP was heavily handicapped by its historically repressive policies and legislative record, the DP had a more prolabor image because of its 1946 platform and its brief parliamentary record. This prolabor image as well as economic slowdown and rising unemployment at the end of the 1940s drove workers to the side of the DP. In 1950 the DP won the national elections by championing individual rights against the repressive RPP-controlled state and political participation by all through the electoral system. It remained in power until 1960.[15]

The 1950s was a period of rural transformation and rapid rural-urban migration. In response to mechanization and favorable agricultural prices, there was a significant expansion of agricultural commodity production, which strengthened small producers and upset much of the sharecropping relationships. At the same time, there was increasing urban demand for labor, especially in the manufacturing, construction, and service sectors. Living conditions in urban areas were becoming relatively more attractive

even when the workers were living on the margins in *gecekondu* neighborhoods devoid of basic infrastructure and services.[16] Between 1950 and 1960
the urbanization rate rose from 25 to 32 percent. The size of the urban
working class grew significantly during this decade. In 1950 there were
374,000 workers covered by the labor law (3 percent of the labor force), 16
percent of whom were unionized. By 1960 these figures had grown to
825,000 workers (6 percent of the labor force) and 34 percent, respectively.
These workers had not yet wholly severed their ties with rural areas. In general, urban workers still owned land in villages, tilled by either family members or tenant farmers. Most urban workers timed their annual vacations
to help harvest and bring back food supplies for their own consumption.
The persistence of these ties, and their strengthening via the transfer of savings to villages to be used in purchasing land or agricultural machinery, ar-
guably slowed down or reversed the process of separation from the land.

During the 1950s, the DP government passed new legislation that included laws on paid weekends, holidays, and annual vacations; lunch
breaks; and disability, old age, and other benefits. Over the decade real
wages increased by 15 percent, a notable increase after the stagnation of
the previous decades under RPP rule.[17] These improvements, in combination with the ineffectiveness of the fledgling unions, helped the state foster
a benevolent image and keep the labor movement under control.

One of the most important players in the history of the Turkish labor
movement, the Confederation of Turkish Workers' Unions (Türk-Is) was
founded in 1952 in the midst of the Cold War with the financial, educational, and training assistance of USAID, the AFL-CIO, ICFTU (International Confederation of Free Trade Unions) and the U.S. embassy. Many
Türk-Is leaders and unionists were invited to the United States for training
purposes. USAID financial contributions were critical for Türk-Is because
of the chronic financial frailty of unions during the 1950s.[18] The nonpolit-
ical—so-called American-type—unionism of Türk-Is may be traced to
the influence of these organizations and their close association with Türk-
Is for years to come. Türk-Is's unionism was premised on the harmony of
class interests, which opposed class-based politics and fitted neatly with
the nationalistic ideology.

The Türk-Is leadership strove for economic gains through solicitation
and lobbying of legislators and the government without actively pursuing
the right to strike in spite of the fact that the DP had promised to legislate
this right if it came to power. One explanation for Türk-Is's submissive-
ness during the 1950s centers on its co-optation by the ruling political
party. The DP actively tried to control the leadership of the labor unions.

Unions whose leadership supported the minority RPP were either threatened with temporary shutdowns for engaging in "political" activity or were harassed by fines that kept them in constant financial trouble. Union leaders who supported the DP, however, were coddled and often rewarded by being elected as representatives in the National Assembly in the DP ranks. Türk-Is leadership vacillated between support for DP and RPP until 1957 but afterward remained loyal to the DP. Ironically, after 1957, repression of the unions increased as the DP government tried to shut down the regional labor organizations and rank-and-file support for the DP diminished.[19]

A more charitable interpretation of Türk-Is's strategy is that this was the best course available under the circumstances. Most industrial activity was in SEEs, and Türk-Is-affiliated unions were predominantly in the public sector. Since the state was the major employer, unions were able to get pay raises for the rank and file by being on good terms with those who held the political power. A ban on strikes and restrictions on political activity limited the power of unions to confront employers, including the largest one, the government.[20] In addition, the absence of an automatic checkoff for union dues and politically motivated fines levied by the government kept unions financially vulnerable. Thus, confrontation was hardly an option for unions. The clientelistic relationship between the DP government and Türk-Is foreshadowed the future right-wing governments' attempts to create a corporatist exchange. The government offered to provide the exclusive right of representation to Türk-Is in return for the latter's pledge to moderate the exercise of labor rights.[21]

In 1960, the DP, which had grown increasingly authoritarian and intolerant of political opposition, was toppled by a military coup supported by the urban middle class. The labor movement did not contribute to the ouster of the DP. Following the coup, Türk-Is leaders immediately denounced the undemocratic policies of the DP regime, announced their support for the military, and expelled their president—who was also serving as a DP representative in the parliament—from the confederation.

1961–1980: Consolidation of the Working Class and the Crisis of Import-Substitution Industrialization

The 1961–1980 period was the most significant phase in the history of the Turkish labor movement. It was a legal turning point for the working class because the 1961 constitution altered the legal framework and expanded democratic and labor rights. Economically, the period was characterized by rapid economic growth, industrialization, and growth of the industrial working class.

The new constitution guaranteed the rights to organize, form unions, bargain collectively, and strike. The 1963 laws on unions, collective bargaining, strike, and lockout imposed some restrictions on exercising these rights. Nonunion, general, political, and solidarity strikes were banned; so also were work slowdowns. Although lockouts were not recognized by the constitution, the new legislation allowed employers to use them. Nonetheless, these legal changes brought Turkey more in line with the ILO conventions and labor standards in other OECD (Organization for Economic Cooperation and Development) countries.

The working class had little to do with the framing of the new constitution. Some union leaders were involved in drafting the constitution not because of demands of the working class but rather because of the paternalistic stance of the political leaders and intellectuals who held power after the 1960 coup. These people believed that it was beneficial for society as a whole for the working class to avoid the prolonged class conflicts that characterized the attainment of the basic rights that had become standard in the West.[22] Moreover, the labor demonstrations that took place between 1961 and 1963 could have influenced only the 1963 laws, which elaborated on the constitutionally recognized rights.

Under the new political-legal framework, ISI was regenerated from the early 1960s onward. The scope of ISI quickly expanded to the production of durable consumer goods and intermediate goods in private as well as state enterprises. Domestic market-oriented industrial production grew at an annual average rate of 6.5 percent over the period, although there were interruptions due to foreign exchange crises in the early and late 1970s.

Parallel to industrialization, there were significant developments in the labor market. First, as the rural-urban shift accelerated, an established urban working class emerged.[23] Rising real wages and improvements in the *gecekondu* standard of living raised the number of permanent industrial workers and weakened their ties with their villages. By the late 1970s, the nonwage incomes of urban wage earners became insignificant, indicating that the separation of urban workers from the land and the means of production was complete. But the extent of dispossession in rural areas in the 1970s is not known because of the prevalence of petty commodity production and because of access to seasonal jobs, especially in construction, in the urban areas.[24]

The second significant labor market development of this period was labor migration to Western Europe to meet the shortage of unskilled, low-paid labor. Rapid emigration in the 1960s, mainly to West Germany, slowed and eventually ceased in the mid-1970s amid worldwide economic stagnation. Initially this migration was presumed to be only temporary, but it became permanent as families joined workers. These workers' remittances significantly affected the Turkish economy and class differentiation. They single-handedly helped the economy weather the foreign exchange crisis of the early 1970s; they helped strengthen small family farms, postponed their dissolution, or gave impetus to large-scale mechanized farming; and they often allowed for the growth of nonagricultural activities in both rural and urban areas.[25]

The third characteristic of the labor market in this period was the relatively low employment creation in manufacturing. Most jobs created were in the service sector and in the informal sector.[26] This trend is explained by the substitution of capital for labor as real wages rose and by the extension of import substitution in the 1970s to the more capital-intensive industries.[27] An associated development was that, as elsewhere, ISI utilized predominantly male labor and did not create many work opportunities for women.[28] The outcome was a male labor movement from leadership to rank and file.

Fourth, a two-tiered labor market structure emerged. The first tier was the modern import-substituting, protected industrial sector, where unionization spread and real wages rose. The second tier of small-scale firms produced intermediate goods and services for the modern sector and cheap consumer goods. These firms were subject to intense competition and low profit margins. This sector was characterized by an informal labor market, where workers were transitory and unorganized, and real wages were low.

Fifth, although private manufacturing grew, the state also expanded its role in manufacturing, especially in intermediate and capital goods production, which meant that about one-half of the industrial labor force was employed in the public sector. This sector was subject to political interference and often turned into a generator of jobs for the supporters of the ruling political party. This rampant featherbedding caused divisions among workers along lines of political party affiliation. Since the conservative Justice Party (JP) or conservative coalitions were in power for much of this period, the ranks of public-sector workers swelled with right-wing partisans, which impeded the emergence of a class- or economic interest–based movement. Furthermore, public-sector workers received higher wages and benefits without much struggle because the public sector was not constrained to be profitable. By contrast, greater militancy distinguished the private-sector workers, who had to drive harder bargains.[29] These characteristics shaped the potential for labor activism in the two sectors.

The political process of ISI was marked by a populism whereby the state took an active role in the distribution of income and the extension of the market.[30] A high real wage was a prerequisite for expanding the domestic market and for ensuring a contented working class. As the largest employer, the state set a high-wage pattern in SEEs. The capitalist class did not raise objections to this regime as long as national income grew at a rapid enough pace. Urban real wages almost doubled from 1960 to 1977, which was an unprecedented rise.[31]

Populism also guaranteed industrialists access to cheap credit, foreign exchange, and tax incentives, which more than counterbalanced wage growth.[32] Without competition from imports, firms were also able to maintain profitability by passing on wage increases to consumers in the form of higher prices.[33] The state also appeased the mass of small agricultural producers, who were incorporated into the expanding domestic market as consumers via favorable agricultural support prices.

By the mid-1970s the limits of ISI were reached; foreign exchange and fiscal crises loomed, hampering the state's distributive functions. After 1977 money wages no longer kept up with accelerating inflation, and real wages declined by 25 percent between 1977 and 1980. In the last years of the decade, disputes between labor and capital and strike activity intensified with an increasing number of workdays lost to strikes.[34]

Flourishing of the Labor Movement

In the liberal atmosphere of the 1960s the political spectrum widened. In 1961, the socialist Turkish Workers' Party (TWP) was formed by leaders of eleven unions, most of which were affiliated with Türk-Is. The party's leadership was composed of union leaders, workers, and intellectuals. Türk-Is voiced vigorous opposition to TWP's formation because its left-wing politics contradicted Türk-Is's proclaimed principles, which disavowed class conflict. Turk-Is leaders joined right-wing politicians in red-baiting TWP. TWP nevertheless gathered significant support in the 1965 elections and elected 15 (of 450) representatives to the National Assembly, the largest contingent of left-wing unionists and intellectuals ever in the parliament. This outcome did not indicate the political awakening of the Turkish working class, however. TWP won only 3 percent of the popular vote, and with the exception of Istanbul, its support was from Alawite and Kurdish constituencies in the least industrialized eastern and southeastern provinces. By 1970, the political effectiveness of TWP waned due to changes in the election system, the founding of another radical party (the Unity Party of Turkey, supported by the Alawite sect), the leftward shift of the RPP, and intra-TWP disputes.[35]

In this period Türk-Is remained the largest labor union confederation. In 1964, Türk-Is articulated its "above political parties" position on the grounds that the existing political parties were not trustworthy and that the Turkish working class was not mature enough to form its own political party.[36] Its leadership, however, supported the right-of-center JP, the successor of the DP, which came to power in the 1965 elections. Several union leaders were elected as representatives in the parliament on the JP lists and led the fight against TWP and RPP in the parliament, championing the ideology of harmony between workers' and employers' interests. Although Türk-Is leaders contemplated the right to stage a general strike, which was banned by law, they never actively pursued the issue even when some RPP representatives favored its legalization.

Türk-Is was not an organization with strict central control, and its leadership and principles came under frequent attack from affiliated unions. Many of these unions acted autonomously in formulating their political strategies.[37] Yet these opposition groups were not able to change the stance of the Türk-Is leadership. Instead, the Türk-Is leadership moved further to the right as a result of the departure, expulsion, or marginalization of the opposition groups.

The most important development on the unionization front was the founding of the Confederation of Revolutionary Workers Unions (DISK) in 1967 by socialist leaders of unions splintered from Türk-Is who were committed to political struggle and active support for political parties sympathetic to workers' interests. There was significant overlap between the founding members of DISK and TWP, and TWP became the voice for DISK in the parliament until its demise in the early 1970s. DISK remained the most active and progressive labor organization until 1980 in spite of the fractious struggles for leadership in the 1970s, which at times produced undemocratic, sectarian practices within the confederation.

Competition between the Türk-Is- and DISK-affiliated unions over membership was intense. Since Türk-Is was already well established in the public sector, DISK made inroads mostly among workers in the private sector. The rivalry between the two confederations reached its peak in 1970 during the parliamentary and public debates over the amendment to the unions law. The amendment aimed to bring the growing and increasingly political labor movement under control by granting Türk-Is the exclusive right to represent labor and some access to policymaking.[38] Its most contentious part was the requirement that to be active nationally, a union or a confederation's membership should exceed one-third of the workers covered by the social security system in its own work branch. Such a rule would have prevented the smaller emerging unions from challenging the preexisting ones. The spokesman of the JP government openly announced that the real motive of the amendment was to eliminate DISK. The General Assembly passed the amendment in spite of the opposition from the TWP and the RPP and sent it to the Senate. Four days later, mass demonstrations known as the June 15–16 incidents took place in Istanbul and Izmit in response to the amendment. Although DISK had initially planned the demonstrations, they started spontaneously in Istanbul out of the control of DISK leaders and with the participation of hundreds of thousands of workers. The significance of this event lies as much in its sheer magnitude as in its expression of the rank and file's outright rejection of the corporatism favored by conservative politicians, union leaders, and business. Political discontent rather than economic concerns motivated the workers. Authorities responded by mobilizing the security forces and the army, and martial law was declared on June 16. In clashes with the security forces, five people died and hundreds were wounded. Twenty-one DISK leaders were arrested for inciting these events but were later released. Although workers were subdued, their discontent was not suppressed and strikes continued. The amendment became law after the Senate passed it in July 1970. Although it had kept quiet during the debates, Türk-Is openly expressed its support for the amendment when TWP and RPP appealed it to the Constitutional Court, where it was struck down in 1972.

Militant leftist university students misread the June 15–16 events as the signal of the readiness of the working class for an armed revolutionary struggle to establish socialism. These students started an urban guerrilla campaign and created a pretext for military intervention, which decimated the left and the labor movement.[39]The intervention began when the General Staff of the armed forces gave an ultimatum to the president of the republic on March 12, 1971, which led to the resignation of the prime minister, Süleyman Demirel, and to the formation of a series of civilian interim governments under the close supervision of the military. Both Türk-Is and DISK initially endorsed the military intervention, but the new regime proved to be hostile to the labor movement. It closed down the TWP and harassed and persecuted the DISK leaders under spurious allegations. The unions law was once again amended, this time to ban union-ization of civil servants. Strikes required the permission of the martial law commander. There was a dramatic decline in the number of strikes and an increase in the number of lockouts between 1972 and 1974.[40] In 1972 and 1973, real wages declined for the first time since the 1950s.

In the early 1970s yet another internal opposition to the Türk-Is leadership emerged, known as the Social Democratic movement. The Social Democrats acknowledged class conflict, but they viewed the paternalistic state as a safeguard of workers' well-being and an arbiter of class conflict. The Social Democratic union leaders supported the left-of-center RPP, and several were elected to the parliament as RPP representatives in the 1973 elections.[41] The Social Democratic movement gained momentum after 1972, reportedly supported by more than 40 percent of the Türk-Is rank and file as well as by some independent unions. Meanwhile the Türk-Is leadership had gradually become critical of the interim regime, reacting to the suppression of the labor movement and deterioration in the standard of living of the working class. In a largely symbolic gesture, it abandoned its own above-political-parties principle in 1976. But the leadership continued the policy of not endorsing political parties and refused to form a new labor party. It also did not tolerate the Social Democratic internal opposition.[42] In 1976 and 1977, the two largest groups of Social Democratic opposition broke off from Türk-Is and joined DISK.

The RPP evolved into a center-left party under the leadership of Bülent Ecevit in the 1970s, who gave voice to the problems of workers and attracted the rank and file and the unions. Although RPP leaders expressed interest in establishing ties with unions and although many unionists (both Social Democrats and DISK members) became active in the party, relations between the party and unions were strained: RPP was ambivalent toward DISK as a class-based organization.[43] Moreover, the economic-austerity measures implemented by the RPP in 1978 were strongly opposed by DISK. Türk-Is began supporting the RPP after the party's success in the 1977 elections; when it demanded exclusive representation rights, however, the RPP declined in order not to alienate DISK. Consequently, Ecevit's attempts to build a coalition with labor within the RPP failed.[44]

Two smaller union confederations formed in this period were the Confederation of Right Workers Unions (Hak-Is), which was associated with the religious-fundamentalist National Salvation Party (NSP), and the Confederation of Nationalist Workers Unions (MISK), which was associated with the ultranationalist pan-Turkist National Movement Party (NMP).[45]

Hak-Is was organized mostly in state enterprises that were controlled by the NSP while it was a coalition partner in the cabinet, and it tried to attract the Türk-Is-affiliated workers. The MISK platform was based on the principle of the commonality of employer and employee interests on the basis of nationality and xenophobia. The fact that both parties were either members of the National Front coalitions or supporters of minority governments between 1975–1980 strengthened these confederations.

In the 1960–1980 period there was a significant increase in unionization. The State Planning Organization puts the number of unionized workers at the end of the 1970s at around 1.5 to 2 million.[46] Türk-Is and DISK accounted for between 800,000 and 1,000,000 and between 400,000 and 600,000 union members, respectively.[47] The State Planning Organization also estimates that 43 percent of the labor force was unionized in 1967 and that this number rose to 57 percent by 1977. Thirty percent of all the wage and salaried workers, all public-sector industries, and all establishments with more than 100 workers were unionized. Unionization did not necessarily help create a working-class identity, however, because traditional networks of kinship, religious sectarianism, regional origin, and ethnicity through which people found entry-level jobs as well as party affiliation survived as sources of division among the workers.[48] Between 1960 and 1980, bread-and-butter issues, namely wages and severance pay, were the greatest concerns of the labor unions in collective bargaining. Although unions attained their goals in these areas, this narrow focus was detrimental to working-class interests. First, it led to the eclipse of other concerns, such as improvement of working conditions, control over the labor process, participation in political activity, education, and legislative changes for meaningful job security or unemployment compensation.

Second, the economic gains made, such as in severance pay, proved to be mixed blessings for workers. Workers viewed severance pay as a substitute for unemployment insurance or job guarantees and pressured unions to negotiate generous compensation. In practice high severance pay led employers to raise labor turnover in order to eliminate the higher paid senior workers and in turn keep severance payments low.[49]

The centrality of collective bargaining to union activity also forced unions to devote their resources to interunion competition over certification issued by the Ministry of Labor. The ministry used size to determine which union it would certify to bargain collectively at each workplace. Unions created fake membership rosters and engaged in prolonged court battles, both of which delayed collective bargaining. Since the ministry made no effort to determine the legitimate representative of the workers, certification was not always granted to the rightful union, which in turn fueled worker mistrust and cynicism toward unions.

The relative ease of collective bargaining in comparison to striving for substantive economic and political rights explains how it became the main union activity. Divisions amongst unions and the publicity over collective-bargaining agreements as a tool in interunion competition also contributed to the neglect of work on the legislative front. Efforts in the latter area were further hampered by the fact that Türk-Is and, to a lesser extent, DISK were not centralized labor organizations and lacked the discipline necessary for mass action and that close ties between unions and political parties did not exist.[50]

1980–1990: Structural Adjustment, Repression, and the Response of Labor

Economic and political adjustments to dismantle ISI and to roll back democratic and labor rights obtained in the previous two decades began in 1980. Facing severe balance-of-payments problems, declining production, and galloping inflation, the government passed a set of economic policy measures on January 24, 1980, following the recommendations of the World Bank and the IMF. These measures targeted the ISI strategy as the source of economic ills and reoriented the economy toward an outward-oriented, export-led growth path. The adjustment required contracting the domestic market and lowering the costs of production via reductions in real wages. The feasibility of these policies and a clear break with the earlier populist economic regime were doubtful given the likely opposition from labor and other social groups that were to bear the burden of adjustment. Under the pretext of putting an end to escalating political strife and violence, the military removed these political obstacles with its September 12, 1980, coup, which suspended the parliament, closed political parties, and curbed union activities. The January 24 program was implemented by the military-dominated cabinet; its architect, Turgut Özal, became the vice-premier responsible for economic affairs.

The military rulers suspended collective bargaining. Between 1981 and 1984 wages were determined exclusively by the Supreme Arbitration Board, which made its decisions on the basis of the government's target inflation rate.[51] Since the actual rate of inflation was always above the target, real wages declined by 17 percent between 1980 and 1986. Wages did not regain their peak 1977 level until 1990.[52]

Structural adjustment in the Turkish economy had significant effects on the labor market structure. Pressures on industries to become competitive internationally gave rise to the expansion of subcontracting by large manufacturing establishments. There were also attempts to reorganize the operation of SEEs according to profitability principles, trim employment, and shut down or privatize some SEEs. Finally, erosion of agricultural incomes due to unfavorable agricultural prices under the new economic strategy gave impetus to accelerated rural-urban migration.[53] These developments, together with workers' attempts to achieve an adequate standard of living, gave rise to the growth of casual, temporary wage employment and self-employment and to increasing informalization of the urban labor market.[54] The ranks of the informal sector were swelled by population growth, rural-urban migration, and absorption of formal-sector workers and members of their families. Working people associated with the informal sector defied working-class characterization and were not disposed to unionization: They saw themselves not as members of a working class but as temporary wage workers, the self-employed, small property holders, even entrepreneurs or just housewives or daughters.[55]

The increase in urban women's labor force participation rates since 1982 is most likely explained by the economic squeeze on the working class and the increasing availability of work under subcontracting arrangements either in small workshops or at home. In view of the invisibility of most of these workers in official statistics, it is difficult to ascertain whether these changes in the employment structure have given rise to a "feminization" of manufacturing employment overall. In the large-scale manufacturing sector, however, there was no feminization of employment under way under the new export-oriented growth strategy, and the traditional industrial working class remained predominantly male.[56]

Repression and Labor's Response

One of the first actions of the 1980 military regime was to crush the labor movement. Unions were accused of a variety of sinister deeds ranging from engaging in terrorist activities and sabotaging the economy via strikes to greedy wage demands that led to inflation and social inequity.[57] Activities of DISK, Hak-Is, and MISK were suspended. In 1981, lawsuits were brought against leaders of DISK and affiliated unions, which covered some 1,400 individuals. They were accused of advocating the domination of one social class over another and attempting to establish the dictatorship of the proletariat and to destroy the constitutional system. DISK property was confiscated well before the end of the trial, and its imprisoned leaders were tortured. In 1986, 264 union leaders were sentenced to up to ten years in prison. These sentences were appealed and reversed by the higher court. DISK resumed its operation again only in 1991.

Hak-Is and MISK were allowed to continue their activities shortly after their suspension in 1980. While the left was subject to persecution, 1980s governments, military and civilian, openly or implicitly supported the Islamic and the ultranationalist movements. These groups gained ground in state institutions throughout the 1980s.[58]

The 1981 constitution, drafted with the help of the Confederation of Turkish Employers Unions, is a testimony to the antilabor bias of the military junta. It banned unions from pursuing political goals, engaging in political activity, and cooperating with political parties, associations, and public and professional organizations.[59] Strikes were legal only when disagreement arose over ongoing collective-bargaining negotiations, not when employers did not abide by an existing agreement. General, solidarity, and political strikes and work slowdowns were also banned.

The unions and the strike, lockout, and collective-bargaining laws of 1983 imposed further restrictions on the labor movement. Some highlights of these laws reveal the straitjacket the labor movement was forced into.[60] To engage in collective bargaining, a union had to obtain membership of 10 percent of workers employed in a branch of industry and 50 percent of workers employed in a given establishment; collective bargaining would not begin until the Ministry of Labor issued certification; only workers who belonged to a union that could bargain collectively could strike; public officials, civil servants, teachers, and workers under the age of sixteen were not allowed to unionize (and hence to strike); individual membership in a union required notarization and notification of the employer within fifteen days; unions were forbidden to engage in political activities; union leaders running for local or national office were suspended from their union positions and, if elected, removed from their positions; · workers with fewer than ten years in a branch of industry could not run for union office; strikes in banking, transportation, petroleum production and distribution, utilities, and educational institutions were banned; the government had the authority to postpone any strike and submit the conflict to the Supreme Arbitration Board; leaders of unions and confederations were not to take part in governing bodies of political parties.[61]

Besides outright repression of union activity, the government and the private firms also used other means to defeat unionization and union activity in the 1980s. First, there were systematic attempts to denigrate unions in the eyes of workers or to make them appear superfluous. The crudest tactic was the junta leader's attempts in the early 1980s to slander all unionists routinely at mass rallies and in radio and television speeches. There were more subtle schemes as well. One was the increasing reliance on subcontracting by private to nonunion workplaces. The other was the emergence after 1984 of contractual workers in the SEEs who were employed for fixed but renewable contract terms. These, at least initially, enjoyed higher wages and salaries but were not allowed to unionize and engage in collective bargaining. In addition, many workers were recategorized as civil servants in the public sector and as a part of management in the private sectors, depriving them of the right to unionize and bargain collectively.

Predictably, Türk-Is was originally supportive of the military regime. It lent its general secretary to the government as the minister of labor and endorsed the 1981 constitution, which drew criticism from international labor organizations. ILO determined that the post-1980 labor legislation, in particular those laws pertaining to political activity, was in conflict with the ILO conventions.[62] ICFTU and the European Trade Unions Confederation distanced themselves from Türk-Is while providing moral support to DISK.

Türk-Is's initial conciliatory stance toward the military regime in the early 1980s gradually turned into condemnation of the economic and social policies pursued by the military and the subsequent civilian Motherland Party (MP) governments. After 1985, in the absence of DISK and in response to growing worker discontent, Türk-Is started becoming more centralized and militant. In the 1987 and 1988 referenda, which turned into votes of confidence for the ruling MP, Türk-Is openly opposed the MP positions. Within the confederation, Türk-Is leaders started questioning the wisdom of their association with right-wing international labor organizations such as the Asia-America Free Labor Institute.[63]

Hak-Is also continued its operations throughout the 1980s. However, Islam as a working-class ideology had a limited appeal. In order to retain its members, Hak-Is sought to establish ties with the ruling MP in the late 1980s and tried to obtain favorable outcomes in collective bargaining in the public sector. MISK faded away as a result of worker disinterest and legislative changes on unions.[64] In 1991 the embattled DISK finally resumed its activities, facing the formidable task of rebuilding after a decade of forced separation from union activity. Whether it will regain its powerful role in the labor movement is yet to be seen.

Lackluster performance of unions in defending workers' rights in the early 1980s and, even worse, their support for the military regime and the new antilabor constitution, resulted in growing worker distrust of unions. Relentless antiunion propaganda by the military and MP governments, and policies such as the creation of the category of contractual workers, also contributed to workers' alienation from unions and the weakening of their union ties. Within this atmosphere workers sought other solutions to their problems: They participated in lotteries (betting and all kinds of games of chance reached unprecedented levels); more family members participated in the labor force in order to make ends meet; and, especially after 1986, innovative methods of labor organizing and resistance emerged.

Developments in the labor movement after 1986 indicate that the activism of workers was far ahead of what the unions were able or willing to undertake. They also signify the declining importance of unions as the organizational vehicle of the labor movement. In the midst of the restrictive milieu, facing many obstacles to staging strikes, workers found various alternatives at the grassroots level to make their voices heard and attract public attention. These included visiting physicians en masse in order to effect work slowdowns, refusing overtime work, staging hunger strikes and lunch boycotts, refusing to shave beards, walking barefoot, handclapping before lunch, and holding rallies.[65] Most of these protests were organized and carried out by workplace committees established by the workers, and not under the direct leadership of unions. These workplace committees failed to establish close ties with unions because of the undemocratic, hierarchical structure and practices of the latter.[66]

These alternative forms of protest also accompanied strikes that increased after 1987 and peaked in spring 1989. The most important strikes were at two public-sector establishments, SEKA in Izmit (paper and paper products) and Zonguldak Coalmines. These labor actions had several features that distinguished them from those before 1980. Workers were now highly politicized, and they recognized that their struggle was against not only the employer but also a state that passed and implemented antilabor legislation. These were relatively spontaneous movements organized not with but in spite of Türk-Is. Workers' protests often targeted Türk-Is leaders alongside the employers and the government.[67] Pre-1980 political divisions among workers weakened as cooperation, including financial assistance networks, expanded. There was also rising support for the labor movement among other social groups, such as shopkeepers and civil servants, who recognized that their economic troubles were not separable from those of the workers.[68] In the 1990s, civil servants whose real earnings had deteriorated continuously also demanded the right to unionize and joined the protests.

The legality of these activities was dubious, but the government was often unable to implement the laws against strikes and demonstrations.

The magnitude of the movement, open support for it by the opposition left-of-center Social Democrat Peoples Party (SDPP) and right-of-center True Path Party (TPP), and the declining popularity of the ruling MP prevented the government from taking punitive actions.

Working-class opposition to the ruling MP was significant in the 1991 elections, which produced the center-right TPP and the center-left SDPP coalition. Workers who blamed the military regime and the following MP governments for their deteriorating living standards had high hopes, expecting a major social and political turnaround. These hopes were dashed, however. Attempts by the coalition's left-wing partner to remove restrictive labor laws were squelched by the right-wing parties.

After 1989, following the rise in strike activity, there were wage hikes in both the public and private sectors. Higher wages were the outcome not only of rising labor activism, union activity, and responsiveness of the last MP government to popular discontent but also of the initial willingness of the private-sector employers, enjoying high profits for nearly a decade, to maintain peaceful industrial relations.[69] Continuing rises in real wages, however, eventually led to employer complaints in the private sector, dismissal of workers, and the further spread of subcontracting.[70] That there was no such flexibility in the public sector, however, exacerbated the fiscal crisis and ultimately led to the implementation of a new set of austerity measures in April 1994 by the coalition government.

The momentum of the late 1980s needed new forms of organization and leadership to turn the grassroots labor activism into a mass movement capable of confronting the capitalist class and the government in order to alter the legal and economic framework set up after 1980. In the absence of such a mass movement, individual actions, at best, improve conditions temporarily for isolated pockets of the working class. Neither unions nor the three left-of-center parties have assumed a leadership role as yet. The latter, preoccupied with inter- and intraparty bickering, lost their credibility and sank in the polls, decimating the left parliamentary opposition in 1993–1994. Unions have no legal way of participating in the political process and also lack credibility in the eyes of workers. The major weakness of the current labor movement is this leadership vacuum.

Bolstered by the state during the 1980s as an instrument against the left, Islamic fundamentalism is now poised to fill this vacuum and shape the future of the labor movement. The religious fundamentalist Welfare Party (WP), the heir to the NSP of the 1970s, took advantage of the changing structure of the working class in the 1980s as well as labor's discontent with the post-1991 coalition government. Besides harping on the alleged deterioration of values and morals, the WP successfully appropriated the Turkish left's antiimperialist slogans of the 1960s and 1970s against the IMF and the World Bank and blamed the external powers and their domestic "collaborators"—which included other parties—as sources of economic and social problems. It also adopted the earlier populist rhetoric of the DP and JP, which espoused the individual's rights and freedoms (with emphasis on religious) vis-à-vis the (secular) state. The informal sector provided an electoral base for the WP. It campaigned in the 1994 local elections under the class-neutral slogan of "just system" and was able to win in the bedrock of the traditional Turkish working class—the industrial regions of Istanbul and Kocaeli. A study of voting patterns between 1987 and 1991 shows that blue-collar households that had moved relatively recently from rural areas or provincial centers were one of the primary supporters of the WP.[71] It is too early to tell whether the support for the WP is a protest vote or a sign of the rising appeal of Islamic fundamentalism among the working class, but it is an unmistakable manifestation of the leadership vacuum in the labor movement.

The alternative ideology from the right is ultranationalism, once promoted primarily by the pan-Turkist NMP. Since 1923 nationalism has been used to veil class conflict. In its current incarnation, this ideology promotes an authoritarian state in the political arena and free reign of capitalism in the economy. The former component has been popular among the provincial petty bourgeoisie and urban marginals since the 1970s. Ultranationalism is increasingly finding approval among the non-fundamentalist conservative politicians and businessmen, especially against the backdrop of the escalating Kurdish insurgency in eastern Turkey. This ideology may become the common denominator for the nonfundamentalist conservative political parties that are committed to the post-1980 economic model and for the capitalist class in its demands for a docile, low-wage labor force. Both of these oppose changes in the restrictive legal framework toward expansion of labor's rights and democratization. It is yet to be seen whether chauvinistic nationalism will become more influential among the working class as the informal sector expands and whether it will fragment the working class along ethnic lines.

Conclusion

Whether workers' rights were given from above by the government or won through hard-fought struggles has been a central and emotional debate within the Turkish left.[72] Our examination shows that the labor movement was hardly influential in the broadening of democratic rights and the acquisition of workers' rights in the turning points of the 1946 transition to a multiparty system, the 1950 elections, and the 1960 coup.

It was the paternalistic state that recognized and broadened workers' rights even in the absence of a strong labor movement. Several considerations motivated those in political power. The recognition of a limited set of workers' rights in the late 1940s and the 1950s is attributable to the ruling parties' desire to tame and harness labor and to control it as an electoral bloc. Post-1961 prolabor changes in legislation were the outcome of attempts by paternalistic-progressive groups among the drafters of the 1961 constitution and in the subsequent government who wanted the Turkish working class to enjoy the labor rights that had become standard in the West.

We have traced the sources of the lack of agitation by the working class for the expansion of labor rights and its limited struggle against labor repression to the interaction of the ISI strategy with inherited paternalistic state traditions and to the nonfeudal, smallholder structure in agriculture. There was limited proletarianization under the state-led ISI until the early 1960s, when labor rights were obtained. Isikli argues that the Turkish working class received the right to bargain collectively at an earlier stage compared to its Western counterparts, and its scale of unionization was large in proportion to its size and power.[73] Thus, it lacked the experience and maturity of its Western counterparts, requisite to the development of class identity and consciousness.

The lack of cohesion of workers around class interests was a persistent problem of the Turkish labor movement. Workers identified themselves often by ethnic, religious, regional, or political party affiliation rather than as members of the same class. The state's extensive involvement in industrial production under ISI and the consequent division between public- and private-sector workers and bargaining patterns also hindered unified action. Even when it had growing strength in numbers, the labor movement did not act in a unified way to obtain the right to stage general strikes, to have unemployment insurance, or to remove the ban on political activity by unions. The majority of unionized workers were associated with Türk-Is and were absent at the peak of labor militancy on June 15–16, 1970. Due to unwilling or weak leadership and loose central control, union confederations were incapable of articulating and pursuing long-term economic and political objectives. The pursuit of short-term economic gains that could be met within the ISI framework, then, became the primary function of unions to the exclusion of political, legislative, and educational concerns.

The absence of class cohesion is also revealed by the post-1980 unraveling of the labor movement. The military junta did not meet much resistance when it jailed labor leaders, terminated union activity, and passed legislation that abolished the rights obtained in the 1960–1980 period. Workers' responses, or the lack thereof, are attributable in large part to the formidable power of the military. Many individual workers may have also overlooked the economic and political ramifications of the new political system and supported the junta in anticipation of an end to urban terrorism. Nonetheless, the military's successful neutralization of the labor movement was in no small measure due to persistent intraclass divisions, lack of leadership, and cynicism among workers about unions.

By contrast, the labor activism that erupted after 1987 revealed more unity and political consciousness than ever. Unions were the followers of this movement rather than its architects. This spontaneity may be taken to be the indicator of rising class consciousness, a maturing of the labor movement, and labor's transformation into an active agent of social change. Indeed, Ahmad concludes an essay on the Turkish labor movement on a cautiously optimistic note in light of these events.[74] However, this grassroots activism came into being at a time when the very existence of the traditional industrial working class was threatened by ongoing economic adjustments. Moreover, the growth of the informal sector recasts the identity and political choices of the working class. In view of these changes and with the benefit of hindsight, we conclude that prospects for a regenerated working-class movement in Turkey are uncertain. As anticipated by Bianchi in the late 1970s, the current rapid social change in Turkey and the attendant cleavages within the political right and the left render the societal corporatist solution to manage conflict of interest no longer viable.[75] If the working-class movement can coalesce within itself and with other progressive groups and political parties of the left, it can form a powerful bloc for democratization and for the expansion of economic and political rights. The increasingly diversified and ambiguous nature of the working class and the obsolescence of unions are only two of the hurdles on the path of this project. In the absence of leadership to articulate objectives and to shape and develop the means toward these ends for the whole working class, the spontaneous growth of labor action may dissipate and members of the working class may find themselves at the mercy or even supportive of either the secular-ultranationalist or the religious variants of state authoritarianism.

Notes

We would like to thank Korkut Ertürk, Ellis Goldberg, and Peter Philips for comments and suggestions.

1. We do not contend that this model is the norm from which Turkish experience deviates; indeed, the classic model may be a special case. For our purposes it serves as a theoretical benchmark and an entry point to the analysis of labor and labor movements.

2. Feroz Ahmad, "The Development of Working-Class Consciousness in Turkey," in Zachary Lockman (ed.), *Workers and Working Classes in the Middle East* (Albany: SUNY Press, 1994).

3. Çaglar Keyder, *Ulusal kalkinmaciligin iflasi* (Istanbul: Metis Yayinlari, 1993), 75–77.

4. The average size of a manufacturing establishment was only 2.3 workers. Even in 1927, more than 70 percent of the establishments employed less than four workers. Alpaslan Isikli, "Wage Labor and Unionization," in I. C. Schick and A. Tonak (eds.), *Turkey in Transition: New Perspectives* (New York and Oxford: Oxford University Press, 1987), 312.

5. Sevket Pamuk, "War, State Economic Policies and Resistance by Agricultural Producers in Turkey, 1939–1945," *New Perspectives on Turkey* 2, 1. (Spring 1988): 19–36.

6. Yildirim Koç, "Türkiye'de ücretlilerin mali durumu," *11. Tez*, no. 2 (1986): 163–164; Yildirim Koç, "Isçi haklari ve sendikacilik," *11. Tez*, no. 5 (1987):45.

7. Sevket Pamuk, "Long Term Trends in Urban Real Wages in Turkey, 1850–1990," in P. Sholliers and V. Zamagni (eds.), *Labour's Reward, Real Wages and Economic Change in Nineteenth and Twentieth Century Europe* (Cheltenham, UK: Edward Elgar, 1994).

8. Koç, "Isçi haklari," 64.

9. See Isikli, "Wage Labor and Unionization," 310; and Ahmad, "Working-Class Consciousness in Turkey."

10. Alpaslan Isikli, *Sendikacilik ve siyaset*, 4th ed. (Istanbul: Imge Kitabevi, 1990), 314.

11. Bans on the rights to unionize, bargain collectively, and strike remained in place in spite of the fact that Turkey had become an ILO member in 1932 and ratified ILO conventions.

12. See Koç, "Isçi haklari," 65; and Isikli, "Wage Labor and Unionization," 314.

13. Sehmus Güzel, "Türkiye'de isçi hareketi ve tarihi," *11. Tez*, no. 8 (1988), draws the opposite conclusion.

14. The RPP's other attempts to gather electoral support in the late 1940s included new legislation on occupational diseases, work injuries, and maternity benefits and the establishment of the Ministry of Labor.

15. For a discussion of the appeal of the DP to the electorate, especially the peasantry, see Resat Kasaba, "Populism and Democracy in Turkey," in Ellis Goldberg, et al. (eds.), *Rules and Rights in the Middle East* (Seattle: University of Washington Press, 1993).

16. *Gecekondu* means "landed overnight." The living standards in these neighborhoods, however, were never as poor as those in the notorious slums of the Third World (such as the *favelas* in Brazil or the slums of Manila).

17. Pamuk, "Long Term Trends."

18. Yildirim Koç, "Sendikalarin bagimsizligi, ABD ve türk-is," *11. Tez*, no. 3 (1986):254–257.

19. Isikli, *Sendikacilik ve siyaset*, 325.

20. Robert Bianchi, *Interest Groups and Political Development in Turkey* (Princeton: Princeton University Press, 1984), 215.

21. Ibid.

22. Alpaslan Isikli, "Türkiye'de isçi hareketinin bati isçi hareketi karsisinda özgünlügü," *11. Tez*, no. 5 (1987):26–27.

23. During the 1960–1980 period the urbanization rate rose from 32 to 44 percent and the share of agriculture in the economically active population declined from 75 to 58 percent.

24. Koç, "Türkiye'de ücretlilerin," 166–168.

25. Some immigrant workers also used their savings to set up their own businesses upon their return rather than take up wage employment. The impetus in the 1980s was retirement or financial incentives provided by the West German government.

26. Between 1960 and 1980, the share of manufacturing in the economically active population rose from 6.8 to 11 percent; the share of services in the economically active population tripled from 5.2 to 15.6 percent.

27. See Fikret Senses, "Labour Market Response to Structural Adjustment and Institutional Pressures: The Turkish Case," *METU Studies in Development* 21, 3 (1994).

28. Between 1964 and 1982, women's share of manufacturing employment in large workplaces remained relatively constant, about 20 percent in the private sector and 14 percent in the public sector. The difference between the two sectors is explained by different sectoral characteristics, such as greater capital intensity in public-sector production. See Nilüfer Çagatay and Günseli Berik, "Transition to Export-led Growth in Turkey: Is There a Feminization of Employment?" *Review of Radical Political Economics* 22, 1 (1990).

29. Bianchi, *Interest Groups*, 230.

30. For a detailed account of the role of the state in the management of the economy see Çaglar Keyder, "Economic Development and Crisis: 1950–80," in Schick and Tonak, *Turkey in Transition*.

31. However, we should note that especially in the public sector, productivity growth outstripped wage growth in this period, leading to an actual decline in the share of wages in national income. See Korkut Boratav, "Import Substitution and Income Distribution Under a Populist Regime: The Case of Turkey," *Development Policy Review* 4, 127 (1986); and Nurcan Özkaplan, *Sendikalar ve ekonomik etkileri: Türkiye üzerine bir deneme* (Istanbul: Kavram, 1994), 109.

32. Boratav, "Import Substitution and Income Distribution," 127–128.

33. This is not to say that employers always acquiesced to unionization and union demands. Employers often fired militant workers who chose unions of which they did not approve; they were fully cognizant of the fact that it was costly for workers to sue and that even if employers were found guilty, fines were small. See Sükran Ketenci, "Isçiler ve Çalisma yasami: 1980'lerde sinirlar ve sorunlar," in *Birakiniz Yapsinlar birakiniz geçsinler: türkiye ekonomisi 1980–1985* (Istanbul: Bilgi, 1985), 161–163.

34. In 1980, there was a record level of 227 strikes (30 in the public sector and 197 in the private sector) involving 36,216 workers, with 5,778,205 workdays lost. See Özkaplan, *Sendikalar ve ekonomik erkileri*, 124.

35. Ahmet Samim, "The Left," in Schick and Tonak, *Turkey in Transition*.

36. Isikli, *Sendikacilik ve siyaset*, 354–355.

37. In the 1960s and 1970s, a number of Türk-Is-affiliated union leaders were elected representatives in the RPP. See ibid., 342.

38. Bianchi, *Interest Groups*, 247–248.

39. See Samim, "The Left," 159.

40. There were 14 strikes in 1972, 22 in 1973, and 45 in 1974, in contrast to the peak level of 101 in 1970 and 97 in 1971.

41. Yildirim Koç, "Türkiye'de sosyal demokrasi, ve sendikacilik," *11. Tez*, no. 4:126–127; Isikli, *Sendikacilik ve siyaset*, 374, 377–379; Bianchi, *Interest Groups*, 239.

42. Isikli, *Sendikacilik ve siyaset*, 46–47.

43. Koç, "Türkiye'de sosyal demokrasi," 126–127.

44. Bianchi, *Interest Groups*, 247–248.

45. The Turkish word "Hak" means both "right" and "God."

46. Isikli, "Wage Labor and Unionization," 322. These estimates are much lower than the official statistics on union membership reported by the Ministry of Labor, which reached 5.7 million by 1980. Post-1967 (after the formation of DISK) official statistics on unionization are misleading because membership in more than one union was allowed and unions inflated their rosters with fake members in order to gain certification from the Ministry of Labor.

47. Alpaslan Isikli, "DISK sendikal tercihini bati avrupa sendikaciligi olarak yapmistir," *11. Tez*, no. 7:322.

48. Bianchi, *Interest Groups*, 191. On the social significance of these traditional networks see also Kasaba, "Populism and Democracy," 58–59.

49. Ketenci, "Isçiler ve çalisma yasami," 163–164.

50. Koç, "Isçi haklari," 59–60.

51. There were no strikes between 1981 and 1983 and only 4 in 1984, in contrast to the peak number of 227 strikes in 1980.

52. In order to show evenhandedness, the military regime initially also banned the dismissal of workers, but this restriction was removed subsequently.

53. Between 1980 and 1990, the urbanization rate rose from 44 to 59 percent. The share of agriculture in the economically active population continued its decline, from 58 to 52 percent; manufacturing and services increased their shares, from 11 to 12.6 percent and from 15.6 to 17.3 percent, respectively.

54. Keyder, *Ulusal kalkinmaciligin iflasi*, 75–77.

55. Despite their increasing entry into wage employment, due to the intermittent, short-term, low-income, and oftentimes home-based nature of their employment, the 1980s and 1990s cohort of women workers are unlikely to identify themselves as "workers." See Jenny B. White, "Linking the Urban Poor to the World Market: Women and Work in Istanbul," *Middle East Report*, no. 173 (1991); and E. Mine Çinar, "Unskilled Urban Migrant Women and Disguised Employment: Home-working Women in Istanbul, Turkey," *World Development* 22, 3 (1994).

56. Nilüfer Çagatay and Günseli Berik, "What Has Export-Oriented Manufacturing Meant for Turkish Women?" in P. Sparr (ed.), *Mortgaging Women's Lives: Feminist Critiques of Structural Adjustment* (London: Zed Press, 1994).

57. These charges were made in spite of the fact that real wages had been declining since 1977. Assassinations of union leaders (including the president of DISK) and prolabor intellectuals and the armed attacks on the May 1 demonstrators, whose perpetrators were never found, also indicate that the working class was more a target of terrorist activities in the late 1970s than a supporter.

58. The asymmetry was so glaring that the jailed leader of the ultranationalist NMP, Alpaslan Türkes, complained: "Our ideas are in power, but we are in jail."

59. Isikli, *Sendikacilik ve siyaset*, 22.

60. For details of the post-1980 legislation see Ketenci, "*Isçiler ve çalisma yasami*"; and Sehmus Güzel, "1980 sonrasinda isçi haklarinda gerilemeler," *11. Tez*, no. 5 (1987).

61. Post-1980 legislation was not limited to these restrictions. A variety of other laws, including the martial law, penal code, labor law, meeting and demonstration law, free trade zones law, state security court law, and associations law, further restricted the freedom to organize and unionize.

62. Isikli, *Sendikacilik ve siyaset*, 24.

63. Ibid., 27.

64. Yildirim Koç, *Türkiye isçi sinifi tarihinden yapraklar* (Istanbul: Ataol Yayincilik, 1992), 314–329.

65. Yildirim Koç, *Günümüzde isçi sinifi ve sendikalar* (Istanbul: Metis Yayinlari, 1989), 67–84.

66. Yildirim Koç, *Isçi sinifi ve sendikacilik hareketinin güncel sorunlari* (Istanbul: Ataol Yayincilik, 1991).

67. Ahmad, "Working Class Consciousness in Turkey," 157–158.

68. Koç, *Isçi sinifi ve sendikacilik.*

69. Senses, "Labour Market Response," 50.

70. Ibid., 55; Özkaplan, *Sendikalar ve ekonomik erkileri.*

71. These blue-collar workers were born in provincial centers or villages, and their fathers were farmers or agricultural workers. Interestingly, medium to large employers emerged as the other important supporter of the WP. Korkut Boratav, Bahattin Aksit, and Bilsay Kuruc, *Political Economy of Structural Adjustment* (Turkish Social Science Association, 1993), 167.

72. The debate over these questions leads to sterile polemics when it is reduced to caricatures such as "The Turkish working class was indulged by benevolent governments and therefore failed to mature enough to be willing and capable of exercising the rights provided in the 1961–1980 period" (and the sometimes implied corollary that it does not deserve these rights) or "Worker rights were obtained as a result of struggles by the Turkish working class, which fought heroically against the powers that tried to repress it every step of the way." Indeed, many participants in the debate attempt to distance themselves, albeit not always successfully, from the crude versions of these theses and acknowledge the complexity of the dynamics of acquisition of workers' rights. See, for instance, the exchange between Güzel ("Türkiye'de isçi hareketi,") and Koç ("Isçi haklari tartismasi") in *11. Tez*, no. 8 (1988).

73. Isikli, "Wage Labor and Unionization."

74. Ahmad, "Working-Class Consciousness in Turkey."

75. Bianchi, *Interest Groups*, 342.

Making History, but Not of Their Own Choosing: Workers and the Labor Movement in Iran

Valentine M. Moghadam

The historiography and sociology of the labor movement and the working class in Iran have been the focus mainly of left-wing and Marxist scholarship.[1] These writings often sought to establish a relationship between the formation of the working class and the development of capitalism in Iran, the links between the labor movement and the strength of communist parties, and the role of the working class in the 1978–1979 Iranian Revolution and afterward.

There was a political motivation to these studies, one that sought to establish the viability of the socialist project as an alternative to both monarchism and Islamism. The 1970s and 1980s were especially productive for Marxist scholarship, but the 1990s have seen a number of studies that contribute to the scholarship even while criticizing some of the earlier writings.[2] Non-Marxist scholarship on Iranian labor also provides detailed descriptions of labor unions and the social conditions within which they operated.[3] Recurrent themes in the literature are the horrific conditions of the working class, the organizing efforts of the left, periodic bouts of labor militancy, and state repression. Primary sources include the detailed reports of British labor attachés in the 1940s and early 1950s on the trade unions and the Tudeh Party, compiled in the British Foreign Office Records; reports by the labor attachés of the U.S. embassy; and the documents by socialist and labor leaders compiled by Chosroe Chaquerie.

This scholarship is less prolific than labor studies in other countries, and we lack the rich materials that exist on the laboring classes of, for example, England, France, and Germany. The existing literature does, however, provide the basis for a social history of the Iranian labor movement and an analysis of its travails, which is my object here.

Iran experienced a social revolution that culminated in the establishment of the Islamic Republic in February 1979. During the 1980s the scholarship on the revolution provided differing analyses of its causes and of the social forces involved. Because so many studies now sought to underscore the centrality of the Shi'i clergy in the making of the revolution or to emphasize cultural, religious, and ideological variables in the causes, course, and outcome of the revolution, those who wrote within the Marxist or socialist tradition were implicitly and sometimes overtly challenged to provide alternative explanations or to defend the Marxist categories of class, capitalism, and class conflict. For example, Said Amir Arjomand expressly rules out a role for workers in the Iranian Revolution and is highly critical of the Iranian left (and others, including the entire middle class) for irrationally paving the way for Khomeini by rejecting the shah.[4] The prolabor point of view has therefore had to contend with and respond to this trend by clarifying the role of the left and by, once again, documenting the importance of the workers' movement.[5] Within the left there has also been a debate, especially concerning the role and significance of the workers' councils during and after the revolution. This debate, which I discuss further on, has involved, among others, myself, Assef Bayat, and Saeed Rahnema.

Here I examine the trajectory of the labor movement in Iran in the twentieth century with an emphasis on left-wing organizing efforts, industrialization patterns, and the power of the state. The labor movement and trade unionism began in Iran when communists attempted to organize labor in the first half of the twentieth century in the context of state-led industrialization. Trade unionism, labor militancy, and left-wing organizing correlated with the weakness of the state. The course of independent trade unionism and labor militancy was interrupted at least twice, once by Reza Shah in the 1930s and then by the Shah-CIA coup d'état of 1953.

From the 1950s to the 1970s Iran was characterized by an increasingly strong and centralized imperial state system, import-substitution industrialization, accelerated oil production and exports, importation of technology and industrial products, and large expenditures on military imports. Among the implications for the labor force were the growth of a modern industrial proletariat in key industries (steel, oil, transportation, public utilities), strict state regulation of labor unions, expansion of small-scale manufacturing, and the creation of a female labor force in the small-scale manufacturing sector and in the government-public sector. Rising oil revenues and investment in infrastructure development and in manufacturing greatly accelerated the process of urban industrialization, rural transformation, and proletarianization.

Industrial transformation and proletarianization resulted in growing labor militancy in the 1970s. The labor movement was adversely affected by the uneven pattern of development, including the persistence of traditional means and relations of production, the small size of the modern working class, and the absence of independent labor organizations and continuous trade unionism. I will show that workers played a significant role in the Iranian Revolution of 1977–1979, but the pattern of industrialization and proletarianization had retarded the development of a strong working-class movement and led many workers to identify with Islamic populism. This is the sense in which the Iranian labor movement made history in late-twentieth-century Iran, but within a historical legacy of a discontinuous movement and the structural constraints of uneven socioeconomic development.

The Reza Shah Era

The roots of the Iranian working class lie in halfhearted modernization efforts of the Qajar rulers in the nineteenth century, but expansion of the industrial working class occurred only in the 1930s. Industrial workers remained a tiny proportion of an overwhelmingly agrarian society. The first socialist movement in the Middle East—and the first communist party in Asia—emerged in Iran. The first trade unions in Iran organized the embryonic working class in 1906, and by 1922 over 20,000 workers were unionized under socialist leadership. The migration of thousands of workers from the Baku oil fields and other industries in Russia after the 1917 revolution contributed to the political development of the nascent Iranian working class. This led to the growth of a trade union movement in Iran that was so active in the 1920s that Willem Floor calls the years 1918–1925 "the golden age" of the Iranian labor movement.

Reza Shah initiated reforms that resulted in the establishment of a centralized army and state bureaucracy, the development of modern industry, heavy investments in infrastructure (especially railroads and communications), and the establishment of secular educational institutions. State projects included the Trans-Iranian Railway, new ports, 12,000 miles of roads, and modern factories. Foreign investment was not entirely discouraged, but neither was it courted. Because capital investment from indigenous private sources was difficult to arrange in a context where bazaar attitudes were prevalent, Reza Shah used the state as an active investor.

In 1925 Iran had fewer than 20 modern industrial plants, only 5 of which had more than fifty workers. By 1941 the country had over 346 modern industrial plants, which included 146 major installations such as textile mills, match factories, sugar refineries, chemical plants, modern glassworks, and tea- and tobacco-processing plants. All industrial enterprises, with the exception of a few privately owned textile mills, were owned and operated by the state. As a result of this industrialization drive, the number of workers employed in large modern factories increased from fewer than 1,000 in 1925 to more than 50,000 in 1941.[6]

The working class further expanded when the oil labor force grew from 20,000 to nearly 31,000, but also when many small workshops, especially shoe factories, carpentry stores, and tailoring shops, merged to form larger workshops employing over 30 workers. By 1941 wage earners in the large modern factories, transportation, fishing, and the oil installations totaled over 170,000. Roughly half of these were textile workers, and state-financed textile factories remained the largest. The rest of the labor force was either in agriculture or in small cottage industries. Thus, at this time the industrial working class constituted about 2 percent of the total labor force.[7]

Workers initiated strikes over wages, but working conditions and disputes were frequently decided by repression. In 1931 Reza Shah turned against the trade unions and their leaders and banned "collectivist" discourse and organizing altogether. This labor law had no provisions for strikes or trade unions but was limited to working conditions in industrial establishments. The working class was subject to repression but grew rapidly as a result of Reza Shah's policies. In Gilan, Mashhad, Tabriz, Abadan, Tehran, and Isfahan, the Communist Party of Iran (CPI) organized unions and workers protested against the unjust conditions of the workplace. Floor writes that the passage of an anticommunist bill in June 1931 that forbade the formation of trade unions, and the arrest of more than 2,000 CPI or suspected CPI members, "had grave results for the activities of the unions which, as we have seen, were in fact creations of the CPI."[8]

Floor argues that size and composition affected working-class capacities. There were few factories employing more than 500 workers and "a considerable share of the industrial labor force had not been divorced from its traditional agricultural and pastoral pursuits." The prevalence of female and child labor, especially in the textiles (including rug-making) industry and the high rates of illiteracy also served to explain the absence of independent labor organizations.[9]

Reza Shah's rapprochement with the Axis led the Allied powers to occupy Iran in 1941 and force him to abdicate in favor of his son, Mohammad Reza Pahlavi. The interregnum was remarkable in many ways. First, it was a period of relative political freedom with a proliferation of political parties and lively publications. Second, trade unionism revived and, due primarily to the efforts of the Tudeh (Communist) Party, expanded into the largest labor confederation in Asia. Third, Iranian industry, particularly the manufacturing sector, grew considerably. As a consequence, Iran's first development plan was implemented in 1949. Fourth, the oil sector took on greater significance, and the first plan was to be financed chiefly by oil revenues. Fifth, the growth of industry and the labor movement in Azerbaijan converged with the long-standing national question to create an autonomous republic led by an indigenous progressive party, the Fergheh Demokrat. Finally, a nationalist movement emerged largely to contest control over Iranian oil. An intense struggle with profound implications for postwar geopolitical hegemony and for the labor movement, democratization, and modernization took place between Iran, Britain, and the United States.

The Oil Industry and the Labor Movement, 1941–1953

The oil industry played an important role in the history of industrialization and the labor movement in Iran. Iranian oil was discovered in 1908 by a British company. To ensure an adequate supply for its fleet, the British government purchased a majority share in the Anglo-Persian Oil Company in 1914. Although the name was changed to the Anglo-Iranian Oil Company (AIOC) in 1938, it remained an essentially British enterprise. During World War II, as military demand rose, both producing and refining facilities were enlarged with U.S. lend-lease funds. After the war, production continued its rapid expansion, rising to more than 70,000 barrels per day by the beginning of 1951 and accounting for nearly half of all Middle East production at that time.[10]

The oil industry was still quite labor intensive in 1951, when the number of oil workers in the Khuzestan oil fields had reached 55,000. A further 15,000 were working for employers who received contract work from AIOC. Khuzestan was one of the least urbanized areas of Iran at the time, but as a result of oil no fewer than eight separate towns came into existence.

The largest, Abadan, site of the refinery, grew from a fishing village of a few hundred in 1900 to a city of 170,000 in the late 1940s. Virtually the whole population depended directly or indirectly on the oil company for employment. Abadan, like the oil industry itself, was entirely an enclave. There was not even a bridge connecting Abadan with Khorramshahr—merely a ferry.

The workforce in the oil industry was segmented into three groups. The majority were unskilled laborers recruited locally from the Arab tribes of Khuzestan or from the Bakhtiari nomads of the surrounding mountains. At the end of 1949 an estimated 33,000 out of 38,000 employees at Abadan were wage earners of this kind; in the fields themselves, 15,000 out of 17,000 fell into this category. Unskilled workers were involved in construction, maintenance, transportation, loading, and work on pipelines. The production and refining processes were sufficiently automated even then such that only a small number of skilled workers were required who were frequently recruited from Tehran and Isfahan.

The next group was a layer of technical and clerical workers, many of whom were first brought from India. As Iranian nationalist protests increased, the company established technical schools, trained a larger number of local personnel, and recruited Iranians for these jobs. On top was a level of managerial and engineering staff. At first, these were mainly British, but gradually Iranian engineers replaced them. After the nationalization of oil the number of foreign personnel in the oil industry fell substantially.[11]

Labor organizers and radical intellectuals released from prison in 1941 almost immediately set about reviving the trade union movement. During 1942, they focused their energies on the factories and workshops of Tehran, the coalfields nearby, and the textile mills of Mazanderan and Gilan. During 1943, they turned their attention to winning over independent unions that had sprung up in Tabriz, Mashhad, Rasht, and among textile workers in Isfahan. In May 1944, the CCFTU was formed.[12] The British labour attaché wrote that "33 Unions with a total of 275,000 are affiliated to the Central Council of Iranian Trade Unions." Almost every trade was represented in the membership lists, from oil workers (45,000), railwaymen (20,000), and spinners and weavers (40,000) to "carpets (home workers)" (20,000) and workers in public baths (1,500).[13] The leadership of the early labor movement was not primarily workers, for as Habib Ladjevardi notes, "Not only were all the founders of the Central Council members of the Tudeh Party, but three-fourths of them were intellectuals rather than workers."[14]

During the 1940s, the CCFTU was a vital and militant union. Apart from the general relaxation following Reza Shah's abdication, several factors favored trade union organization: (1) the need for collective action to secure wage increases; (2) employers' concessions to organized labor to avoid shutdowns because wartime profits were high; (3) an increase in industrial employment; (4) the exposure of Iranian labor, in the areas occupied by Soviet forces, to communist labor organizers; and (5) fear of layoffs following the war when unemployment was widespread. Floor provides another reason: "The new class of managers . . . were, with few exceptions, totally indifferent to the safety and health of their workers." He cites a British observer: "The employers feel somewhat outraged that such important persons as themselves should be treated in this disrespectful way by mere workers."[15]

The right of workers to organize was first recognized by the labor law of 1946. Until 1944, the Civil Employment Act of 1922 and a series of laws dealing with workmen's compensation in various industries were the sole labor legislation. In 1944, the Directorate General of Labor was established within the Ministry of Trade and Industry. In 1946 the first general labor law was promulgated by the Council of Ministers. The law covered almost every aspect of the working conditions of laborers in Iran and made detailed provisions in respect of hours of work, rest and recreation, holidays and leave, sickness and unemployment insurance, conditions of work inside the factories, safety measures, employment of women and children, minimum wage, trade unions, strikes, and settlement of disputes. Article 15 established a tripartite High Labor Council, and Article 16 described the Workers' Aid Fund and Insurance.

The law was "hastily drafted and established by decree following a serious general strike,"[16] and it was circumvented by employers as much as possible. An American labor observer wrote that "Iranian employers look upon the labor laws with contempt and as manifestations of government weakness."[17]

The labor movement peaked in May and June 1946, when oil workers went on strike. In July Khuzestan was engulfed by a general strike of 65,000 workers that has been called the largest industrial strike in Middle Eastern history.[18] In the summer of that year when a Tudeh leader became minister of trade and industry, the CCFTU claimed 335,000 members and it became a member of the communist-led World Federation of Trade Unions (WFTU). The central government and various social groups reacted with anxiety and hostility. Tribal leaders in the south, spurred by the AIOC, agitated against the Tudeh Party and the CCFTU. Tudeh Party sympathy for Azerbaijani autonomy heightened government suspicions. Forced to choose sides, the central government moved against the Tudeh

Party and the CCFTU in October 1946. Repression culminated in the banning of the party and the union in 1949 following an assassination attempt on the shah.[19]

Four significant factors undermined the labor movement. The underdeveloped nature of Iranian society, characterized by an industrial labor force that constituted a tiny percentage of the population, was one reason. The ability of the central government to deploy the army against striking workers and the revolt of the large tribes, especially the Qashqa'i against the "atheistic" Tudeh Party are two more. Finally, the isolation of the Arab population from Tudeh and trade union activities increased its susceptibility to the machinations of its chiefs and sheikhs. For all its apparent strength, the labor movement could not oppose the intrigues and subterfuges of the various interregnum governments. When the Tudeh Party was banned and its most active cadres imprisoned or forced underground, the labor movement was unable to carry on—until 1951.

In March 1951 oil workers struck to protest a cut in wages unilaterally ordered by the AIOC. By April 1, most of the 45,000 workers were out. AIOC rescinded the cuts, but when workers returned, company managers declared they would not be paid for the three weeks they had been absent. A general strike was called throughout Khuzestan, and the demand escalated to nationalize the oil industry. The popularity of the Tudeh Party was sufficient to gain a crowd of 100,000 on one occasion, whereas the National Front had attracted only 10,000.

Nationalist concentration on oil was stimulated by the AIOC's payment of more in British taxes than in royalties, by Iran's lack of control over the AIOC's accounting procedures, by royalty terms hit by inflation, and by the better terms offered by U.S. companies in Saudi Arabia and Venezuela. Nor were workers satisfied with their conditions. British embassy reports describe their complaints regarding the minimum wage, high rents, and inadequate supplies of food. In 1950 the International Labor Organization (ILO), at the invitation of the Iranian government, sent a mission to investigate labor conditions in the AIOC. The report was not conclusive, although working conditions would later be cited in partial justification for the nationalization of the petroleum industry in 1951.[20]

In March 1951 the Majlis (unicameral parliament) nationalized AIOC's operations. As in the late Qajar protest movements, the oil nationalization movement represented the bazaar classes of merchants and guildspeople, along with an anti-imperialist ulama and a liberal section of the landed classes, represented, for example, by Muhammad Mossadegh, who became premier in May. As in the 1979 revolution, the movement was joined by members of the new middle and working classes and by the majority of

Iranian intellectuals. The government created the National Iranian Oil Company (NIOC) to take over the nationalized properties, including the Abadan refinery, then the world's largest, as well as the oil fields. The new company immediately encountered the refusal of the established international oil companies to process or market nationalized oil. Despite the consequent loss of a major source of revenue and employment, by 1952 about 10,000 more factories of all sizes had been established in the country than existed in 1948.[21] Mossadegh's government had encouraged small indigenous industries by introducing protective measures and a favorable exchange policy raising the domestic prices of imported commodities. As a result, the manufacturing industry began a period of rapid growth.

Nonetheless, the active opposition of the British and the ensuing problems played into the hands of Dr. Mossadegh's domestic enemies. The crisis culminated in the coup d'état of August 1953, which overthrew the Mossadegh government, outlawed the Tudeh Party, and returned Mohammad Reza Pahlavi to the throne with greatly enhanced powers. Despite the fall of Mossadegh, Iranian oil remained in the possession of the state as the National Iranian Oil Company. On October 30, 1954, British Petroleum, the Compagnie Française des Pétroles, Royal Dutch/ Shell, Standard Oil of New Jersey, Socony-Vacuum Oil, Standard Oil of California, Gulf Oil, and the Texas Oil Company reached an agreement to market Iranian oil. Informally they were called "the Consortium."

Labor After the Coup

The labor situation changed drastically following the overthrow of Mossadegh and the restoration of royal power. In September 1953, the Office of the Military Governor of Tehran—predecessor to SAVAK (the secret police)—announced that a Tudeh Party network and a cache of weapons had been found. In October 1954 the first of a series of executions of Tudeh army officers began. In March 1955 some thirty-five leaders of the Tehran Provincial Council of the CCFTU were arrested.[22] Factories began to be policed, and in the virulently anti-Tudeh and anti–National Front atmosphere, the incidence of strikes plummeted. The government finally moved to disband all labor organizations in 1957.

Ladjevardi notes that while the United States was promoting collective-bargaining unions as an alternative to politically partisan unions, the Iranian government was busy discouraging independent unions and collective bargaining altogether.[23] A U.S. Department of Labor report described industrial relations in Iran in 1955 thus: "Because of the great surplus of labor, the weakness of local trade unions, and the large social gap between the industrial employer and his workers, the employer determines the terms of employment almost unilaterally. . . . There is no known case of a comprehensive collective agreement between an employer and a union."[24] In 1958 the government began to register employee syndicates that could meet certain requirements. In 1959 a comprehensive law was enacted that covered almost exclusively permanent industrial workers in firms with more than ten employees.

The minimum wage for unskilled workers (excluding agricultural and domestic workers) that had been established by the 1946 labor law was not significantly altered under the 1959 law. Although the labor law also stated that employers, "for the purpose of wages," must classify the jobs of their factories, the extent of compliance with this requirement was unclear.[25] The issue of job classifications figured prominently in later labor disputes.

In the late 1950s, unemployment went up dramatically, especially among oil and construction workers. By 1963, estimates of unemployment ranged from a low of 5 percent of the labor force to a high of 35 percent. The official explanation for the contraction of the oil labor force in the 1950s stresses technical innovation. However, many production workers became redundant because Iran, which had previously exported refined products, now contracted to sell only crude oil. The labor force was also reduced for political reasons; workers who had been active in the trade union movement of the 1940s or during the Mossadegh era were dismissed.[26]

The deaths, exile, or imprisonment of Tudeh leaders should not lead to an underestimation of their role in the labor movement and trade unions. On January 6, 1949, the British labor attaché reported, "The Tudeh Trade Union probably gains in reputation amongst the workers, not only for voicing [workers' "justifiable"] grievances (the ESKI Union rarely has such courage), but also for its apparent contacts with, and interest in, employment problems throughout Persia." Later, an American official conceded, "The only true labor leaders this country ever produced, the only workers' representatives who were willing to go out on a limb on behalf of labor, were for the most part unfortunately Tudeh Party members, some perhaps driven to that extreme by economic and social adversity of a kind that can only be compared with conditions in England almost a century ago."[27]

A Demographic Profile

In November 1956, Iran's first population census, undertaken with U.S. assistance, showed a total of 18.9 million persons, 31 percent urban and

69 percent rural. The census revealed ten cities with a population of 100,000 or more; Tehran had 1.5 million. Enough rural-urban migration occurred so that in 1956 only half the population of Tehran had been born in the census district in which it lived. About one-sixth of the workforce was in industrial employment, but over half (56 percent) remained in the agricultural sector. When employment in agricultural processing industries was included, fully 77 percent of Iran's population was directly dependent on agricultural production. Seasonal unemployment resulted in considerable back-and-forth movement with labor migrating into cities in search of work after the harvest was over and moving back to the country as spring arrived.

Women constituted 9.7 percent of the employed workers in 1956, but their participation rate was only 6 percent (compared with 55 percent for males). Female participation varied quite widely across sectors, from 4 percent in the agricultural labor force (clearly a function of undercounting) to about 17 percent in nonagricultural occupations. Women made up almost 25 percent of all workers in the manufacturing and service occupations. Of those employed in the nonagricultural sector, 65 percent were in manufacturing industries, principally textiles, and 33 percent in service industries, mostly as domestic servants. Fewer than 10 percent of professional and technical jobs were held by women.[28]

Capitalist Development and Class Formation

The mid-1950s were boom years. Import-substitution industrialization (ISI) was the development strategy, characterized by state protection of domestic industries and augmented by cheap government credit and U.S. aid. Between 1951 and 1961, investment expanded primarily in food processing, textiles and other light consumer products, and construction materials. As transnational corporations were not dominant in these industries, they played a minor role in Iran in this period. These industries were not new to Iran and did not require sophisticated technologies. The industrial entrepreneurs—who at this time came mainly from the traditional merchant class—could acquire the necessary technology from foreign machinery suppliers and saw little advantage in pursuing joint ventures with foreign capital.[29]

By 1961, manufacturing—exclusive of the cottage industries on the one hand and the oil industry on the other—comprised 8,928 enterprises employing 129,931 workers. The main industries were textiles, food products, metal products, and nonmetallic mineral products (mosaic tiles, bricks, cement).

Many Iranian analysts locate the beginnings of concerted capitalist development in Iran in the White Revolution, a series of economic, political, and administrative reforms that were initiated in 1961. The White Revolution entailed land reform, nationalization of forests, electoral reforms, franchise for women, denationalization of some state industries, literacy corps, and profit sharing for workers in large industrial establishments. Land reform was designed to create a broad national market and to provide a popular base for the shah's regime. The land reform not only achieved both these aims but also accelerated the process of proletarianization. Like land reform, the profit-sharing measure was motivated by both political and economic considerations. Politically, its purpose was to win workers' support for the regime and increase their identification with management. Economically, it was designed to tie workers to one place and encourage productivity.

This strategy was facilitated by the massive oil revenues that accrued to the state as a result of the 1954 oil agreement. There was some assistance from foreign capital (primarily U.S., West European, and Japanese transnational firms), though its share of gross domestic fixed capital formation and of gross national product was insignificant relative to state and private Iranian investment. In the decade 1965–1975, especially through the Third and Fourth National Development Plans, much progress was made in the development of infrastructure. This included road construction and the creation of a base level of heavy industry and large-scale, capital-intensive plants held predominantly by state-controlled organizations. There was also a conscious policy of regionalization of industry during the Fourth Plan period. The main industrial centers became Tehran and environs, Tabriz, Isfahan, Shiraz, Abadan, and Ahvaz, where petrodollars bought highly sophisticated means of production, including a steel complex in Isfahan, two machine tool plants in Tabriz and Arak, and a petrochemicals complex in Shahpour. They also brought in thousands of foreign managers, administrators, supervisors, advisers, technicians, and even skilled and semiskilled workers to run the operations. The massive oil revenues accruing to the state after the 1973 oil crisis prompted the shah to revise the Fifth Plan and accelerate the pattern of investment in industrial activities.[30]

Modernization resulted in a significant alteration in the structure of the economy, the pace of economic change, and the living standards of many Iranians. The rapid industrialization strategy created a layer of skilled workers whose incomes rose in order to develop the home market. Between 1962 and 1973 the mean net earnings of all employees in various branches of industry improved by 37.2 percent in real terms—a rate of growth of about 2.9 percent per annum. The more modern and dynamic sectors (such as basic metals, chemicals, and electrical machinery) bene-fited from the highest rates of growth in wages, whereas traditional branches (such as textiles and wearing apparel, wood and furniture, rub-ber and nonelectrical machinery) registered more modest performances. Even unskilled construction workers saw wages improved by nearly 71 percent in real terms during this period. Unemployment was almost nonexistent.[31] Many development analysts singled out Iran for praise, and Iran's own leader was confident that it would catch up with Japan by the end of the decade.[32]

Land reform had implications not only for the expansion of the urban industrial labor force but for the labor movement and for working-class consciousness, as noted by Bayat, Rahnema, and myself. In the 1960s, rural-urban migration transferred about 400,000 job seekers to the towns from rural areas.[33] Bayat writes, "Coming from the misery of village life, these workers would view factory employment in positive terms: in its job security, regular income, economic betterment, health insurance, fringe benefits and prestige. . . . One could even detect among these workers a certain degree of "rationality" rather than "false consciousness.""[34]

The villagers may have preferred factory life to village life, but once in the factory, "they were now concerned with the misery of factory life: fac-tory discipline, wages, conditions of work, housing problems, inflation, authoritarianism, discrimination, and so on."[35] According to Bayat, these conditions and workers' awareness of them allowed an "industrial con-sciousness" to develop, which led to the rise of protest actions and strikes beginning in the early 1970s.

Throughout the shah's rule, the government exerted tight control over the industrial labor force in the large sector, especially by forming numer-ous and dispersed syndicates. Many authors have described the state-run unions and the proliferation of SAVAK agents, military officers, and in-formers within the unions and factories alike.[36] In the oil sector alone, there were 26 state-controlled unions. The automotive sector had 7. By 1976 there were about 600 trade unions and 20 confederacies, but their existence was largely nominal.[37] Syndicates operated on a factory-by-factory basis, not industrywide or regionally. The number of syndicates, or factory-based labor unions, rose from about 30 in the early 1960s to al-most 400 and possibly 500 by 1972.[38]

During the Pahlavi era many workers' representatives at the shop-floor level were officially employed by SAVAK, the secret police. The government

also controlled workplace organization by means of the militarization of
many factories, particularly those employing over 500 workers. Here, retired army officers were often placed in security positions.[39] Small wonder,
then, that most workers were hostile toward the syndicates. Far from iden-
tifying with unions, workers with grievances would often turn to the Ministry of Labor for recourse.

The structure of the working population reflects the country's level of
development. In Iran in 1976, 19 percent of the working population was
engaged in manufacturing, a figure higher than in many developing countries. The occupational structure changed toward greater concentration in
the category "production-related workers, transport equipment operators
and laborers"—34 percent of the total. The self-employed population decreased to 30 percent (from 37 percent in the 1966 census), and the
salaried population increased to 48 percent of the measured labor force.

Women's labor force involvement had increased as well, and their share
of the salaried manufacturing workforce grew to 18 percent. Nevertheless,
the manufacturing workforce and production-related occupations remained overwhelmingly male. Small wonder that the labor movement in
Iran, as in many countries north and south, was a male movement.

Industrial Development and Working-Class Differentiation

Alongside modern manufacturing and a modern industrial workforce a
large, traditional manufacturing sector persisted. Many people were engaged in such handicraft industries as metalsmithing, carpet weaving, and
the production of leather and wood products. Traditionally manufactured
consumer goods ranged from luxury goods to cheap consumer goods for
those who could not afford either imported goods or their locally produced substitutes. Such industries were mostly operated in Iran's traditional urban markets, the so-called bazaar. Although the workshop sector
(and indeed petty trade, small-scale retailing, and other economic activities known as informal or traditional) predates capitalism proper in Iran,
it has been conserved and strengthened. This sector is functional because
it engages in the repair, maintenance, and production of goods and services in ways that need not conflict with the modern industrial or service
sector. It is also functional because it absorbs the surplus population at little or no cost to the state and to capital.[40]

Tens of thousands of workers were involved in spinning and weaving,
much of this in the rural areas. Traditionally food, beverages, and tobacco

had been the second largest manufacturing sector, but by 1976 second place had been taken by metal products, machinery, and equipment industries. This represented an important shift in the distribution of the labor force and in the composition of manufactures. Most of the 250,000 manufacturing units were extremely small and employed fewer than ten workers, with an average size of three. It thus appeared that a typical industrial worker in Iran was either self-employed, engaged in a family business, or otherwise employed in a small workshop.[41]

A persistent characteristic of Iranian manufacturing—discussed at length by Floor regarding the pre-shah era—was the role of female labor. Carpets and handicrafts were produced in rural workshops, primarily by women, and these women were counted as production-related workers. Although the 1976 census listed 19.7 percent of production workers as female, women constituted only 8 percent of salaried production workers. This suggests a high proportion of unpaid family and otherwise nonregular women workers.

Because manufacturing was thus both modern and traditional, the industrial labor force itself was highly differentiated. The differentiation of the urban industrial labor force of manufacturing corresponds to what is known in the Marxist literature as the division between production characterized by the *formal* subsumption of labor to capital (formal subsumption is equivalent to the informal sector) and that characterized by the *real* subsumption of labor to capital. The fundamental difference in the organization of the labor process is what distinguishes the two sectors. In the former, production is unmechanized and personal; patriarchal relations dominate, hours are long, and remuneration is low; but workers have some control over their tools and their products. In contrast, the concentrated proletariat in advanced production units work with sophisticated machinery and under modern managerial control, are organized into syndicates, and benefit from higher wages, health insurance, housing allowances, pension plans, and profit sharing. In Iran, such workers made up only a very small percentage of the formal manufacturing sector.[42]

This profile of Iran's working class raised questions about class consciousness that have been addressed by Marxists and non-Marxists.[43] Which workers (in the informal or the formal sector) would be more likely to identify with traditional religious values and practices and which with secular and socialist ideas? Did the history of state repression, the absence of independent trade unions or workers' parties, and a discontinuous pattern of labor organization inhibit the emergence of class consciousness? Would the relatively privileged industrial workers in the large and key sectors become a conservative "labor aristocracy"?

Because the state's policies were regarded as a source of worker passivity, analysts were completely unprepared for workers' militancy during the revolution. Fred Halliday, who was completing a book just before the revolution but after the beginning of a wave of strikes, could therefore write: "It would, for any observer, be naive to undervalue the limits of the strike movement which has a mainly economic as opposed to political character. No workers' movement will be able to emerge under conditions of severe repression such as exist in Iran."[44] Nor did he anticipate the speed with which the shah's regime would disintegrate and the left would move into the factories and influence strike committees and workers' councils.

Labor Control and Resistance

The early 1970s was a period when working-class militancy once again broke out through strikes, demonstrations, slowdowns, and absenteeism to protest wages, profit sharing, and job classifications. Less frequent were protests over dismissals, the presence of semimilitary personnel in the units, and mandatory attendance at official celebrations. These actions in the early 1970s were for the most part illegal and unreported. Because they were also sporadic and dispersed, the authorities more easily suppressed them. Information on the earlier strikes comes from activist sources and, for the later strikes, from newspaper accounts.[45] Halliday notes that the number of strikes reported rose from "a handful in 1971–3" to as many as twenty or thirty per year in 1975.[46] One of the most dramatic incidents during this period was the strike by textile workers of the Chit-e Jahan factory in Karaj (north of Tehran) for higher wages. The owner of the textile factory called in the police rather than negotiate with the workers, and several workers were killed in the ensuing confrontation.

From the mid-1970s, there was a noticeable pattern in Iranian industrial labor disputes: Workers demanded higher wages and more benefits and refused to work as long, as meticulously, and for as little pay as before. In many instances, the authorities quickly gave in to workers' demands for wage increases. Increasingly, the protests also focused on profit sharing and job classifications–protests that indicated a questioning and challenging of managerial control and authority in the workplace and its capacity to reorganize production at will.

In 1975, in an attempt to stem working-class agitation and bolster productivity, the regime announced a divestiture scheme that applied to enterprises of ten or more workers (excluding the oil, railway, and tobacco industries). The 1963 profit-sharing law had evolved into little more than annual bonuses, and as such it ceased to link workers' identity to management. Under the new workers' shares measure, workers were to receive up to 20 percent of the firm's profits (an additional 29 percent to be later divested to public ownership). This was to be distributed according to seniority and wages. Here the shah's regime attempted to replicate in the cities what it had accomplished in the rural areas with the land-redistribution program of the 1960s: creating a privileged layer of the labor force that could be counted on for support. The law excluded the small manufacturing firms and therefore bypassed over 70 percent of the industrial workforce. A skeptical American official opined: "This law becomes just another entry in the statute books of Iran, and will very probably be talked about; but little implementation or enforcement is expected, for a country that cannot enforce its minimum wage laws that have existed for many years, its tax laws, etc., offers little prospect of being able to enforce a very controversial workers' profit-sharing law."[47]

In 1977 the latent contradictions in Iran's oil-based development strategy and dictatorial political structure came to the fore, shattering the facade of economic miracle and social stability. The housing crisis erupted with considerable force as both middle-class victims of the enormous income gap and skyrocketing rents and the shantytown dwellers in the outskirts of Tehran began to protest living conditions. Clashes between police and lower-income people who were violating zoning laws paralleled open criticisms by the intelligentsia against political repression and censorship. *Bazaaris* and shopkeepers, targets of an official antiprofiteering campaign, turned to their traditional allies, Shiite clergymen, for support. A populist alliance was in the making.[48]

Labor in the Iranian Revolution

During autumn 1978, the urban centers in Iran were engulfed by street demonstrations and workplace strikes against the Pahlavi regime. Massive street demonstrations combined with a general strike that included the government sector as well as the bazaar and other private-sector institutions did much to demoralize the Pahlavi state. For example, Central Bank employees occupied a sensitive position in the economic system and seemed to be fully conscious of this. They devised creative ways of sabotaging financial activities, such as withholding deposit and withdrawal slips. In autumn 1978, rejecting the inviolate tenet of secrecy in banking, they released the names of those wealthy individuals who had withdrawn large sums of money or transferred their accounts to foreign banks. In the industrial sector, other key strikes were waged by railroad workers and electrical workers, resulting in bottlenecks and blackouts that added to the state's incapacity.

As the general strike gained momentum and numerous factories and bureaucratic organizations ceased operation, workers formed strike committees that coordinated the strikes and drew up demands that increasingly came to have a political orientation. The demands graduated from higher wages to independent working-class organizations to release of political prisoners and the trial of corrupt and repressive officials.[49] As the once mighty Pahlavi state crumbled, more and more power over its institutions came to be vested in the strike committees. These strike committees gradually evolved into workers' councils (*shura*), which spread throughout the urban centers during and immediately after the revolution. The breakup of the highly centralized Pahlavi state resulted in a decentralized network of local, grassroots, and workplace committees and councils. These developments led to much left-wing speculation that the revolution contained socialist and democratic elements in spite of the pervasive Islamic discourse and preponderant role of clerics.

The first indication that the labor force was turning overtly against the regime was in July 1978, when construction workers (many of whom had lost jobs when a recession was induced in 1976) joined the anti-shah street demonstrations, swelling the ranks of the protesters into the hundreds of thousands. Strikes gained momentum in mid-September, when oil refinery workers in Tehran, Isfahan, Shiraz, Abadan, and Tabriz struck to protest martial law. The strikes by the Tabriz industrial workers in the large plants, especially in the machine-tool and tractor-assembly plants, quickly became part of the revolutionary folklore. On November 4, 1978, the workers of the machine-tool and tractor-assembly plants in Tabriz issued a statement in which they demanded that the existing workers' organizations and yellow unions be dismantled, that genuine workers' councils and other working-class organizations be formed to "defend the rights and social prestige of the workers," and that there be no intervention by the authorities in the factories' internal affairs.[50]

In the oil fields, production workers, joined by technicians and sympathetic engineers, refused to pump oil beyond what was needed for domestic consumption. When the military began to appropriate that for its own use, workers refused to pump anything at all. At one point, Ayatollah

Khomeini urged the oil workers to resume production "for the sake of the people." The workers refused, arguing that the oil was being used by the military. All the striking industrial workers, but most notably the oil workers, displayed considerable imagination, courage, and militancy in their tactics against the regime.[51]

Although the Pahlavi regime was still formally intact, workers refused to carry out the directives of the government, of managers, and of owners. As the regime crumbled and managers and owners became powerless or fled, workers resumed production and managed distribution. By this time, strike committees had evolved into workplace councils, a new form of working-class organization.

Skilled workers and technicians in the military sector played an important part in the general social conflict that engulfed Iran in 1978–1979. In the air force, revolutionary committees emerged from the *homafar*, a special category of technical personnel whose social background was rural or urban working class or lower middle class. These revolutionary committees first mutinied at the main air force base in Tehran and then, in conjunction with guerrillas from the communist Fedaii and the leftist Islamic Mojahedin, fought and defeated the shah's elite Imperial Guard (the so-called Immortals) during the armed insurrection of February 9–11, 1979.[52]

The most advanced section of the Iranian labor force, that is, the workers in modern industry (oil, petrochemicals, manufacturing, utilities such as electricity and railroads), were the last social stratum to join the general strike that spread throughout 1978. Is the labor aristocracy thesis correct, and were the industrial workers more conservative, less "revolutionary"? The answer is complex and requires recognition that they had a great deal to lose, having only recently acquired stable employment and security of means. This may explain why, in some plants where the owners and managers had fled, workers formed councils to continue production at a time when Ayatollah Khomeini and his supporters were calling for strikes. It was, perhaps, due to their privileged position and also to their relative "youth" that the modern industrial workers of Tehran, Tabriz, and Isfahan and the famous oil workers of the southern refineries were the last to join the revolution.

What was the role of left-wing organizations in the emergence of the labor opposition? In 1977, under pressure from the Carter administration in the United States the Pahlavi regime released some political prisoners—who promptly went on to resume political agitation. As the Pahlavi regime weakened and political prisoners were released, the left made a rapid comeback and quickly influenced the direction of labor militancy. "Javad" a Tabriz working-class militant I interviewed in Paris in 1985, emphasized the role of the left in the Tabriz industrial strikes, pointing out that the slogans and placards were written by leftist workers like himself. (At the time, he was a Peykar supporter.)[53] The leftist groups, such as Peykar and Fedaii, were very active in Arak and Tabriz, recruiting workers, encouraging and organizing the strikes, and so on. Industrial workers may have been the last social group to join the revolution, but when they did decide to turn against the state, they took a rather militant stance.

The Workers' Councils

Iranian scholars and activists have disagreed on the nature of the workers' councils, the role of the left, and the workers' capacity for self-organization. Bayat writes that

> the *shuras*, or factory committees (or councils) were a particular form of workers' organization that emerged in Iranian industry following the overthrow of the shah's dictatorship in 1979. They were shop-floor organizations whose elected executive committee represented all the employees of a factory (blue- and white-collar) and/or an industrial group, irrespective of their trade, skill or gender. Their major concern was to achieve workers' control.[54]

In 1980, I compared the councils with the Russian soviets and emphasized their political and economic demands.[55] Rahnema argues that the councils were not solely workers' organizations, for they included salaried employees ranging from office clerks to senior employees, supervisors, engineers, and, in some cases, middle managers. Rahnema is especially critical of Bayat's "overestimation of the role of workers and underestimation of the role and influence of the 'intellectuals' and the left-wing organizations in the movement." In fact, he states that "pushing for showras was a premature move, particularly on the part of the left, who gradually came to influence a large number of these organizations . . . the showras, with their slogan for worker control, were doomed to failure."[56] Although I agree with Rahnema's insistence on the need for trade unionism and industrial democracy, I do not agree that the councils were in any way "premature." They were, rather, the product of a particular historical conjuncture and, moreover, vibrant organizations that could very well have evolved into nationwide labor unions—had conditions been more propitious.

Councils were established in nearly every large and modern industrial plant in the period immediately following the February 1979 revolution. By all accounts workers were overwhelmingly enthusiastic about the councils. A new work environment had emerged that was fundamentally different from that before the revolution, when there was no criticism, no open airing of grievances, enormous wage differentials between blue- and white-collar workers, no participation in finances or production goals, and a rigid and authoritarian division of labor within the factory. Many councils proceeded to draw up constitutions stipulating the duty of the councils to intervene in all aspects of the factory's operations. A typical council, for example, at the General Motors plant in Tehran, had twenty-one elected members, composed of fifteen manual workers and six office staff, one of whom worked full time for the council. It met in full every two weeks and had subcommittees to deal with production control, finance, buying and selling, education, discipline, arbitration, and sports. The full council countersigned all documents and inspected the books.[57]

The tremendous power displayed by Iranian workers during the anti-shah struggle and their political as well as economic demands were acknowledged by the new authorities in various ways—recognition of councils, acceptance of salary adjustments, concessions to demands that work on nuclear power plants cease and that shipments of oil to Israel and South Africa stop. Announcing the unilateral abrogation of the agreement under which the Iranian Oil Participants (the former Consortium) acted as purchasers of the bulk of Iranian oil, the new chairman and managing director of the National Iranian Oil Company said in a speech to NIOC employees on February 28, 1979: "We tell those companies that were imposed on us in the past that it is better for them to withdraw, because if they refuse, the workers will kick them out."[58]

May Day 1979 was a major public festival in cities throughout Iran. Interestingly enough, it was celebrated not only by the left and workers' groups associated with them but by the Islamic populists as well, an indication of their recognition of the workers' role in the revolution. Another indication was that even before May Day 1979, the minimum wage of workers was more than doubled by the Ministry of Labor, and employers were gradually forced to reemploy discharged workers and to place seasonal workers on the regular payroll.[59]

To understand the rise and decline of the councils movement, it is useful to distinguish four phases. The first stage began with the downfall of the shah, when strike committees evolved into councils and these new working-class organs sprang up in nearly all factories. This first phase, characterized by the expansion of the councils movement despite official discouragement, covered most of 1979 until the occupation of the U.S. embassy in November. During this period, not only were there factory councils but students' councils were formed in high schools and universities throughout Iran, and peasants' councils were established in Kurdestan and Turkaman Sahra.

The second phase began after the U.S. embassy was occupied and Prime Minister Mehdi Bazargan resigned. This period was characterized by a more concerted effort on the part of the authorities to undermine the independent councils. Both the new president, Abolhassan Bani-Sadr, and his partners and rivals within the Islamic Republic Party (IRP) were involved in this effort. During this period, the Turkaman councils were violently smashed, the students' councils in the universities were suppressed, and the regime attempted to transform the councils by appointing managers and by creating Islamic associations. This period continued until the Iran-Iraq War, which ushered in a new stage. This third period saw the gradual decline of Bani-Sadr and his liberal-technocratic associations and the ascendancy of the IRP. It also witnessed the increasing power of the Islamic associations as rivals to the workers' councils and growing pressure on industrial workers to increase production and otherwise participate in the war effort. It continued until June 1981. The last stage began with Bani-Sadr's ousting and included the internal war against the left, the full takeover of the autonomous functions of the councils, and an attempt to codify new and Islamically inspired labor relations.

A brief description of the immediate economic situation illustrates the power of the councils and the consequent need of the new authorities to confront them. In 1979 the government began a program of nationalization that eventually covered about 85 percent of all firms and legalized the de facto expropriations by the workers' councils. Workers welcomed this and demanded further nationalizations. Subsequently, insurance companies and banks were also nationalized. Although investment was cut back, the government was forced to channel considerable capital into wages.

In 1979–1980 there was, for the first time, a negative growth rate. This was the inevitable result of the revolutionary disruptions, the unavailability of raw materials and spare parts, and the capital flight of 1977–1979, but a Central Bank report cited worker discipline as a major problem as well.[60] The liberal managers sent in by the provisional government were encountering serious difficulties with the workers' councils and were not receiving much cooperation from their clerical allies. They were expected to fire all personnel connected with the shah's regime, share power with the workers' councils (or the parallel Islamic councils), and keep the unit operating without reviving old contracts with foreign corporations.

In 1980–1981 the government declared a $2.28 billion loss in state-owned industrial units. The decline in industrial output was not accompanied by a corresponding decline in industrial employment or in wages. Despite the sharp fall in labor productivity, real wages increased substantially in 1979 and 1980.[61] This was because the councils had doubled wages in many factories for blue-collar workers while reducing salaries of white-collar personnel by one-third or even one-half. The political power of the councils during this period prevented redundancies and factory closures.

Both the Islamic and liberal wings of the new regime decided they were not prepared to share power with the councils, although their respective approaches to the councils differed. The Islamists used a combination of force and concession to co-opt or transform the councils. Force was used with councils dominated by leftists. The revolutionary air force personnel committees were the first to be disarmed and dismantled by what was still widely perceived as the "revolutionary" and "popular" regime. This was followed by the purging of radical leftists from the oil fields, and in time, from most of the factories and production units.

The oil workers' councils were rather quickly transformed into consultative bodies. This process was apparently facilitated by their links with the "anti-imperialist" clerics and distrust of the liberal capitalist associates and appointees of Bazargan. The Tudeh Party had been influential among the oil workers since the 1940s, and the party's active support of the new regime, and particularly its enthusiasm for the clerical wing, may have helped to diminish militancy among the oil workers. Councils influenced by the Tudeh Party developed a supportive view of the new regime, especially the radical-populist Islamic wing. Oil workers supported the Islamic Republic Party's radical new domestic and foreign policies such as ending supplies to South Africa, Israel, and the United States. Ayatollah Khomeini himself was given to proworker statements such as the following in his May Day speech of 1981: "One day of your life is worth all the lives of the capitalists and the feudalists put together."[62]

There were other obstacles to a united working-class movement: ideological differences among workers and a certain underdevelopment of culture and consciousness. "Javad," the Tabriz militant I interviewed, stressed problems internal to the workers' movement in addition to regime repression. As he put it, "We had all kinds of workers: Left, Right, religious, progressive, reactionary." The new authorities seized upon these ideological differences and encouraged antileft activities. As Javad said, "We easily put up posters in universities, but not in the factories. We found that the workers' consciousness was at odds with our received ideology. It did not match the formulae we had learned." He also stressed the "backwardness" of workers, particularly in terms of an emphasis on religious observance, an undeveloped working-class consciousness, the absence of a democratic culture, and pervasive sexism. Javad therefore felt that a cultural transformation of the workers was as important as their political development and economic well-being.[63]

The Islamic populism of the new regime disarmed those on the left who were trying, in 1979 and 1980, to formulate new strategies and programs for Iranian society. It was also fairly successful in attracting the support of large sections of the working class. Thus the incipient project for democratization—as embodied in the workers' councils—was subverted. Perhaps the biggest blow to the councils movement was the disunity of the left and especially the split that took place within the Fedaii organization in April 1980.[64]

In 1983 the minister of labor, Ahmad Tavakoli, who had earlier issued a ban on the formation of new councils (even progovernment ones), caused an outcry with the labor law he had drafted. The law stipulated ideological preconditions for membership in the councils, placed the Islamic councils under strict supervision by the Ministry of Labor, and imposed severe restrictions on the individual and collective rights of the workers. It was so biased in favor of management and caused such a controversy that Tavakoli was dismissed. These concessions notwithstanding, in the period following the decline of the workers' councils and with the diversion of economic resources away from productive investments, the working class experienced unemployment and disorganization.

Although the labor movement was influential in the immediate postrevolutionary improvements in income distribution, distributional inequality has increased steadily since.[65] It is entirely conceivable that if the workers' councils had survived as strong and independent bodies with the role in decisionmaking and management that they had initially sought, income distribution would not have deteriorated.

The labor law that was finally adopted in 1991 recognizes worker organizations, specifically "Islamic associations" and "Islamic labor councils," but assigns significant control over them to the Interior Ministry and the Ministry of Labor and Social Affairs. This control is justified by reference to the values and objectives of the Islamic Republic Party.

Class and Gender: A Note on Women Workers

We have seen earlier that the labor movement was a male movement, as so few women were part of the industrial labor force. We have also seen that with the expansion of Iran's modern industry, more and more women were seeking employment in textiles and food-processing factories, as well as in government offices, hospitals, and schools. But employed women from working-class and middle-class families found themselves at odds with the cultural orientation of the Islamic component of the revolution, especially with the new Islamic state established in February 1979. It appears that female employment was viewed unfavorably by traditional sections of the urban population and that female domesticity was the ideal for rural migrants, lower-middle-class families, and some workers. This is captured in a conversation related by Kaveh Afrasiabi that took place in early February 1979 with a striking worker named Alimorad. The latter had just returned from Shahr-e Now (the red-light district in downtown Tehran), which had been destroyed by a fire set by Islamist militants.

> "We burnt it all. Cleansed the city," he said.
> "And women?" I asked.
> "Many were incinerated [jozghaleh shodand]."
> "Who are you? Where do you come from?" I asked him. . . . "Why do you support the revolution?"
> "Islam, freedom, poverty, oppression [zolm]," he answered without hesitation.
> "What else?" I insisted.
> "Dignity [heisiat]."
> "Dignity?"
> "Yes brother, Shah took our dignity. He took man's right from him. My wife is now working. What is left of family when the wife works?"
> "And what is your expectation of Islam?"
> "Islam is our dignity. I want to bring bread on my own—to have a wife at home to cook and nurse the children, God and Islam willing."[66]

Such attitudes were behind the early legislation pertaining to women. The 1979 constitution spelled out the place of women in the ideal Islamic society that the new leadership was trying to establish: within the family, through the "precious foundation of motherhood," rearing committed Muslims. Motherhood and domesticity were described as socially valuable, and the age of consent was lowered to fifteen (or thirteen, in some accounts). The Islamic Republic of Iran emphasized the distinctiveness of male and female roles, a preference for the privatization of female roles, the desirability of sex segregation in public places, and the necessity of modesty in dress and demeanor and in media images.[67]

In the first two years of the Islamic Republic government, policies were enacted that adversely affected women and curtailed their participation in the public sphere. These policies resulted, in the first instance, in the loss of employment by elite women and all women associated with the Pahlavi state. Various retirement programs allowed women who had worked as little as fifteen years to retire without loss of entitlements. Later, another law was passed allowing working couples to enjoy the full benefit of the wife's salary if she decided to stay at home. Women with working husbands were told to forgo employment to open up positions for men. Many day-care centers that had been opened in various factories and government agencies under the previous regime were closed.

The main victims of the regime's new policies and gender attitudes were working-class women, whose employment in modern industry declined dramatically in postrevolutionary Iran. In the years following the revolution, female employment in modern industry decreased relative to the prerevolutionary situation and to employment in government agencies and ministries. Women continued to work in the large industrial establishments, but their participation in modern-sector industrial activity was almost insignificant.

Data in the 1976 census indicate that women earning wages and salaries in public- and private-sector manufacturing and mining-quarrying made up between 20 and 27 percent of the total. In 1983, however, the 40,000 female wage and salary earners in urban factory employment in 1983 represented a mere 6 percent of the total. Clearly there had been a sharp decline in female factory employment. There was a further decline in industrial work by women, although the *Statistical Yearbook 1364* (1985–1986) showed a decrease in industrial employment for both men and women, indicating the weakness of this sector of the economy. Compared with 1976, when the female share of manufacturing was reported to be 38 percent, in 1986 it had declined to 14.5 percent; the majority of these women were not regular wage workers.

Conclusions

The major achievement of the labor movement in Iran was its role in the 1978–1979 revolution and the part it played in the councils movement. Trade unionism dates from 1906, and the labor movement was able to carve a role for itself especially in the period 1920–1925. It was, however, unable to structurally change labor relations. This was partly due to its political aims, partly due to the small, fragmented, and noncohesive labor force. Small artisanal establishments were the main feature of the Iranian manufacturing sector until 1970. These establishments were preindustrial in nature, often family businesses, and labor relations were steeped in tradition. Another reason was the hostility of the state led by Reza Shah, which turned against the trade unions and its leadership.

In the period between the two dictatorships (1941–1953), a communist movement emerged in Iran that actively organized workers into what became the largest trade union in Asia. Capitalist development in Iran had produced a new social class, industrial workers with the capacity to paralyze production and precipitate political crises through militant strikes. But the labor movement suffered its second historic defeat in 1953, when the coup d'état against the Mossadegh government suppressed the Tudeh Party and the National Front (communist and nationalist organizations, respectively) and dismantled Iran's large and militant labor confederation. These breaks in the socialist movement and labor history—the cumulative effects of defeats and setbacks to socialists and to workers—are important factors in assessing the capacity for working-class organization and struggle in the immediate postrevolutionary period.

As modern manufacturing expanded in the 1960s, industrial workers assumed a strategic role in the economy and in the society. This allowed them to play a pivotal role in the revolution, to articulate new demands, and to create new forms of organization. Nevertheless, the process of industrialization had not supplanted preexisting forms of economic activity. Neither had a discourse evolved that posited democratization and modernization as essential goals. Moreover, during the period of accelerated industrialization, urban working-class ranks were inundated by illiterate or poorly educated and organizationally inexperienced immigrants from the countryside. The labor movement lacked cohesion and leadership and, due to the existing structural and subjective forces, did not forge a strong and lasting labor organization. Many workers were attracted to the radical Islamic populism of the Islamist movement. Workers did make history, but under conditions that did not allow for the flourishing of the labor movement.

Following the revolution there were class and gender conflicts among the state, organized workers, women, and the left. The fate of the independent workers' councils, the new discourses and policies on female labor force participation, and the decline of the left occurred in the context of the centralizing efforts of the new state, the regime's initial populism, the cultural project of Islamization, and the pursuit of the war with Iraq. These and other economic and political developments in the 1980s had distinct effects on the labor movement and on the structure of the labor force. As the 1986 census clearly shows, the contraction of the industrial labor force and the expansion of self-employment and the informal sector were features of the 1980s.

And what of the prospects for a renewal of the labor movement in Iran? If the proletarian revolution is no longer a serious proposition, leftists continue to argue that industrial democracy is an essential part of the equation that makes up modernity and economic development for Iran. Moreover, a workers' party or a labor party could unite those in various occupations and professions who are concerned about labor standards, patterns of decisionmaking, the distribution of income, social solidarity, and definitions of citizenship. This is a road not yet taken in Iran and not outside the realm of possibility.

Notes

1. Ervand Abrahamian, *Iran Between Two Revolutions* (Princeton: Princeton University Press, 1982). Assef Bayat, "Workers' Control After the Revolution," *MERIP Reports*, no. 113 (March/April 1983); *Workers and Revolution in Iran* (London: Zed Books, 1987); "Capital Accumulation, Political Control and Labour Organization in Iran, 1965–75," *Middle Eastern Studies* 25, 2 (April 1989). Seyyid Ali Mirsepassi, "Historical and Structural Development of the Politics of Production in Modern Iran, 1926–1978," Ph.D. dissertation, American University, Washington, D.C., 1985. T. Jalil, *Workers of Iran: Repression and the Fight for* Democratic Trade Unions (London: Campaign for the Restoration of Trade Union Rights in Iran, 1976). Ahmad Ghotbi, *Workers Say No to the Shah: Labour Law and Strikes in Iran* (London: Committee to Restore Trade Union Rights in Iran [CRTURI], 1977). C. Chaquerie, *Historical Documents on the Labour Movement in Iran*, 7 vols. (Florence: Mazdak, 1974–1978). Fred Halliday, *Iran: Dictatorship and Development* (Harmondsworth: Penguin, 1979). Hassan Hakimian, "Industrialization and the Standard of Living of the Working Class in Iran, 1960–1979," *Development and Change* 19, 1 (January 1988); *Labour Transfer and Economic Development: Theoretical Perspectives and Case Studies from Iran* (London: Harvester Wheatsheaf, 1990). Misagh Parsa, *Social Origins of the Iranian Revolution* (New Brunswick: Rutgers University Press, 1989). Essays by the present author include Shahrzad Azad [V. M. Moghadam], "Workers' and Peasants' Councils in Iran," *Monthly Review* 32, 5 (October 1980); Valentine M. Moghadam, "Workers' Councils in the Iranian Revolution," *Against the Current* 3, 2 (Spring 1985); "Accumula-

tion Strategy and Class Formation: The Formation of the Industrial Labor Force in Iran, 1962–1977," Ph.D. dissertation, American University, Department of Sociology, Washington, D.C., 1986; "Industrial Development, Culture, and Working Class Politics: A Case Study of Tabriz Industrial Workers in the Iranian Revolution," *International Sociology* 2, 2 (June 1987); "Industrialization Strategy and Labour's Response: The Case of the Workers' Councils in Iran," in Roger Southall (ed.), *Trade Unions and the New Industrialization of the Third World* (London: Zed Books, 1988).

2. For example, Saeed Rahnema, "Work Councils in Iran: The Illusion of Worker Control," *Economic and Industrial Democracy* 13 (1992):69–94.

3. See Willem Floor, "Labour Unions, Law and Conditions in Iran 1900–1941," Durham University Occasional Papers Series no. 26, Durham, England, 1985; Habib Ladjevardi, *Labor Unions and Autocracy in Iran* (Albany: SUNY Press, 1985).

4. Said Amir Arjomand, *The Turban for the Crown: Iran's Islamic Revolution* (New York: Oxford University Press, 1988), 108.

5. Among those who have done so are Moghadam, "Industrial Development, Culture, and Working Class Politics," 151–176; Parsa, *Social Origins of the Iranian Revolution*, esp. ch. 5; Farideh Farhi, "Class Struggles, the State, and Revolutions in Iran," in Berch Bergeroglu (ed.), *Power and Stability in the Middle East* (London: Zed Books, 1989); Ali Mirsepassi-Ashtiani and Val Moghadam, "The Left and Political Islam in Iran: A Retrospect and Prospects," *Radical History Review* 51 (1991); Mansour Moaddel, "Class Struggle in Post-Revolutionary Iran," *International Journal of Middle East Studies* 23, 3 (August 1991):317–343; Ervand Abrahamian, *Khomeinism: Essays on the Islamic Republic* (Berkeley: University of California Press, 1993), esp. ch. 3.

6. See Abrahamian, *Iran Between Two Revolutions*, ch. 3; and Floor, "Labour Unions." This paragraph also draws on information from the Ministry of Labor (1948) and from F. Daftary and M. Borghey, *Multinational Enterprises and Employment in Iran* (Geneva: ILO, 1976), 9.

7. Floor, "Labour Unions," 14–15, 59–60; Abrahamian, *Iran Between Two Revolutions*, 213.

8. Floor, "Labour Unions," 57.

9. Ibid., 58.

10. Exxon, "Middle East Oil and Gas," Exxon Background Series, New York, 1984, 6.

11. Information from L. P. Elwell-Sutton, *Persian Oil: A Study in Power Politics* (London: Lawrence and Wisehart, 1955), ch. 8; Charles Issawi (ed.), *The Economic History of Iran 1800–1919* (Chicago: University of Chicago Press, 1972), 48–49; Halliday, *Iran*, 98.

12. Central Council of Federated Trade Unions. Ladjevardi uses the acronym CUC.

13. British Foreign Office Records, London, "The Tudeh Party and Iranian Trade Unions," September 1946. This and several other reports have been reproduced in an appendix in Mirsepassi, *Historical and Structural Development* (see note 1).

14. Ladjevardi, *Labor Unions and Autocracy in Iran*, 32.

15. Cited in Floor, "Labour Unions," 61–62.

16. U.S. Department of Labor, *Summary of the Labor Situation in Iran* (Washington, D.C.: Department of Labor, October 1955), 11.

17. Cited in Ladjevardi, *Labor Unions and Autocracy in Iran*, 42.

18. Abrahamian, *Iran Between Two Revolutions*, 299.

19. This is described in a lengthy reported dated July 18, 1949, by K. J. Hird, British Embassy labour attaché, "Labour Developments Six Months Ended June 1949."

20. International Labor Organization, *Labour Conditions in the Oil Industry in Iran* (Geneva: ILO, 1950); see also Nikki R. Keddie, "Oil, Economic Policy, and Social Conflict in Iran," *Race and Class*, Special Issue on the Iranian Revolution 20, 1 (1979):17.

21. Julian Bharier, *Economic Development in Iran 1900–1970* (London: Oxford University Press, 1971), 184.

22. Ladjevardi, *Labor Unions and Autocracy in Iran*, 201.

23. Ibid., 212.

24. U.S. Department of Labor, *Labor Law and Practice in Iran* (Washington, D.C.: GPO, 1964), 10.

25. Ibid., 45, 46, 47.

26. Information from my father and uncle, government employees at the time.

27. Cited in Ladjevardi, *Labor Unions and Autocracy in Iran*, 200.

28. Information from the U.S. Department of Labor, *Labor Law and Practice in Iran,* (1964), 24. For labor force data on Iran drawn from the 1956, 1966, 1976, and 1986 censuses, see International Labor Organization, *Yearbook of Labour Statistics: Retrospective Edition on Population Censuses 1945–89* (Geneva: ILO, 1990), Table 2B, 571.

29. It soon became clear, however, that many of the new industrial plants could not survive without further government aid. A period of recession thus followed the initial boom. See Keith McLachlan, "The Iranian Economy, 1960–1976," in H. Amirsadeghi (ed.), *Twentieth Century Iran* (London: Heinemann, 1977), 131; Vahid Nowshirvani and Robert Bildner, "Direct Foreign Investment in the Non-Oil Sectors of the Iranian Economy," *Iranian Studies* 6, 2–3 (Spring/Summer 1973):77.

30. A good discussion of the shah's industrialization policy is in McLachlan, "The Iranian Economy," 129–169. See also Massoud Karshenas, *Oil, State and Industrialization in Iran* (Cambridge: Cambridge University Press, 1990), chs. 5–8.

31. Hakimian, "Industrialization and the Standard of Living," 9. According to Ahmad Ashraf, nearly 1 million unskilled Afghan workers were working in Iran after 1973 (personal communication, New York, February 1985). Iranian skilled labor was in short supply and much in demand. See also Halliday, *Iran*, ch. 7; and Robert Graham, *Iran: The Illusion of Power* (New York: St. Martin's Press, 1979), chs. 6 and 7.

32. See Sanjaya Lall, *Developing Countries in the International Economy* (London: Macmillan, 1981), p. 219. In a 1978 study, the Organization for Economic Cooperation and Development (OECD) predicted a shift of production of standard car models to countries such as Brazil, Argentina, Mexico, South Korea, and Iran.

33. ILO, *Employment and Income Policies for Iran* (Geneva: ILO, 1973).

34. Bayat, "Capital Accumulation," 200–201.

35. Ibid., 202.

36. See, for example, Halliday, *Iran*, 205; Bayat, *Workers and Revolution in Iran*, 59–63; Ladjevardi, *Labor Unions and Autocracy in Iran*, 213–215. Also, personal communication from my father, an engineer with the National Railways and then the Heavy Machineries Division of the Ministry of Roads and Transportation.

37. ILO, *Labour Legislation, Practice and Policy*. See also Halliday, *Iran*, 203–204; Ladjevardi, Labor Unions and Autocracy in Iran, 239.

38. Halliday, *Iran*, 204; Ladjevardi, *Labor Unions and Autocracy in Iran*, 239.

39. The role of SAVAK in factories is also stressed in U.S. Department of Labor, *Labor Law and Practice in Iran*, 28. It seems clear that in the factories, machinery was more modern than was management and supervision. In the early 1979s there was much discussion on the need to improve and modernize managerial and supervisory methods, and a management institute affiliated with Harvard was planned. See Gail Cook Johnson, *High-Level Manpower in Iran* (New York: Praeger, 1980), esp. 43. By 1978 the division of labor in factories and other organizations was based less on scientific management than on the presence of SAVAK and retired or active military personnel, and high-level manpower was determined primarily by family ties, connections, and educational achievement.

40. Nevertheless, inasmuch as the workshop sector was not a beneficiary of state largesse and because of preferential treatment of large firms and the government's attempt to regulate the bazaar's productive financial and commercial operations, competition and resentment grew.

41. Ministry of Economy, *Report on the Results of the Annual Industrial Survey in 1967* (Tehran: Bureau of Statistics, 1967); A.C.R. Wheeler, *The Development of Industrial Development in Iran before 1353 (1974–1975)* (Geneva: Population and Manpower Bureau [ILO] 1976), 14.

42. These features of Iranian manufacturing and of the industrial working class have been highlighted also by Halliday and by Rahnema. See Halliday, *Iran,* ch. 7; and Rahnema, "Work Councils in Iran."

43. For other contexts, see Peter McGee, "Labor Mobility in Fragmented Labor Markets, the Role of Circulatory Migration in Rural-Urban Relations in Asia," in H. Safa (ed.), *Toward a Political Economy of Urbanization in Third World Countries* (Delhi: Oxford University Press, 1982); Michael Burawoy, *The Politics of Production* (London: Verso, 1985); John Humphrey, *Capitalist Control and Workers' Struggle in the Brazilian Auto Industry* (Princeton: Princeton University Press, 1982); John Goldthorpe et al., *The Affluent Worker: Political Attitudes and Behaviour* (Cam-

bridge: Cambridge University Press, 1968). A recent article raises some of these questions in the Indian context. See Pravin Patel, "Trade Union Participation and Development of Class Consciousness," *Economic and Political Weekly* (September 3, 1994):2368–2377.

44. Halliday, *Iran*, 209.

45. See Jalil, *Workers of Iran*; Ghotbi, *Workers Say No to the Shah*; Bayat, *Workers and Revolution in Iran*, 85–89.

46. Halliday, *Iran*, 206.

47. Cited in Ladjevardi, *Labor Unions and Autocracy in Iran*, 238–239.

48. The populist alliance was based on the convergence of all urban classes and social strata in the anti-shah struggle: the urban poor, traditional petty bourgeoisie, new petty bourgeoisie, working class, clergy, students, and *bazaaris*. The main slogan of the populist alliance was "Independence, freedom, Islamic Republic." After the shah's downfall, the alliance began to break down. For a full account and analysis see my chapter "Revolutions and Regimes: Populism and Social Transformation in Iran," in Philo Wasburn (ed.), *Research in Political Sociology*, vol. 6 (Greenwich, Conn.: JAI Press, 1993).

49. See Ahmad Ashraf and Ali Banuazizi, "The State, Classes and Modes of Mobilization in the Iranian Revolution," *State, Culture and Society* 1, 3 (1985).

50. "Resolution of the Workers of the Machine Tool and Tractor Assembly Plants of Tabriz," (November 4, 1978). Reprinted in Organization of Iranian People's Fedaii Guerrillas, "The OIPFG Salute the Advanced Workers of the Soil, Machine Tool and Tractor Assembly Industries" (leaflet), Tehran, 15 Aban 1357 (November 6, 1978) (translated by the Iranian Students Association in the United States). See Azad, "Workers' and Peasants' Councils in Iran," 16.

51. A fascinating firsthand account of the oil workers' strike is a document entitled "How We Went on Strike and Paralyzed the Shah's Regime." It was carried in *MERIP Reports*, (March/April 1979) and in Peter Nore and Terisa Turner (eds.), *Oil and Class Struggle* (London: Zed Press, 1980), 293–301.

52. In 1972–1974 I taught English to homafar at the Imperial Air Force Language School. For a detailed description of these events, see Ervand Abrahamian's concluding chapters in *Iran Between Two Revolutions*; see also Parsa, *Social Origins of the Iranian Revolution*, esp. chs. 5, 6, 8.

53. See Moghadam, "Industrial Development, Culture, and Working Class Politics."

54. Bayat, *Workers and Revolution in Iran*, 100.

55. Azad, "Workers' and Peasants' Councils in Iran," 14–29.

56. Rahnema, "Work Councils in Iran," 69–70, 81.

57. Chris Goodey, "Factory Councils in Iran," *MERIP Reports* (June 1980).

58. *Middle East Survey* (Nicosia) 22 (March 5, 1979):8.

59. Cited in Ladjevardi, *Labor Unions and Autocracy in Iran*, 249.

60. Javad Salehi-Isfahani, "Economic Consequences of the Iranian Revolution,"

paper presented at the fifteenth annual meeting of the Middle East Studies Association of North America, Philadelphia, November 1982.

61. Massoud Karshenas and Hashem Pesaran, "Islamic Government and the Iranian Economy," paper presented at the eighteenth annual meeting of the Middle East Studies Association of North America, Chicago, November 1, 1983.

62. Quoted in Bayat, *Workers and Revolution in Iran*, 185.

63. See Moghadam, "Industrial Development, Culture, and Working Class Politics," 169–170.

64. An interview with two Rah-e Kargar members (London, September 23, 1994), one of whom had been with the Fedaii in 1979–1980, confirmed this.

65. Sohrab Behdad, "Winners and Losers of the Iranian Revolution: A Study of Income Distribution," *International Journal of Middle East Studies* 21, 3 (August 1989); Hooshang Amirahmadi, *Revolution and Economic Transition: The Iranian Experience* (Albany: SUNY Press, 1990), esp. 194–203.

66. Kaveh Afrasiabi, "The State and Populism in Iran," Ph.D. dissertation, Boston University Department of Political Science, 1987, 307.

67. For details on women and gender issues in postrevolutionary Iran with a comparative glance at the Pahlavi era, see ch. 6 in V. M. Moghadam, *Modernizing Women: Gender and Social Change in the Middle East* (Boulder: Lynne Rienner, 1993).

5

Labor in Syria: The Emergence of New Identities

Elisabeth Longuenesse

The socialist world has collapsed, the communist parties have been transformed. These events, along with the divisions and marginalization of the working classes in the West (which is itself one of the main causes of the crisis in the trade union movement), force historians toward a reinterpretation of recent events. The transformations of the dominant paradigms in the social sciences also push us in the direction of at least rethinking our interpretations so as to refine them (if we do not radically revise them).

Raymond Hinnebusch, Yahya Sadowski, Alasdair Drysdale, Philip Khoury, Michel Seurat, Elizabeth Picard, and, more recently, Volker Perthes and Steven Heydemann have contributed to a better comprehension of the political and social reality of Syria.[1] They have done so collectively precisely because they shared neither analytic frameworks nor underlying assumptions. As for Syrian publications, all are still small in number and remain more or less constrained to recount an institutional political history that ends in 1958. The publication in Syria, since the 1980s, of a number of autobiographical or memoiristic accounts has nevertheless added important new sources of information.

Unfortunately, the study of labor and labor movements has only slightly benefited from these advances. The number of works that deal explicitly with the Syrian labor movement is rather small because the subject itself appears to have little importance for most analysts for historical, political, and theoretical reasons.[2]

In the following pages I present some reflections on what we do know as well as on problems of interpretation. In the first section of this chapter I attempt a broad historical survey from the dissolution of the late

Ottoman precapitalist socioeconomic structures through the creation of new economic and social structures. The second section provides, from a sociological perspective, an account of more recent transformations. These transformations include the roles of industrial production and the working class in contemporary Syria and the institution of trade unionism since the coming to power of the Ba'th Party.

The Decline of Handicrafts and the Growth of Industry

Syria was long a center of handicraft production. Beginning with the second half of the nineteenth century, traditional industry underwent an initial decline due to competition from cheaper foreign products. It was around this time that the first steam-powered silk-spinning machines appeared. Western penetration of Syria was accompanied by the development of communications, roads, and railroads, which allowed more and more numerous commercial networks to arise.[3]

Just before World War I, Syrian industry appeared primarily as artisanal workshops and handicraft production. Large enterprises were rare: Only a few dozen businesses had more than fifty employees. The most numerous producers were spinners, but there were soapmakers, saddlers, oil crushers, and mill workers. The artisanal character of most production did not prevent these enterprises from modernizing their equipment and introducing new techniques. It was just in this way that the knitting industry emerged as a sudden and successful new branch of textile production just after the war.

World War I, followed by the parceling out of the Ottoman Empire, dealt a blow to the Syrian economy by cutting its links with its larger market. French domination and the increased access of foreign producers aggravated the crisis of traditional productive structures. Most authors agree, for example, that the number of looms dropped by 80 percent between 1910 and 1930.[4] According to one report the number of artisans and handicraft workers dropped by half between 1913 and 1937.[5]

Until 1928 artisanal production was predominant in Syria. Capitalist workshops with a relatively large number of workers were nothing more than a group of artisans working together on equipment little more advanced than they would have used alone. The division of labor was rudimentary and labor organization virtually absent.

In the 1930s artisanal and mechanized industry began to exist side by side. The first large mechanized establishment, the Dummar cement factory, was founded in 1928. The second, a textile factory, was created in Aleppo in 1933. Thereafter an industrial proletariat came into existence and workers' strikes appeared for the first time in the country, heralding class conflict that would deepen. Although Jacques Berque's "factory affecting the heart" was not yet a dominant economic or cultural artifact, it symbolized a new civilization and foretold profound economic, social, and cultural transformations.[6]

Industrialization occurred in two ways: by the direct creation of new enterprises and by the renewal and mechanization of old ones in which the outmoded instruments of production were replaced by machines. A 1934 study by the International Labor Organization listed 306 modern factories, of which 81 were in Beirut, 71 in Aleppo, and 63 in Damascus. These factories were quite small, employing overall between 5,600 and 5,800 workers; 1,700 of these were in Aleppo and 1,300 in Damascus. [7]

Not until after independence, in 1946, do we see a true industrial take-off. The rupture of economic relations with the outside during World War II, when coupled with the growth of domestic demand due to the presence of foreign troops, stimulated the local market. It also encouraged the accumulation of wealth, the reopening of artisanal workshops, and investment in the creation of new firms. Industries using local raw materials developed in textile and food production. Wealth accumulated during the war provided funds for more investment after the war, when the collapse of the European economies also limited their competitive capacity. Beginning in 1944–1945 more and more new firms were created, and in 1946 the largest textile factory in Syria was created, the Khumassiyyah firm.[8]

The first ten years of independence were marked by a flurry of industrialization and particularly by the establishment of large joint-stock firms. The same families were often owners of different firms, and investments were such that the sectoral pattern of industrialization remained largely the same as before the war: textile and food production.

The Workers

Not until the turn of the twentieth century can we observe both a polarization of social relations of production and the embryonic development of the working class. On the one hand, we see the introduction of capitalist relations of production inside modern firms where the owner is—at least initially—usually a foreigner and the worker is of local nationality.[9] On the other, we see the decline of traditional structures of production (due to competition from foreign commodities) lead to a crystallization of new relationships between artisan owners and journeymen workers. The old upward mobility from journeyman to owner was increasingly blocked. This second phenomenon was slow and led to the polarization of class relations only in the 1930s. The first phenomenon, however, was brutally swift but of limited importance in a society still primarily precapitalist.

The decline of artisanal production nevertheless implies an inexorable reduction in the number of workers employed in traditional industry. This reduction was never fully balanced by an increase in employment in the modern industrial sector. In Aleppo, for example, the number of looms, which had dropped to 2,200 in 1931, increased to 6,500 in 1933. The number of workers in the textile industry in Aleppo, however, declined continuously between 1910 and 1930 from 40,000 to 25,000.[10] In Homs, the decline was even steeper: from 20,000 or 25,000 workers to 4,500 or 5,000 in the same period.[11]

More generally, between 1913 and 1937 the number of workers in all industry, traditional and modern alike, dropped from 309,000 to 203,000.[12] Apparently the growth of employment in the modern sector did not make up for jobs lost in the traditional sector, even understanding that it is difficult to fix firmly a boundary between the traditional and modern industry.[13] It is also striking that the workforce itself changed; we find fewer women, less homework, and less piecework.

The statistics are too unreliable to give a clear idea of the working-class population in the country as a whole.[14] They do, however, suggest two types of conclusions. First, the decline of the crafts and the development of industrial production reveal a structural transformation of the working-class population. The process may well have been slower in Syria than in Egypt, Turkey, or even Lebanon and Palestine, but it was nevertheless profound and irreversible. Second, the overall decline in the size of the working class indicates a relative decline in the importance of production in the overall economy. Until the nineteenth century, the artisanal and laboring population probably was as significant in demographic terms as the peasantry. The continuous decline of this sector and the accompanying transformation of social relationships are signs of the upheavals that Syria was to undergo from the mid-nineteenth century on.

The crisis of 1930 only accelerated this decline as the sharp drop in the prices of imported goods aggravated the brutal competition to which local enterprise was exposed and thereby increased the number of bankruptcies. Craftspeople were especially hard hit, and unemployment increased with consequent hunger and misery. In 1931 the high commissioner listed 14,250 unemployed in Damascus, 30,000 in Aleppo, 9,400 in Hama, and 5,200 in Homs.[15] Other sources place the number of unemployed at 150,000, or between 15 and 20 percent of the economically active population, in the two territories under French Mandatory control: Lebanon and Syria.[16]

Both processes of change continued after independence. Between 1937 and 1957, the number of individuals in traditional industry are reported to have dropped from 170,000 to 30,000; those in the modern sector slightly more than doubled from 33,000 to 70,000.[17] Other sources give somewhat different measures, but whatever sets of data are used, the same picture emerges: an inexorable decline in the number of employees in the artisanal sector and a much slower increase in the number in modern industry.[18]

Artisanal industry underwent another kind of change as well: the creation of the small firm. Some industries were disappearing, but there was also the creation of a sector of truly small but relatively mechanized firms that employed dozens of workers. One obvious example was the knitting industry with its many establishments employing twenty or thirty workers. Initially concentrated in old Damascus, knitting spread to new industrial districts.[19] Alongside these small firms, some of the modern enterprises employed quite a large number of workers. At least ten firms in the cement, textile, and food-preparation sectors of the economy may have had 500 or more employees.[20]

The careful analyses of Louis Massignon, Jean Gaulmier, and Syrians writing shortly after independence such as Youssef Helbaoui, Aziz Allouni, and Bagh all describe the larger social processes I have sketched.[21] Such transformations went hand in hand with changes in the urban environment and in the countryside. The growth of the nationalist movement, the birth of new political parties, and the crystallization of the workers' movement were all expressions of these changes.

The National Movement and the Origins of Trade Unionism

Only gradually did associations of workers disengage themselves from the corporate structures inherited from the Arab-Islamic city and the Ottoman era. In 1912 an Ottoman law was passed that aimed to transform the corporation by making it an open and advisory organization exclusively for owners. The new corporate structure was to be under strict administrative control of the state; its internal laws required approval by the municipal authorities. This law remained a dead letter during the Ottoman period, but the French Mandatory authorities revived it and enforced it so that the two systems coexisted until 1935.[22]

Louis Massignon's 1927 list of Damascene corporations and associations clearly reveals the coexistence of traditional trades (whose structures had not changed for centuries) beside modern professions, which appropriated and transformed the old associational models.[23] At the margin one can also see the evidence of European penetration: Capitalist production had imposed radically new activities and an uprooted proletariat appeared whose members had broken their ties with the rural or urban worlds from which they had come. It is not surprising that the first strikes appeared among the railway workers in 1908.[24] Strikes became far more common during the 1920s, especially in 1926 after the Syrian revolt of 1925. Strikes, usually over low wages, occurred in several sectors of the economy: notably in textiles, but also in the railways, the urban tramways, printing, and among tobacco workers.[25]

The history of the origins of Syrian trade unions remains to be written, although several works have laid the broad foundations. Among these are the dissertation of Shafiq Sanadiki (1949), which deals with the Syrian trade union movement, and the work of Abdalla Hanna twenty years later. Jacques Couland's book on the Lebanese trade union movement throws some indirect light on Syrian history.[26] Archival materials are scarce and difficult to consult, for they are scattered among private hands and working-class organizations that are themselves largely international and thus outside Syria. The Mandatory archives themselves have not yet been employed.

In the Mandatory period it is often difficult to distinguish between guildlike associations and more explicitly working-class ones. The official historiography of the Syrian trade union movement lists the knitting union as the first workers' union in the modern sense of the term. It is said to have been formed in 1925 by Subhi al-Khatib, later president of the first federation of Syrian trade unions, which was founded in 1939. Both Sanadiki and Hanna give this version, which is also widely disseminated in the trade union publications. The printing workers might, however, date to 1924 and thus be the oldest union.

The issue here is not purely idiosyncratic but rather reveals how political engagements inform historical reconstruction. The printers' union was part of an early minority of Syrian unions with explicitly revolutionary leadership, and it (along with the waterworks, electricity, and petroleum production) established relations with the Red International of Labor Unions. Subhi al-Khatib's knitters' union was, in contrast, led by moderate reformers. The current reconstruction of events by Sanadiki and Hanna has an apologetic character because it provides al-Khatib with an early and important role in the creation of the first confederation of trade unions (General Confederation of Trade Unions), whose president he remained until he was ousted by a leftist coalition led by communists in 1957.

In 1929, Massignon

> observed through the Syrian interior a remarkable revival of the traditional corporate spirit; thus in Damascus more than 16 trades have printed constitutions and continue to name *syndics* officially recognized by the municipality. . . . While this reorganization occurs in the Syrian interior, on the Lebanese coast which is undergoing massive Europeanization we can see only a disquieting individual leveling which is manifest in the creation of three or four unions which could possibly turn to communism as has already occurred in the Palestinian coast areas.[27]

In the context of colonial domination, workers and owners were led to struggle together against a common enemy, the Mandatory regime, so as to protect local production.[28] Gaulmier's description of the trade union movement in Hama is a riveting illustration.[29] It was this that led Massignon later to write, "The journeymen were seduced by the idea of trade unions which the Mandatory power could not accept without apprehension in the Levant . . . and the Syrian petty-bourgeois nationalists knew how to profit (against both the Mandate and against the Communists) from the favorable impression among the journeymen of trade unions."[30]

Working-class conflicts, and their tendency to reinforce trade union institutions, really begin with the Great Depression in 1930, whose repercussions were harshly felt in Syria. Strikes, primarily in the textile sector, were numerous in Aleppo, Homs, and Damascus between 1930 and 1933. In 1932 in Aleppo, 50,000 people demonstrated before the offices of the high commissioner against competition from Japanese textiles. In the footwear industry, workers, artisans, and owners all struggled against the entry of products from the Czechoslovak firm Bata into the market. In Beirut, in contrast, the footwear industry was already dominated by capitalist enterprises, and a working-class conflict more purely over wages occurred.[31]

In the Syrian heartland, strikes expressed both the political conflict with the Mandatory authorities and their policies and the economic conflict over higher wages. They were spontaneous, but their outbreak usually aided the creation of permanent labor organizations.

In 1935, as the level of conflict grew, the authorities decided to abolish the 1912 Ottoman legislation and to replace it with a new law governing professional associations. The new law turned out to be mere window dressing that did not fundamentally change the relations between owners and workers.[32] New trade unions remained subject to stringent administrative control, and a list of professions authorized to establish unions was promulgated. For the most part, these were mixed unions that included owners and workers even as conflicts between them became increasingly acute. Trade unions continued to be formed despite the law, however, and modification of the new law became an increasingly pressing demand for the unions.

The Popular Front came to power in France in 1936 and gave a significant push to popular movements in Syria. In 1936 the First Workers' Congress was formed in Damascus with Subhi al-Khatib as its president.[33] In February 1938, the Federation of Aleppo Unions was formed and comprised twenty-two unions under the presidency of Mustafa Jalab, leader of the shoe workers' union. The Federation of Homs Unions was formed at the same time, and shortly thereafter the General Confederation of Trade Unions was formed when the federations of Damascus, Aleppo, and Homs joined together.[34]

The watchwords of the trade unions were the abrogation of the 1935 law, better conditions and pay, the eight-hour day, restriction of the employer's right to fire without warning, and elaboration of a complete labor law. On May 29, 1938, a general strike was called to demand a new labor law. The strike was widely observed; twenty-four unions participated in Damascus alone.[35] The outbreak of World War II put social issues on the back burner. Although Syria officially was made independent in 1943, French troops did not finally withdraw until April 17, 1946—celebrated as Independence Day—and only then did parliamentary life resume. A labor law was finally enacted in June 1948 after more than a year of strikes, demonstrations, and petitions. In principle the workers had won the right to form unions and a limited right to strike as well as a minimum wage, the eight-hour day, a weekly day off, and an annual paid vacation. They also won indemnification in case of firing, layoff, accidents, or work-related illness. Not until the Syro-Egyptian union of 1958 would the law be fully applied.

To place working-class activism in the context of the larger social and political transformations in Syria, we must recognize that the movement remained quite marginal. It was hardly able to speak in its own name politically, and its spokesmen were usually attorneys or members of other liberal professions. These professionals used the workers and their demands as a means to advance their own political ambitions. The winning of a labor law at the dawn of independence was thus a concession given to workers and also a sign of the importance of their support during the earlier struggles. In the years to come this alliance broke up, and workers met growing hostility from their erstwhile allies.

The Struggle for Recognition, 1946–1958

Although the first decade of Syrian independence can be characterized as one of growing social conflict, these years have not so far been the object of specialized research. Steven Heydemann has suggested that these are crucial years if we wish to understand the Egyptian-Syrian union of 1958 or the Ba'th's later coming to power. From the very beginning of this period, when the social cleavages were still largely masked by the struggle for independence, the development of national capitalism was accompanied by the growing intervention of the state in the economy. Measures were taken early on to protect local industry, to limit the activities of the state, and to "Syrianize" industry. Enterprises that had been controlled by the French state passed under the control of the Syrian state, including mines, the post office, the ports and railway systems, customs, and the tobacco monopoly. Among foreign firms nationalized were the water and electricity companies of Aleppo (1951), those of Homs and Hama (1953), and the Railway Company of Damascus, Hawran and Extensions (1955). Yahya Sadowski underlines the elite consensus that existed regarding the necessary role of the state: "The twin pillars of state formation and economic development comprised a publicly shared vision of Syria's future."[36]

At the same time, the alliance that had been sealed with the popular classes in the struggle for independence was ruptured. The Syrian bourgeoisie, which had generally profited from World War II, no longer required the political support of the working class. Confronted with the ever more pressing demands of the workers, the employers organized themselves and formed the first federation of business associations in 1949 in Damascus and elsewhere in the following years.[37]

The creation of trade unions confronted many obstacles and was subjected to strict legal control. Ministerial authorization was required for any union, and the leaders were required to register with the authorities. Forming unions was especially difficult in the large enterprises, whether foreign or domestically owned. Owners used any means, including firing workers who attempted to organize unions, to obstruct the process. The right to create unions and the right of unions to engage in action freely was thus a constant theme in the struggles of the 1950s. Not until the years between 1954 and 1958, after the collapse of the Shishakli dictatorship, did the workers at such large enterprises as Khumassiyyah and the Societé de Filature et Tissage in Damascus succeed in creating unions.[38] Paradoxically, therefore, during this rather lengthy period, trade union activity developed in small enterprises more than in large ones because of the greater freedom of action in that area of the economy and the long traditions of struggle that had their roots there.

The 1950s were a period of numerous strikes in Damascus (textiles, matches, bus company), Aleppo (textiles), Homs and Hama (electricity), and Banias (petroleum) against dismissals and for annual vacations and better salaries.[39] In 1954 workers in mechanized weaving undertook one of the longest strikes of this period (fifty days) and succeeded in winning higher salaries and a uniform wage scale. At the end of this strike the National Assembly enacted a law enlarging the right to strike.[40] In 1956 5,000 workers in the Iraq Petroleum Company went on strike for two weeks and won a salary increase of 16 percent.[41]

Even if conflicts increased during these years, however, the union movement remained relatively small and poorly rooted. In 1947, there were only forty-six unions with a membership of about 6,000 workers. The growth in the postwar period was so rapid that the number of members tripled in three years. Such growth would imply a remarkable degree of popular mobilization if it were in fact correct, but unfortunately this does not appear to be the case. According to Willard Beling, a certain number of these unions existed only on paper.[42] Ibrahim Bakri suggests that the state sought a counterweight to the influence of militant trade unions. After the war it encouraged the formation of unions in many professions and trades as a means of extending its influence in the absence of any link to large industrial undertakings.[43] The degree of militancy among unions varied by sector and place, and many unions limited themselves to mutual aid and relief work. Some played a purely intermediate role in social conflicts, and, of course, many unions had only a formal existence.

The trade union movement was, however, the site of a conflict among various political currents for influence and therefore reflected the political conflicts in the country as a whole. Within the movement were representatives of the nationalist parties, the Muslim Brothers, the communists, and, above all beginning in 1954, the Ba'thists. Until 1957 the General Confederation of Trade Unions was dominated by the moderate current of its president, Subhi al-Khatib. Al-Khatib was a member of the small Cooperative Socialist Party, which Patrick Seale has described as a "right-wing Islamic Party."[44] Several unions with radical leaders joined the World Federation of Trade Unions (WFTU) while remaining part of the General Confederation.[45] This minority current was severely repressed by the dictatorial regimes that lasted until 1954.

At the beginning of 1957, the fall of Adib Shishakli and the installation of a democratic coalition created favorable conditions for leftist political initiatives. Subhi al-Khatib was ousted from the presidency of the Syrian confederation by a group composed of communists, Ba'thists, and unaffiliated leftists that had gained a slender majority.[46] That the minister of labor and social affairs had been, since 1956, a member of the Ba'th party facilitated such a reversal because the election of trade union leaders at all levels still required ministerial consent. Thanks to this new majority, relations with the WFTU became official, and the Syrian trade union movement participated as a member of both the General Confederation and the Progressive Federation of Damascus.[47]

In 1958 Syria and Egypt were joined in the United Arab Republic (UAR), which lasted until 1961. The Syro-Egyptian union overturned yet again the relationship of forces within the trade union movement. Communists were expelled from unions and their party outlawed. In September 1958, just as unity was being realized, Talaat Thaghlabi, the leader of the Progressive Federation of Damascus, was elected to the leadership of the General Confederation of Trade Unions. The federations of Damascus and Homs were united. Measures to unify the Egyptian and Syrian trade unions were undertaken in 1959. The workers' movement was subjected to a far tighter control than had previously been the case.

The Years of Transition, 1959–1965

To understand the period of Syro-Egyptian unity, it is necessary to keep in mind two major laws that turned economic structures and social relations upside down: the agrarian reform of 1959 and the nationalizations of 1961. The break with the past in the second instance was less sharp than it appears because it was preceded by nationalizations at the beginning of the decade. Badr ed-Din Siba'i has shown that the agrarian reform, by attacking the landowning aristocracy, liberated labor from agricultural servitude and actually created the conditions for capitalist development in this sector.[48] Land reform initially enhanced the attachment of a class of small peasant proprietors to the land. Over time, as it contributed to the employment of modern techniques by this class, it also pushed part of the rural population toward the cities.

From the workers' point of view, even before the nationalizations, the social-affairs decrees of 1959 marked a spectacular advance. The new labor law regulated the length of the workday and overtime pay, granted annual vacations of two or three weeks depending on seniority, limited the hours of women's work, and guaranteed maternal leave. The new social security laws guaranteed coverage for illness and work-related accidents as well as retirement.

At the same time, trade unions were severely restrained. The right to strike was eliminated, the trade union leaderships were more tightly controlled by the Ministry of Labor, and political activity was forbidden. Repression against activists, especially communists, was brutal. The trade union movement had been entirely taken in hand.

The breakup of the UAR in September 1961 had entirely negative repercussions for the labor movement and workers. The social legislation was not revoked, but the nationalizations were immediately annulled. As the workers attempted to defend them, they faced increased repression.

In 1962 the unions demanded that the nationalizations of 1961 be reinstated and that Syro-Egyptian unity be reconstituted. A strike at Khumassiyyah ended in a confrontation with police in which 4 workers were killed and 100 arrested. Nasserists had achieved real popularity in the labor milieu, taking advantage of their association with social legislation and the repression of the communists.[49] Mass political movements swamped the labor movement's particular interests, however. In October 1962 during two days of demonstrations, several newspapers, including that of the Ba'th Party, were shut down. In November trade union leaders were arrested in Aleppo. Conflicts occurred in the schools and at the university. When Ba'thist army officers announced their coup on March 8, 1963, thousands of peasants, workers, and students went out into the streets.[50]

The new regime did not immediately reinstate the nationalizations, however. In 1963 it nationalized the large private banks, but not until 1964 did it announce the first decrees nationalizing industrial enterprises. Between these two events, the strikes and demonstrations of merchants, artisans, independent workers, and small owners in February and April (first at Hama and then throughout the country) required a response from the

Ba'th Party and initiated a progressive radicalization of the regime.[51] The first nationalization decrees, which applied to seven textile firms in Aleppo and Damascus, were undertaken as sanctions against such political resistance. The nationalizations quickly became a weapon in a game with ever increasing stakes against the bourgeoisie and the right, but perhaps also between opposing tendencies in the Ba'th Party. As Hannoyer and Seurat put it, "The nationalizations appear not as measures responding to any particular economic imperative, but rather as a political tool in the hands of the 'regionalists' to prove their own leftism and the right-wing tendencies of the national command."[52]

The oil industry was taken over in December 1964 and a new wave of nationalizations was announced in January 1965. Nationalizations continued throughout the year with occasional adjustments and retreats—when they appeared to have gone too far. By the end of the year 158 enterprises had passed into the hands of the state, and the public sector made up 75 percent of industry as opposed to a previous 25 percent. The nationalizations of 1961 had affected between 12,000 and 15,000 workers, whereas those of 1964–1965 affected an additional 32,000.[53]

For the first few months of the Ba'thist revolution the trade union movement had a pluralist character. After the secession from Egypt, Nasserists and communists were influential; but the Muslim Brothers were also, and the "workers' movement remained a powerful force with which the government had to bargain in order to win its support."[54] The trade union movement rapidly became a pawn in the conflict that was raging within the state and the party itself for political control. In July 1963, the Nasserist Thaghlabi was replaced by the Marxist Khaled al-Hakim, who entered the regional command of the Ba'th Party in September.

The mobilization of the trade union organizations for the confrontations of 1964 was little more than symbolic, according to Elizabeth Picard. The unions were still dominated by the Marxist current, which demanded trade union autonomy in regard to the state. This Marxist wing was progressively eliminated as the conflict within the Ba'th Party grew more intense. A new, more democratic labor law was passed that eliminated earlier repressive practices, reestablished the principle of election to high office, and allowed political activity once again to unions. Hardly had the law been passed before it was suspended for six months. Khaled al-Hakim was ousted from the Ba'th Party in July 1964, and the executive committee of the General Confederation was replaced by eleven activists chosen by the party. The trade union elections in December and January 1964–1965 (and those that followed for the fourteenth congress of the General Confederation to be held in April) were marked by raucous debates and by a mixture of fraud and intimidation that allowed the Ba'thists complete victory. In 1965 the repression affected not only communists but all union activists; it intensified the following year with waves of arrests. The sixteenth congress, held in 1966, marked the definitive subordination of the trade union movement to the Ba'th Party and the state. But "although the confederation entered the conflict of the 1963 revolution with a militant potential hardened by the years of conflict with the bourgeoisie during the rupture with Egypt, inside several months it had lost most of its power."[55]

Trade unionism came to be a completely different thing after 1966. The 1959 law had, it is true, introduced several restrictions to the freedom of action of the unions. The law of 1964 was, at least in appearance, less repressive, although it continued to forbid the right to strike. However, faced with a state that asserted for itself the prerogative to speak for the workers, trade unions no longer had any oppositional task. Henceforth their mission was to contribute to developing production and building a new society by working for "the realization of the aspirations of the Arab people for unity, freedom and socialism, for the protection of work and production, for the creating of skilled manpower . . . which would be capable of assuming national responsibilities and the protection of the material, moral, health and cultural interests of the workers."[56] The following congress would only deepen this new orientation.

Class, Labor Organization, and Trade Unions in Ba'thi Syria

In the 1960s, Syria began to undergo such massive social change that the social landscape since has been turned upside down. The population doubled in twenty years, from 4.5 million to 9 million between 1960 and 1981. According to the CIA, in the mid-1990s it approaches 14 million. The urban fraction of the population has grown from 37 percent to 50 percent, and the modernization of the countryside, the development of education, and the growth of state services has profoundly changed rural lifestyles.

These changes have been at the initiative of a political elite originating in social groups that emerged out of the modernization of the country during the Mandate and early independence. The Ba'thi state issued from a movement that claimed to represent the interests of the entire people and that had, from the very beginning, an ambiguous relationship with society in which were mixed the desire to control, reciprocal manipulation, laxity, and tolerance or even blindness in regard to what happened at the edge of the law.

How, in this context, were socioeconomic institutions articulated and mechanisms of alliance and solidarity induced by the functioning of a new regime? Central to answering this question is the study of the world of labor, which itself questions at the outset the utility of the categorization that underlies it: It appears even more difficult than previously to define a class in the absence of any collective action by its members. How, in the absence of any social expression of such a whole, can we ferret out its interests or the solidarities that might constitute it?

Reasoning in this way privileges the expression of solidarity in regard to social reality. It may also draw out more from Syrian history than it can really provide. Had I chosen to use the workers' struggles between the 1930s and 1950s as a way of understanding later developments, I would implicitly be accepting the hypothesis that the past still weighs on the present. This poses a theoretical problem that deserves a longer discussion, for it would include a reflection on society as a whole as well as in each of its social relationships. Hinnebusch, at odds with the dominant interpretations, argues that one cannot understand Syria without taking into account the variable of class.[57] On the condition of not stopping there, which he is the first to insist upon, I agree.

The World of Labor and the Active Population

Beginning with 1960, we have relatively good figures for Syria thanks to three censuses undertaken in 1960, 1970, and 1981. Additional surveys undertaken in 1984, 1989, and 1991 flesh out the census data and provide useful information down to the mid-1990s, when changes continue to be profound.

From 1960 to 1970 the proportion of the population by sector or by socioprofessional category changed little. By comparison, the division of the population in regard to employment status reveals some massive changes, due mainly to the agrarian reform laws and secondarily to the nationalizations. Independent laborers doubled in absolute numbers and increased from 26 to 38 percent of the population at large. The number of wage workers remained constant and dropped in relative terms by 13 percent. The category of independent laborers corresponds here primarily to peasants who, from agricultural wage laborers, became small owners. An increase in the proportion of unpaid family labor arose from the same cause.

Between the 1970 and 1981 censuses, however, the opposite phenomenon was at work. The proportion of the population active in the agricultural sector dropped in half, as did the absolute number of workers in the sector. The remainder could be found in industry and services, whose numbers nearly doubled, and in construction, which increased threefold. At the same time, the portion of the population taken to be "production workers" doubled in size, growing from 28 percent to 40 percent of the total. Wage workers went from 43 percent to 60 percent of the workforce but remained constant within the category of "production worker" at about three-quarters of the total.

During this decade there was a rapid increase in the degree to which the working population as a whole became wage earners. This development reversed the tendency of the previous decade, when the major economic tendency was the growth of the independent peasantry. This reversal was more a result of the overall reduction in the agricultural population than of an increase in the proportion of wage earners in other parts of the economy.

If we look more closely at the classical proletariat, in the sense of wage earners in productive sectors (extractive or transformative industries, transport, building, public works, and electricity), we see their number double from 258,000 to 543,000; their proportion of the population grew from 17 percent to 26.5 percent of the total. However, these statistics can be misleading. We know that a significant number of the industrial workers, particularly in the public sector, for example, continue to work occasionally in agriculture.

Moonlighting became more common at the end of the decade, but it was already apparent at the beginning of the 1980s. The census data record only the primary activity or (more likely) the official one, which is not always a person's primary source of income. One survey taken in 1980 in a large textile firm confirmed the importance of the second job.[58] Ten years after the inflation that accompanied the policy of economic liberalization had dramatically eroded the purchasing power of wage earners, they could no longer survive without additional sources of income. One official of the same firm estimated in 1986 that the overwhelming majority of the employees had other incomes. The ordinary source was agriculture, which provided both consumption goods such as fruits and vegetables that did not need to be paid for as well as money when such products were sold. By the same token, for a growing part of the agricultural population, wage employment provided a money income that could not be earned from agricultural labor. Thus, although the figures accurately reveal a decline in agriculture's role in the economy as a whole, they may also be interpreted as reflecting the fact that fewer workers declared agriculture as their primary source of income and that more peasant proletarians (employed in both agriculture and industry) were moonlighting.

The relatively low intensity of work in the public sector made the "double day" possible. It may also explain the low wages that made a second income necessary, although because low wages may also induce low productivity, the direction of causation is hard to determine. The relatively greater productivity in the private sector certainly made higher wages possible there while also making a second job far more difficult to manage.

The other major phenomenon of social change was the increase in the level of education. The proportion of children in secondary school went from 28 percent in 1965 to 60 percent in 1985; the proportion of the youth attending universities went from 8 percent to 18 percent over the same period. The proportion of illiteracy dropped from 66 percent in 1960 to 35 percent in 1990. Among the working-class population, the proportion of illiterates dropped from 47 percent in 1960 to 39 percent in 1970 to less than 25.5 percent in 1990. The proportion of this same group with certificates of primary education or more grew from 12 percent to 20 percent to reach 40 percent in 1981. There is every reason to believe it had reached 50 percent by the mid-1990s. This growth in literacy had significant effects on the consciousness and behavior of workers, although these effects may not always be apparent. In a small firm that made chocolate cookies and whose workforce had quadrupled in a dozen years, for example, the personnel director recalled in 1986 that the same women workers who had signed their initial employment contracts without understanding a word of them now discussed every detail.

The Public Sector, the Private Sector, and Labor Relations

The nationalization of the largest industrial enterprises, which followed the agrarian reform by several years, implied a profound restructuring of labor relations. The first consequence, from the workers' point of view, was a clear improvement of the situation of wage earners in the public sector. This was primarily because of the reevaluation of public-sector wages and the effective application of the labor legislation and social insurance schemes, of guaranteed employment, and of protection against firing. The workers understood this clearly, and the conflicts of the years between 1961 and 1965 attest to their mobilization in support of nationalization.

Above all, the cleavage that already existed between wage earners in the large modern enterprises and those in artisanal and semiartisanal enterprises widened. Working conditions, pay, confrontation with owners, all changed in character, and from this followed an evolution of the two categories of workers in very different ways.

It is difficult to ascertain the distribution of workers between these two sectors. If those in the public sector were correctly counted for self-evident reasons, it is far more difficult to determine the number for the private sector, partly because employers tended to undercount their employees (in order to escape social insurance payments) but also because these workers were mobile and a significant proportion of them worked at home or in familial settings.

The first wave of nationalization, in 1961, affected 12,000 to 15,000 industrial workers out of a total of 85,000. By June 1965, the public sector included 158 enterprises with 32,000 workers. Initially the nationalizations spurred on industrial production, which doubled between 1963 and 1969. Existing enterprises thereafter expanded, new ones were created, and in 1970 the number of employees in the public industrial sector amounted to 56,000. This was now 39.7 percent of the wage workers and 28.7 percent of those in industry; a decade later the respective figures were 46 percent and 34 percent.

The nationalizations of 1965 touched enterprises that had barely fifty workers.[59] The private sector began to appear as a residual category. As a matter of fact, however, it still contained thousands of small firms with an artisanal character that were represented in artisans' associations. Until 1970 the growth of the public sector was more rapid than that of the private sector, and the role of the latter in industrial employment dropped from 66 percent in 1966 to 59 percent in 1970. In the next decade, however, this tendency too began to reverse, and in 1972 private manufacturers accounted for 62 percent of employment.[60] In 1970 the Central Statistical Bureau enumerated 33,000 so-called industrial establishments, of which only 550 had more than ten employees; more than a third were in the textile sector.

According to the estimates of the Central Statistical Bureau, the end of the 1980s saw a continuing downward trend in the public sector, whose industrial employees represented only 30.7 percent of the total employed in industry as a whole. A similar story can be told for the creation of firms that moved dramatically upward in 1986 after a slowdown between 1982 and 1984, which itself occurred after an earlier upturn dating from 1981.

Functioning and Evolution of the Public Sector

Syrian industry remains characterized by intermediate industry and the almost total absence of an industry producing the means of production. Of course, the first five-year plans aimed at creating metallurgical and chemical industries using primary resources available in the country itself, such as phosphates and petroleum. Between 1972 and 1992, if we take the increase in the number of unionized workers as a reliable indicator of employment in the public sector, the most important growth occurred in Sweida and Deraa in the south and in Tartous on the northwest coast. Aleppo, Homs, and Damascus, by contrast, grew by far less. The eastern regions such as Raqqa, Hassake, and Dayr al-Zur (despite the creation of some foodstuffs industries, sugar mills, and a paper factory) hardly took part in these economic developments.

Jean Hannoyer has shown in detail, in regard to Dayr al-Zur, the role of the public sector in industrializing a hitherto exclusively agricultural region and the contradictions inherent in the model of development undertaken by the Syrian state. The way in which such projects are put in place and the perverse ways in which individual interests are manifested in clientelism combine to make it impossible to block the influence of other effects that diminish the workforce, such as the attractiveness of the labor markets of the Gulf and especially nearby Saudi Arabia.

New enterprises created by the state were far from being as productive as private ones, and all analyses (including those published in the Syrian press) accentuated the role of the underemployment of productive resources: As early as 1976 one journalist estimated that such plants were used to only 60 percent of capacity (and some far less) and placed the opportunity cost at 45 percent of the gross national product.[61]

Given this history, it is not surprising that the Fifth Plan at the beginning of the 1980s once again emphasized agriculture, self-sufficiency in foodstuffs, and increased productivity in industry rather than the building of new enterprises. Throughout the decade the underutilization of capacity grew worse because of the difficulties in finding raw materials, new machinery, and spare parts and because of energy prices—all of which had significant effects on working conditions and the pay scale. These difficulties grew out of dependence on foreign markets and currency shortages. They were avoided or arrested briefly each time there was an increase in petroleum resources, whether due to price increases of crude petroleum or to the discovery of new fields. The campaigns for self-sufficiency, usually under the slogan of self-reliance, and the campaigns to increase initiative and inventiveness were designed to better exploit existing resources. They brought, at best, slight results. In the end only the loosening of currency exchange regulations and of import-export licensing were able to unblock the situation. It was to this end that the regime undertook economic liberalization in 1985–1986.

Generally speaking, the conditions in which the workforce was mobilized were not those in which one could expect to see the emergence of a working-class consciousness or the crystallization of a common set of interests in any form. Because most of the firms had been in operation for such a short time, most workers had very little seniority and thus little experience in industrial work. To this must be added the factories'placement in a rural setting and the tendency of workers either to retain and till their land or to leave the factory when rural wages increased at harvest time. The extreme instability of a workforce whose turnover could reach 30 percent a year in some enterprises also made it difficult for an industrial workforce to accumulate common experiences.

Last, and perhaps behind everything, was the devaluation of productive work and especially manual labor. The weight of the administrative corps and the privileges it received only increased the demoralization of the workers. Production incentives, which could represent an important part of earnings, were generally higher for the administrators than for those in production. This was because they were equally divided among the administrative staff so that all benefited, whereas among production workers they applied strictly in regard to individual productivity. The best workers could double their incomes, but the least productive (for whatever reason) sometimes earned less than a raw recruit.

The Problems of the Private Sector

The policy of the state in regard to the private sector was in general ambiguous, hesitant, and contradictory. After several difficult years, the rectification movement at the end of 1970 announced a period of easing by the state. This was translated into a slight increase in the creation of firms in the first half of the 1970s. The main difficulties came from import-export regulation that limited access to primary materials, machinery, or assembly kits.[62] Small entrepreneurs used the black market, and prices skyrocketed so that used machines were sometimes more expensive than new ones; some public-sector products doubled or tripled in price when demand was strong or when, as sometimes occurred, the inputs originally destined for the public sector had been sold on the black market.[63] The small firms showed a real dynamism and great nimbleness in profiting from the difficulties of the public sector and the possibilities of export (to the Soviet Union but also to other Arab countries).

Confronted with a public sector that was made up of a small number of large, autonomous, and well-integrated firms, the private sector developed productive structures that were entirely the reverse, depending primarily on an extremely complex system of subcontracting. Between the merchant and the product, there were as many as half a dozen producers, each of which mastered one or more processes of a complete line of production.

The other characteristic of the private sector was the relative importance of family labor and apprentices. This was the expression of an economic strategy to reduce costs, a family strategy of giving children or relatives an interest in the enterprise, and a social strategy of winning the loyalty of a worker by hiring his children. The small firms, then, were essentially familial and headed by men who had acquired their knowledge on the spot by apprenticeship with a parent and by experience. The most traditional only rarely employed outside experts such as engineers. The use of female labor at home was frequent but is hard to measure.

Such strategies of extreme specialization may have been more common in the textile industry than in others, but they appear to have been a common feature of the private sector. This specialization must be seen as a form of adaptation to the particular context of a society under the constant pressure of a strong state that it sought to escape.

In these conditions, labor relations were marked by high levels of paternalism but also by high mobility, at least in the smallest firms. In these situations employment was based on highly personal relations, and the workers were rarely declared, as was required by the labor codes. Problems were resolved more or less amicably based on which side was dominant, the state of the market, or the goodwill of the owner. In the largest firms, however, employers could not ignore the social insurance schemes: All employed workers had to be declared, and all guarantees in the law applied to them. The labor force in large private firms was more stable than in the smaller ones. As for the level of pay, it generally depended on the labor market. Skilled workers were generally better paid in the private sector, but if unskilled, they were generally no better off.[64] Higher wages corresponded to much more intense work, of course.[65]

The years between 1982 and 1986 were dark for the Syrian economy and especially for the private sector. The following years were relatively better, as a series of measures were enacted that eased first imports and exports and then private investment. These measures gave impetus to the creation of new enterprises and allowed an enlargement of those already existing. By 1993 it was possible to find dozens of private firms with 100–200 workers. This was a radically new situation and actually helped to enhance trade union activity.

There are, therefore, still two worlds of work rather than one, and they run according to radically different social and economic constraints. On the one hand are workers in the public sector, more nearly marginalized than exploited in the classic Marxist sense of the word because they are immersed in a system that is subject not to the economic logic of profitability and productivity but to social and political goals. These firms go back and forth between being a public service (many of the middle-level officials are truly service oriented) to an outright prebend, providing opportunities for some of the highest-level directors to control networks through which goods and services are distributed and thus appropriated.

The private sector faces a subtle mix of real pressure for rationalization (and thus exploitation) along with a set of common interests between worker and owner in which everything is ultimately negotiable. Private enterprises not only can provide workers with meaningful compensation but also can bind them to the solidarity of a joint struggle against the state, which is seen as the sole source of problems faced by both workers and owners.

These two worlds, separable for analytic purposes, interpenetrate largely because workers are employed in both during the "double day." It remains to be asked if and how in the consciousness of workers the interests defended in one world affect their sense of the other. A look at trade union organization and its evolution will bring us closer to an answer to this question.

Trade Unions and Politics

The trade union congresses between 1965 and 1974 made the unions ever more bureaucratized, transforming them into conduits for state policy. Still, control by the state was never complete, and diverse political currents, however weak, managed to survive and express themselves. At the end of the 1980s, then, the economic opening and the development of the private sector progressively modified the ways in which the state intervened in the economy; such interventions in turn had significant repercussions on the trade unions.

As early as 1964, new trade union legislation redefined the mission of the trade unions. From that date on they were supposed to "work for the realization of the aspirations of the Arab people for unity, freedom and socialism." The fourteenth congress of the General Confederation reaffirmed this new conception of trade unions, which was the reverse of the principles for which unions were initially formed: The unions formerly had rights; now one spoke of their duties.

This new orientation marked the end of trade union autonomy and the integration or "incorporation" of the unions into a social and political system in which the "mass state" extended its control over society. Seurat and Hannoyer speak of a process of "desocialization" in which the state sought to substitute itself for civil society as the latter became more and more confused with political organization.[66] They take this formulation too far, but it captures the attempt by the new leaders to speak of the people as a form of mystification through which they legitimated their own outlawing of all autonomous expression in civil society.[67] From 1964 to 1968, repression intensified against the activists who did not join the dominant current, and the fifteenth congress, in 1968, marked the definitive closure of the trade unions to pluralist currents.

The introductory report to the fifteenth congress made explicit the concept of complete congruence between the objectives of the regime and those of the working class. The expression of political differences was discouraged so that "the working class [could] realize its historic mission" of building "Arab socialist society."

The new legislation announced in 1968 introduced new rules of the game. It created the trade union committee, which was elected by the general assembly of the workers for the entire plant or group of enterprises with more than fifty employees. More important, it introduced the principle of "democratic centralism," which was a counterweight to the principle of elections at each level because it allowed the higher levels of an institution to strictly control the lower ones. The General Confederation was to be one of the popular organizations dedicated to constraining society. Without officially ceasing to represent the interests of the workers, it gained the new functions of training, isolating, mobilizing, and propagandizing to its members.

Between the fifteenth and sixteenth congresses, the minister of defense, Hafiz al-Asad, came to power in a coup, usually referred to as the corrective movement of November 13, 1970. In February 1971 al-Asad became the president of Syria, a position he retained into the 1990s.

The sixteenth congress refined the reversal of the prior orientation of the unions. It developed the concept of production as a weapon in the struggle for liberation, unity, and socialism. In 1974, during the eighteenth congress, this path led to the idea of "political trade unionism," and the guiding principle of the congress was that "political unionism, as the alternative of the struggle for economic demands, is the foundation of working class unity in the fight for liberation." The major issue for the congress was whether this concept indicated an opposition to, or at least suggested a radical opposition between, economic demands and political commitments. Different points of view were apparently expressed by the head of state and the head of the General Confederation, but was there a real divergence of opinion between them? Hannoyer and Seurat think not: "Two currents may indeed come into conflict within the trade union organization, but it seems more likely that it was the ambiguity inherent in this conception of trade unionism which was expressed. Did not M. Hadid simply play his necessary role as head of a 'popular organization' in expressing to the regime what were the demands of his constituency?"[68] Such an argument appears as well to imply the impossibility of reducing trade unionism completely to a matter of hearing "the master's voice" and of making unions into nothing other than a conduit for state or party policies.

Daily Trade Unionism: Discourses and Practices

The level and manner of trade unionization reflected the development of the conception of unionism. By 1972, if membership remained formally voluntary, it had become more or less compulsory in the public sector, where dues were collected directly by the enterprise from workers' salaries. In the private sector unions remained far weaker; some enterprises were wholly unionized and others not at all.

In 1972, according to official figures, trade union density was 82 percent in the public sector and 32 percent in the private sector. These figures, however, hide some important differences between areas of activity. Basic industry in the public and private sectors was unionized at 91.4 percent and 19.8 percent, respectively. Banking, in contrast, had the highest level of unionization in the private sector, which is indicative of the professional milieu in which the Ba'th Party is most deeply rooted.

Trade unions had branch unions in each province and horizontal federations in each region and were also structured vertically by profession (*niqabah mihaniyyah*). Every plant with more than fifty workers had a trade union committee elected by the general assembly (or congress) of workers in the factory at the time of the General Confederation Congress, which initially occurred every two years but since 1974 has been held every four years.

In practice it appears that after 50 percent of the employees had joined, the firm was considered organized and the owner was responsible for collecting dues for all employees with a checkoff system. The nature of trade unions as transmission belts in the machinery of governmental power encourages us to imagine the complexity of the relationship that workers in the private sector had with such organizations. Trade unions offered workers not only a way of putting pressure on owners but also benefits and social services that made the decision to join far easier.

Trade union elections in such a context rarely offered any surprises. Theoretically all workers had the right to be candidates, whether as individuals or as part of a list. In the overwhelming majority of cases only a single list was presented, and it was composed mainly of members of the Ba'th Party; a few members of allied parties in the National Progressive Front and some "independents" might be added. It did happen on occasion that opposition lists (or more frequently individual candidacies) were presented in opposition to the official list: activists of leftist parties, the Muslim Brothers, or even those without other partisan connections.

Within the plant itself the trade union limited its activity to providing social services and participating in the administration of the enterprise. It was this participation that made Hannoyer and Seurat speak of a "trade unionism transformed from opposition to management," in which the union became just another point in the flow chart of the public sector.[69] The workers' production councils, whose implantation caused so much ink to be spilt in the ensuing years, quickly became nothing more than empty shells.[70] The absence of any real economic demands was consistent, at least in the public sector, with the new conception of trade unionism and the idea that the administration of public-sector firms could, as a matter of principle, be working only in the interests of the workers. The least that can be said is that the resistance of the workers was relatively weak and that this was not due only to repression. Trade unions in the private sector hardly existed, and it is worth remarking that the 1986 trade union congress barely mentioned them. In some cases they played the role of unwelcome guests who forced the owners to respect certain rules and who were then accused by the owners of being responsible for all the ills that plagued the firm.

The one area of activity that does provide surprises is the publication of newspapers at the firm. Because this was considered a cultural and political activity, it occasionally permitted the expression of other than politically ready-made ideas. In these newspapers the expression of demands was more widespread than elsewhere, and criticism was more biting.

Names of officials were never given, which of course limited the range of criticism.

From Corporatism Toward Trade Union Autonomy

The Syrian experience in regard to corporatism has been quite comparable to others and offers an illustration of institutional reciprocity. The previous comments on the trade union press reveal that the absence of democracy does not imply the complete absence of any form of expression or participation. At another level, the trade union organizations functioned as a kind of powerful lobby capable of blocking decisions that appeared contrary to the immediate interests of the workers. This is what appears to have occurred after the passage of the 1992 legislation installing a new medical insurance scheme. Because the workers at the large factories already had free medical care guaranteed by law and paid for by the firm, they refused to accept a new system that would have required them to pay without a corresponding increase in services.[71]

Syria seems quite different, however, in another regard, that is, the previous existence of a real political party, the Ba'th, with a strong ideology and a base of activists that could (even if only weakly at the beginning) penetrate society. Hannoyer and Seurat indicate that the party organization at the bottom of an enterprise could oppose the policies of the director at the top. It is not without importance that in enterprises controlled by the army neither the union nor the party were allowed. At the limit it makes sense to imagine that a return to trade union autonomy implies that the party will also become autonomous.

The twenty-second congress of the General Confederation was held in December 1992, and some unusual conflicts and problems arose. It was not held in November, as had been the case since 1970, because that linked the meeting to the anniversary of the rectification movement. It was said that al-Asad no longer considered this linkage appropriate in the current political situation. One confidential source suggests "a desire by some delegates to distance themselves from the tutelage of the Ba'th party and present themselves as autonomous representatives of the workers confronting the owners."

With the development of the private sector and the multiplication of relatively large enterprises (those with more than a hundred workers), a more muscular trade unionism is set to appear. The fall of the socialist camp in 1991 did not pass unnoticed, and if Syrian leaders still speak of development and construction and of the direction of the labor movement by the Ba'th Party, they no longer speak of socialism. As for the guiding principle of the latest union congress, it was limited to repeating what the president said: "Let us all be workers in this country and let us focus our efforts to build it up, let us fight for freedom, for greatness and prosperity."

Notes

1. Steven Heydemann, "Successful Authoritarianism: The Social and Structural Origins of Populist Authoritarian Rule in Syria, 1946–1963," Ph.D. dissertation, University of Chicago, 1990. Raymond Hinnebusch, *Authoritarian Politics and State Formation in Ba'thist Syria: Army, Party, and Peasant* (Boulder: Westview Press, 1991); "Class and State in Ba'thist Syria," in Richard Antoun and Donald Quataert (eds.), *Syria, Society, Culture and Polity* (Albany: SUNY Press, 1991). Philip Khoury, *Syria Under the French Mandate: The Politics of Arab Nationalism* (London: I. B. Tauris, 1987). Elizabeth Picard, "Clans militaires et pouvoir ba'thiste," *Orient* (Summer 1979):49–62; "Une crise syrienne en 1965: Les syndicats ouvriers face au nouveau régime ba'thiste," *Sou'al: État et Mouvement Ouvrier au Moyen-Orient* (February 1988):82–95; "Infitah économique et transition démocratique en Syrie," in Ricardo Bocco et al. (eds.), *Moyen-Orient fin de siècle migrations, démocratisation, médiations: Enjeux locaux et internationaux* (Paris PUF/IUED, 1994). Volker Perthes, "The Syrian Private Industrial and Commercial Sectors and the State," *International Journal of Middle East Studies* 24, 2 (May 1992). Yahya Sadowski, "Political Power and Economic Organization in Syria: The Course of State Intervention," Ph.D. dissertation, University of California at Los Angeles, 1984. Michel Seurat, "État et industrialisation dans l'Orient arabe: Les fondements socio-historiques," in André Bourguey (ed.), *Industrialisation et changements sociaux dans l'Orient arabe* (Paris: CERMOC, 1984) 27–68.

2. In Arabic, Abdallah Hanna is the only author who has researched and published on labor topics. In European languages there are myself, Hannoyer, Seurat, and Picard. More recent, and from a somewhat different perspective, is the work of Jocelyne Cornand. Abdallah Hanna, *al-harakah al-ummaliyyah fi suriya wa lubnan, 1900–1945* (Damascus: Dar Dimashq, 1973). Jean Hannoyer, "Industrie et changement social en Syrie: Deir ez-Zor et sa région," in Bourgey, *Industrialisation et changements sociaux*, 401–430. Jean Hannoyer and Michel Seurat, *État et secteur public industriel en Syrie* (Beyrouth: CERMOC, 1979). Jocelyne Cornand, "L'artisanat du textile à Alep, survie ou dynamisme 7," *Bulletin d'Études Orientales* 36 (1984); *L'entrepreneur et l'État en Syrie: Le secteur privé du textile Àlep* (Paris: l'Harmattan-Maison de l'Orient Méditerranéen, 1994); Groupe de Recherche sur le Moyen-Orient, "Fabrication et vente des chaussures dans les suwayqa Bab an-Nasr et Ali," in *Monde Arabe Contemporain, Cahiers de Recherche* (Lyons: Maison

de l'Orient Méditerranéen, 1994), 23–42. Elizabeth Longuenesse, "La classe ouvrière en Syrie, une classe en formation," Ph.D. dissertation, University of Paris V, 1977; "Travail et rapports de production en Syrie: Une enquète sur les travailleurs de la bonneterie à Damas," *Bulletin d'Études Orientales* 32–33 (1981); "The Syrian Working Class Today," *MERIP Reports* 134 (July/August 1985); "Secteur public industriel en Syrie," *Maghreb-Machrek*, no. 109 (1987); Groupe de Recherche sur le Moyen-Orient, "Travail et travailleurs dans le secteur public industriel en Syrie, une étude de cas," in *Monde Arabe Contemporain, Cahiers de Recherche* (Lyons: Maison de l'Orient Méditerranéen, 1994), 8–23; "État et syndicalisme en Syrie: Discours et pratiques," *Sou'al: État et Mouvement Ouvrier au Moyen-Orient* (February 1988): 97–130.

3. Charles Issawi, *Economic History of th[e Middle East, 1800–1914* (Chicago: University of Chicago Press, 1966), 248–256.

4. Said Himadeh, *The Economic Organization of Syria* (Beirut: American University Press, 1936), 157; Shafik Sanadiki, "Le mouvement syndical en Syrie," Ph.D. dissertation, University of Paris, 1949; Badr ed-Din Siba'i, *Adwa' 'ala al-ra'smaliyyah al-ajnabiyyah fi suriyah* (Damascus: Dar al-Jamahir, 1967).

5. Khodr Zakariya, "Khasa'is at-tarkib at-tabaqi fi suriya," unpublished study (Damascus, 1974), cited in Longuenesse, "La classe Ouvrière," 36.

6. Rizqallah Hilan, *Culture et développement en Syrie et dans les pays retardés* (Paris: Éditions Anthropos, 1969).

7. International Labor Organization, "Les conditions du travail dans les industries anciennes et modernes en Syrie," *Revue Internationale du Travail* (March 1934).

8. See the list provided by Siba'i, *Adwa' 'ala al-ra'smaliyyah*, 404, as well as the list given by Edmund Asfour in *Syria: Development and Monetary Policy* (Cambridge: Harvard University Press, 1959).

9. These late-nineteenth-century silk-spinning factories usually belonged to English or French investors. See Adnan Farra, *L'industrialisation en Syrie* (Geneva: Université de Genève, 1950).

10. See ILO, "Les conditions du travail."

11. See Siba'i, *Al-ra'smaliyyah*, 248.

12. Cited by Zakariya, "Khasa' is," and also in Longuenesse, "La classe ouvrière en Syrie," 36.

13. Hanna cites the example of shoemaking, where 200 master craftsmen employed 5,000 workers, as an example of a boundary case where artisanal workshops could be found side by side with essentially capitalist firms. *Al-harakah al-ummaliyyah*, 135.

14. Although these figures do indicate tendencies, they are undoubtedly overestimates. A 1934 ILO study ("Les conditions du travail") counted 55,000 laborers and artisans in the fifteen most important cities of Syria and Lebanon of whom fewer than 6,000 worked in modern industry; one Syrian author argues that there were 279,000 laborers of whom more than half were in Aleppo in 1939.

15. Abdallah Hanna, *Al-harakah al-ummaliyyah*, 384–385.

16. Khoury, *Syria Under the French Mandate*, 397.

17. This is drawn from a citation to a League of Nations study by Abdullah al-Azmeh, "L'évolution de la banque commerciale dans le cadre économique de la Syrie," Ph.D. dissertation, University of Lausanne, 1961, 179.

18. Youssef Helbaoui, *La Syrie: Mise en valeur d'un pays sous développé* (Paris: Librairie Générale de Droit et de Jurisprudence, 1956), 111

19. Elisabeth Longuenesse, "Travail et rapports de production en Syrie,"*Bulletin d'Études Orientales* 22–23 (1981):168

20. See Asfour, *Syria*, 133; and Suleiman Bagh, *L'industrie à Damas entre 1928 et 1958: Étude de géographie économique* (Damascus: Editions de l'Université de Damas, 1961), 59.

21. Aziz Allouni, "The Labour Movement in Syria," *Middle East Journal* 13 (1959):64–76. Jean Gaulmier, "Notes sur le mouvement syndicaliste à Hama," *Revue des Études Islamiques* (1932):95–126. Louis Massignon, "La structure du travail à Damas en 1927," *Cahiers Internationaux de Sociologie* 15 (1953): 34–52; "Les travailleurs agricoles et les artisans urbains en Syrie," *Le Monde Colonial Illustré* (1929).

22. See Sanadiki, "Le mouvement syndical en Syrie," 28.

23. Massignon, "La structure du travail à Damas."

24. Eleuthere Elefteriades, *Les chemins de fer en Syrie et au Liban* (Beirut: Imprimerie Catholique, 1944), 313

25. Sanadiki, "Le mouvement syndical en Syrie," 540; and Hanna, *Al-harakah al-ummaliyyah*, 230.

26. Jacques Couland, *Le mouvement syndical au Liban* (Paris: Éditions Sociales, 1977); Sanadiki, "Le mouvement syndical en Syrie."

27. Massignon, "Les travailleurs agricoles," 141.

28. ILO, "Les conditions de travail en Syrie."

29. Gaulmier, "Notes sur le mouvement syndicaliste à Hama," 112.

30. Massignon, "La structure du travail à Damas."

31. See Hanna, *Al-harakah al-ummaliyyah*, ch. 3.

32. For details see Sanadiki, "Le mouvement syndical en Syrie," 57–64.

33. Hanna, *Al-harakah al-ummaliyyah*, 440.

34. According to Sanadiki ("Le mouvement syndical en Syrie"), this occurred in December. Musa Shahhud placed it in March in his *"Al-haraka al-ummaliyyah fi suriya" Revue du Travail et des Affaires Sociales* 2, 1 (January 1950):440, as cited in Hanna, *Al-harakah al-ummaliyyah*, 440.

35. See Hanna, *Al-harakah al-ummaliyyah*, 450.

36. See Sadowski, "Political Power and Economic Organization in Syria," 125–128.

37. Heydemann, "Successful Authoritarianism," 99.

38. See Ibrahim Bakri, "Ba'd zikrayat nidal al-hizb bayna-l-ummal wa fi-l-niqabat," *Al-Akhbar* (Beirut), January 27, 1964, as cited in Longuenesse, "La classe ouvrière en Syrie," 80–82.

39. *Sawt al-Sha'b* (1946 and 1947), as cited in Longuenesse, "La classe ouvrière en Syrie," 80–82.

40. See Longuenesse, "La classe ouvrière en Syrie," 80–82; and Allouni, "The Labour Movement in Syria."

41. *Le mouvement syndical mondial* (May and October 1956 and January 1957).

42. Willard E. Beling, *Pan-Arabism and Labor* (Cambridge: Harvard University Press, 1961), 39.

43. Bakri, "Ba'd zikrayat."

44. Patrick Seale, *The Struggle for Syria* (London: Oxford University Press, 1965).

45. The World Federation of Trade Unions was under communist discipline, and its headquarters was in Prague. It no longer exists.

46. The executive committee was composed of twelve members: seven communists, three socialists, one nationalist, and one without partisan affiliation. See F. Chevallier, "Forces en presence en Syrie d'aujourd'hui," *Orient* 4 (1957):181.

47. Fourth World Congress, *Textes et decisions* (Prague: World Federation Trade Union, 1958), 55.

48. Badr ed-Din Siba'i, *Al-marhalah al-intiqaliyyah fi suriya: 'Ahd al-wahdah, 1958–1961*, (Beirut: Dar Ibn Khaldun, 1975).

49. Hannoyer and Seurat, *État et secteur public industriel en Syrie*, 14.

50. Safouh Akhrass, *Revolutionary Change and Modernization in the Arab World: A Case from Syria* (Damascus: Atlas, 1972), 169–172.

51. J. De Buck, "Les nationalisations en Syrie," *Correspondance d'Orient, Études* 7 (1965): 61–67.

52. Hannoyer and Seurat, *État et secteur public industriel en Syrie*, 11. "Regional command" refers to the Syrian Ba'th Party, which was technically subordinate to a larger pan-Arab, or "national," command.

53. See Yahya Arudaki, *Al-iqtisad as-suri al-hadith*, 2 vols. (Damascus: Wizarat al-Khaqafah, 1972, 1974); Bagh, *L'industrie à Damas*, 253.

54. Picard, "Clans militaires et pouvoir ba'thiste," 83–85.

55. Ibid., 89.

56. See the law of February 29, 1964.

57. See the synthesis I attempted in Richard T. Antoun and Donald Quataert (eds.), *Syria: Society, Culture, and Polity* (Albany: State University of New York Press, 1991).

58. Longuenesse, "Secteur public industriel en Syrie," 1987.

59. According to industrial union statistics, they included a food-preservation company with 90 employees but also an edible-oil refinery in Hama with 51 employees and an electric battery company in Aleppo with 52 employees.

60. Industrial establishment census as cited in Longuenesse, "La classe ouvrière en Syrie," 65. Other figures suggest that public employment rose between 1970 and 1984 and dropped dramatically between 1984 and 1991.

61. Ibid., 145–147.

62. Jocelyne Cornand uses the example of the Aleppo textile industry. *Alep: L'entrepreneur, la ville, l'état* (Paris: l'Harmattan, 1994).

63. Longuenesse, "The Syrian Working Class Today," 16–17.

64. Perthes ("The Syrian Sectors and the State") seems a bit overgeneral when he says that "wages in the private sector, for skilled labor in particular, are considerably higher than in the public sector" (216).

65. One worker explicitly told me this in an interview when he compared pay at the Dibs plant with work in the public sector. Longuenesse, "The Syrian Working Class Today."

66. Hannoyer and Seurat, *État et secteur public industriel en Syrie,* 41.

67. In an analysis of the situation of intellectuals and activists in Tunisia, Abdelqadir Zghal suggests that the elite of the civil society of the preceding period, having attained power, is no longer capable of distinguishing between the state and civil society. See Abdel Qader Zghal, "Le concept de societé civile et la transition vers le multipartisme," in Michel Camau (ed.), *Changements politiques au Maghreb* (Paris: Éditions CNRS, 1991).

68. Hannoyer and Seurat, *État et secteur public industrie en Syrie,* 49–53, but see also my analysis in Longuenesse, "La classe ouvrière en Syrie," 213–216.

69. See Hannoyer and Seurat, *État et secteur public industrie en Syrie,* 41.

70. See Ibid., 53–56; Longuenesse, "La classe ouvrière en Syrie," 219–220; and Bu Ali Yasin, *As-sulta al-ummaliyya ala wasa'il a-intaj* (Damascus: Dar al-Haqaiq, 1979).

71. See M. Ba'th, "A propos de la question de la santé en Syrie," in Brigitte Curmi and Sylvia Chiffoleau (eds.), *Médecins et protection sociale dans le monde arabe,* Les Cahiers du CERMOC, no. 5, 1993.

6

The Labor Movement in Israel:
Ideology and Political Economy

Michael Shalev

Strictly speaking, relatively little social history has been written about Israeli workers. Most labor history narrates the institutional history of the
trade union federation, which has monopolized the representation of Israeli labor since its creation in 1920. Even Anita Shapira, the premier historian of Israeli labor, has concentrated in her published work on the view
from above.[1] Most historians of the Israeli labor movement—and they are
few in number—have political engagements to particular actors within
the partisan structures they describe, loyalties that are sufficiently intense
to leave little room for the less overtly political narratives required by social history. Both Israeli and labor history are usually written with an emphasis on freely chosen ideological commitments, which also militates
against how social historians see social practice and ideology. Because this
chapter must be constructed using the available historiographical materials, I focus on the primary research agenda for several generations of
Israeli scholars and politicians: explaining the distinctive character, success, and longevity of the Histadrut.

What Makes the Histadrut Distinctive?

The Histadrut, Israel's "peak association" of labor, is a formidable Hydra
without peer in the postcommunist world.[2] Much of the Histadrut's distinctiveness, compared with European labor movements, originated in the
specific conditions of its establishment. The Histadrut was a spearhead
of a colonization movement that operated under unusual conditions: A

demographic minority relied heavily on propertyless immigrants to establish its presence in the country. It had no coercive power over the indigenous population and was substantially dependent on external sources of capital.

The story of the Histadrut since sovereignty revolves around the dialectic between this historical inheritance and shifts in the social, political, and economic landscape. The labor organization proved to be remarkably resilient, becoming a deeply embedded pivot in the political economy of Israel. Nevertheless, since the mid-1980s the Histadrut has suffered a series of profound crises culminating in May 1994 with the termination of Labor Party hegemony and with it—perhaps—the beginning of the end of the Histadrut's "exceptionalism."

Far more than just a confederation of trade unions, the Histadrut—whose full title is The General Organization of Israeli Workers—has two other principal branches. It owns, solely or jointly, a vast economic empire that includes the largest bank and the biggest industrial conglomerate in Israel. It also operates two of the country's most important social service funds—the Sick Fund and a group of pension funds—which provide primary health care and superannuation, respectively, to the majority of Israeli households. Its trade union arm effectively has no rivals and until recent years could claim to negotiate (in separate framework agreements for the public and private sectors) on behalf of 85 percent of all wage earners.[3]

The Histadrut's remarkable potency has been due not only to the wide range of functions and resources under its control but also to its organizational character. The subunits of the Histadrut—unions, enterprises, social service funds—are subject to a high degree of formal central control. Until the early 1990s, the Histadrut could claim to speak for approximately two-thirds of all Israeli adults. Members obtain affiliation by directly joining the central organization, which in return provides them with access to its services, only one of which is trade union protection. The Histadrut's elected officials, and traditionally its appointed officers as well, are nominated by political parties that control the Histadrut within an institutional framework that closely parallels the national polity. In practice, from the establishment of the state in 1948, the labor organization and its major divisions were controlled by the same party—the Labor Party and its predecessors—that dominated central and local government. The Histadrut's extraordinary capacities to mobilize workers on behalf of the party, as well as to provide it with money, paid positions, and other bounties, were undoubtedly a central pillar of the party's long period of uncontested dominance, from the mid-1930s to the late 1970s.

The labor organization's historical significance is even more far-reaching than its profound impact on domestic politics. Between 1920 and the establishment of the sovereign State of Israel in 1948, Histadrut functioned as a critical element of Zionism's embryonic "state in the making." The labor organization had special responsibility for assisting immigrant absorption through its labor exchanges, health clinics, housing schemes, and so forth. The Histadrut's contributions to establishing a viable Jewish presence in Palestine and building key parts of the infrastructure of the future state (including, for a time, its military functions) were central to the success of Israeli statemaking. Yet in accordance with the "Labor Zionist" synthesis to which it was ideologically committed, the Histadrut was also faithful to principles of labor solidarity. Its particular commitments revolved around what was termed generality (*klaliyut*, or "comprehensiveness")—meaning the consolidation of all labor-oriented activity under a single roof; and equality (*shivayon*)—the aspiration to achieve not just equal opportunity but similar conditions of life (including wages) for all members of the "working public."

This catalog of glorious achievements is faithful to the self-image of the labor organization and its leaders, as well as to the traditional historiography of the Zionist labor movement.[4] However, it is not indicative of the popular image of the Histadrut, which—since the mid-1980s—has been perceived (especially by younger people) as a bloated, self-serving, oligarchic institution long past its prime. For this reason, because changes in government policy have favored increasing pluralism in the health-care field, and because of the strenuous efforts of non-Histadrut sick funds to recruit the profitable younger segment of the market, Histadrut membership has dropped substantially in recent years. In public life, throughout Israel's history critics from both inside and outside of the labor movement have repeatedly questioned the raison d'être of the Histadrut. Changing conditions also appear to have rendered the Histadrut more of a burden than a political benefit to the Labor Party. A further indication of the Histadrut's problematic status is that with the exception of a handful of historians, it has by and large been ignored by scholars.[5]

In order to make sense of the Histadrut's role over the *longue durée*, we need a more precise grasp of its distinctiveness than has been so far offered. The predominant tendency has been to approach this task from a normative perspective—either sycophantic or malevolent. A more dispassionate approach can most easily be arrived at by adopting a comparative perspective, but which one? Is Israel best compared to other semiperipheral states,[6] other settler states,[7] other Middle Eastern states,[8] or the capitalist and democratic nations of the West, which are the official Israel's preferred reference group? No one answer is necessarily correct, nor is it necessary for all scholars to select the same answer. In my own research I have found comparisons to the West to be fruitful not necessarily because of empirical fit but as a way of framing significant questions.

An obvious starting point is the provision by labor movements in Europe and Russia of precedents for the institutional experiments in Jewish Palestine that resulted in Histadrut as we know it. There are clear "Bolshevik" inspirations for the original centralization, politicization, and multi-functionalism of the Histadrut. Ideologically, though, the Histadrut was from the outset much closer to the spirit of reformist socialism. Consistent with this, the leaders of the Histadrut have for decades been active in the international movement of "free" trade unions, just as their partners in the Labor Party have been active in the Socialist International.

Relations between the union and party wings of the labor movement in Israel, although differing in detail from European counterparts, are fundamentally similar to other class-oriented or German-model movements. Moreover, the institutional features of the Israeli case not only parallel but in many senses exemplify the neocorporatist systems of industrial relations that fascinated comparative political economists in the early 1980s.[9] The Histadrut's exceptional centralization, membership coverage, and functional scope, and the multiple nodes and long time horizons that characterize bargaining between the Histadrut and the state, are quintessentially corporatist. From the perspective of social democratic corporatism, three particularly distinctive issues emerge: the Histadrut's target constituency, the way that it evolved, and its impact on labor relations and public policy.

Historically, the composition of Histadrut membership more closely approximated a national than a class logic. Although never repudiating the principle of class solidarity, the Histadrut was intended from the outset to serve only Jewish workers. Before 1948 its organizational approach to the Arab working class in Palestine rarely went beyond a largely symbolic attempt to sponsor separate-but-equal trade unionism. After 1948, Israel's Palestinian citizens were only gradually incorporated into the labor organization, within what was constructed de facto as a dual institutional structure. Membership has never been offered to the noncitizen residents of the occupied territories, even though the majority of the Palestinian working class in the territories is employed inside Israel's pre-1967 borders and is legally required to pay the Histadrut for alleged services rendered.

Yet within its targeted constituency, the Histadrut is generous to a fault in opening its ranks. Surveys of the Jewish adult public suggest that at least half of the self-employed are Histadrut members. No doubt the major attraction for this group has been access to the Histadrut Sick Fund. Indeed, in that respect there is no real difference between nonworkers and workers.[10]

Broadly speaking, European labor movements evolved from bottom to top and from a market to a political orientation.[11] What are called union peak associations arose as the culmination of a process of aggregation that began with local workers' councils and proceeded to national craft and industrial unions before reaching the so-called confederal level.

The contrast between these patterns of evolution and those that characterized the development of the Histadrut could hardly be greater. Histadrut was formed when the urban industrial sector on which trade unionism thrives was still in a very early stage of development, and except in agriculture, unionism was small-scale and local in character. Creating Histadrut did not signify the vertical integration of trade unionism but instead an attempt to consolidate and expand the workers' instruments of employment and mutual aid, including—in the future—sponsorship of trade unions.

The founders of the Histadrut constituted a coalition between diverse groups and political entrepreneurs among unpropertied Jewish settlers in Palestine: agricultural workers aspiring to found communes with the aid of the Zionist movement; the competing sick funds, labor exchanges, and other services associated with the two main workers' parties; and new immigrants anxious to proceed with the Labor Zionist revolution and dismayed by the petty rivalry that shackled its progress. Far from constituting a station along the road to increasing politicization of an economistic movement, the Histadrut was formed at the initiative of the principal workers' party. The leaders of this party had learned from experience that they could dominate a consolidated workers' movement only by coalition-building and thus by forgoing direct party proprietorship.[12]

The overriding strategic goal that has linked policy and practice in the best known instances of social democratic corporatism—the Scandinavian nations, Sweden in particular—is solidarity. The substantive hallmark of this commitment has, until quite recently, been continuous full employment and comparatively narrow wage differentials. The superficial similarity between the Histadrut's commitment to full employment and the European equivalent, in which peak associations trade wage restraint for job guarantees, should not be accepted at face value. Until the 1990s full employment in Israel was an integral part of the Zionist consensus,

considered indispensable to immigrant absorption and social stability by
all major parties and organized interests. A dramatic deviation from this
stance occurred in the mid-1960s, when a Labor government knowingly
sanctioned a major bout of unemployment and did so with the Histadrut's full support.

That slowdown is a telling exception: The Histadrut's credentials as a
class-oriented labor organization have always been in doubt. The social
and economic policies that Israeli governments pursued during the era of
Labor and Histadrut hegemony exhibit pronounced "dualist" features. In
practice Israel's welfare state has been relatively niggardly. Important elements of it are delegated to political sectors (most notably the Histadrut)
rather than organized on a universal basis by the state; and its overall effect has been to validate rather than mitigate divisions between Oriental
and Ashkenazi Jews and between Jews and Arabs. In the realm of economic policy, Israel failed, for more than a decade following the first oil
price shock in 1973, to adopt effective economic-adjustment policies.
Other corporatist social democracies benefited in these years from centralized wage-fixing and concomitant social consensus, but Israel suffered
from a stagnating economy, a comparatively high incidence of labor disputes, and spiraling inflation.

Can Ideology Resolve the Paradoxes?

At this point, readers may be asking whether the puzzle that I have posed
is only a straw man. Are not differences between Histadrut and comparable labor movements the predictable result of its original multiple commitments to socialism and Zionism? The organization's departures from
Western norms seem easily understood once the role of Zionist ideology
enters the picture. Thus, the Histadrut excluded Arabs and adopted an ex-
aggerated inclusiveness toward Jews because of its determination to advance Jewish immigration and absorption. It was a labor organization that
failed to evolve according to the logic of capitalist industrialization and
democratization because it was, in actuality, the institutional embodiment
of a "settler aristocracy" subsidized by international sympathizers.[13] Accordingly, it is not surprising that after statehood the Histadrut degener-
ated into a tool cynically wielded by apparatchiks. Once essential Zionist
objectives were fulfilled, Histadrut's policies and practices became obviously discordant with those of other social democratic labor movements.

Each of the statements in the preceding paragraph is basically accurate, but in their overall thrust, the statements are seriously misleading. The labor movement's commitment to Zionism is an incontestable historical fact, but it is questionable whether it can explain the movement's distinctive character. To accept this would be to sidestep the fundamental question of what made Jewish labor embrace Zionist priorities so firmly in the first place.

Besides, to argue that socialist Zionism was about Zionism more than socialism is to substitute one ideological motive force for another without questioning the underlying assumption that ideology is capable of explaining social phenomena. This assumption often encapsulates two others: first, that the aspirations of the founding fathers were freely and willfully chosen (rather than adopted during and after the event as a way of making sense of and justifying their actions); and second, that substantive constraints—the problems of making a living, the dynamics of struggling for power—played no determinate role in the directions taken by the labor movement at strategic historical turning points.

I find both assumptions untenable.[14] Labor Zionism and its sympathizers have championed the notion that history is driven by the ideas embraced by visionary leaders, and they have frequently expressed the opinion that social movements can bring about desirable political and social transformations by educating their followers to internalize appropriate values. In the mid-1920s the left sought to interpret Labor Zionism in orthodox socialist terms and provoked a devastating critique by one of the most prominent figures in the nonsocialist Hapoel Hatsair Party, Chaim Arlosoroff.[15] Yet in archetypal fashion Arlosoroff concluded his critique by trying to convince his comrades that socialist aspirations were worth adopting because they helped mobilize the rank and file and added moral authority to the Zionist cause.

Many scholars who work on Israel accept with only occasional reservations the voluntarist perspective that the early development of the Zionist labor movement was the result of its leaders' programmatic commitments.[16] For instance, Shulamit Carmi and Henry Rosenfeld have recognized that ideas can be used cynically.[17] They argue that in the postsovereignty era, David Ben-Gurion and his allies propagated a militaristic, state-aggrandizing ideology that helped consolidate power by marginalizing the left-wing alternative. From a different perspective, S. N. Eisenstadt has argued that in the "postrevolutionary" era after 1948 it was inevitable that Jewish society would enter a less ideological phase simply because the goals of the revolution had now been realized.[18]

The most significant recent invocation of ideology in this vein is a
major work in process by the Israeli political theorist Zeev Sternhell, who
also looks to Europe as the appropriate comparative context.[19] Sternhell
contends that the Histadrut and the Israeli Labor Party failed to generate
the kinds of social and economic outcomes that might be expected of a
progressive labor movement because they were never truly committed to
the program of the European left.[20] Sternhell points out that Ben-Gurion
himself adopted socialism only as an afterthought, and one of the two
parties (not Ben-Gurion's) that merged in 1930 to form the original workers' party, Mapai, was avowedly antisocialist. Socialism was thus merely a
convenient instrument, a shell if you will, for assisting in the mobilization
and consolidation of Jewish workers and their supporters for purposes
that were actually mandated by Zionism.[21]

For Sternhell, the ideology of the Zionist labor movement in the inter-
war period suggests a European parallel, but not social democracy. Rather
he looks to national socialism with its tribal-nationalist outlook, reverence
for productivity, and contempt for "parasites." Even the kibbutz was only a
fig leaf that conveniently absolved the labor leaders from responsibility for
the evident gap between their egalitarian rhetoric and the realities of
Jewish society in Palestine. In this reading, the synthesis between socialism and Zionism was not a synthesis but the capitulation of socialism to
nationalism.

Sternhell is correct about the glaring gap between the so-called con-
structive socialism of national upbuilding favored by Labor Zionism and
the credos favored by both revolutionary and reformist socialists in Europe. Ben-Gurion and his comrades at the peak of the movement indeed
exploited socialist myths to consolidate their authority over Jewish workers and to glorify instrumental struggles for power and money against political rivals associated with the middle classes. Such an interpretation still
lacks a comparable, interest-based explanation of the labor movement's
commitment to Zionism.

The Roots of Labor's Marriage to Zionism

The historical record cannot sustain the assumption that Zionism won
out simply because it was the true belief of the labor movement. Popular
images of Israel's past have obscured the fact that for most of the Jews who
arrived in Palestine during the first half of this century, Zionist motivations were largely irrelevant to the decision to immigrate. In 1880 there

were nearly half a million Arabs and about 24,000 Jews in Palestine. The First Aliyah, or wave of immigration, recognized by modern Zionism occurred shortly before the turn of the century. Motivated primarily by anti-Semitic legislation and pogroms, the newcomers from Russia and Rumania had the effect of doubling the Jewish population. Traditionally Jewish in their outlook, the First Aliyah settlers purchased their own land and worked it using European and subsequently French colonial methods. The 35,000 or so immigrants of the Second Aliyah, emanating mainly from Russia, arrived during the decade before World War I. It is a matter of record that given the harsh conditions they found, the overwhelming majority of these socialist and secular Zionists abandoned the country. A remnant founded and later continued to head the institutions of the Israeli labor movement.

The Allied victory in World War I ended 400 years of Ottoman control of Palestine. With the sanction of a League of Nations mandate, control over Palestine passed to Britain. On the eve of British rule, an official declaration of support was issued for "the establishment in Palestine of a national home for the Jewish people." To the 60,000 Jews remaining in 1919 were added the 35,000 of the Third Aliyah, the first organized Zionist immigration, but in 1923 the ratio of Arabs to Jews was still eight to one. The masses of Jews leaving Russia and Eastern Europe had gravitated mainly to the United States, but America's gates were closed by new, more restrictive immigration legislation in 1924. The first to be affected were the Polish petit bourgeois who formed the core of the Fourth Aliyah, which brought more than 60,000 immigrants to Palestine in the years 1924–1926. A decade later, the biggest wave of prestate immigration by far (190,000 between 1932 and 1936) was prompted by the rise of Nazism and economic depression in Europe and included a large number of German and Austrian refugees.

Many of the activists who led the movement (and later, the state) had reached Palestine as committed socialists in the Second or Third Aliyahs. In the Jewish community in Palestine no less than in Europe, communism appeared ascendant in labor movements during the years immediately following the 1917 revolution in Russia and World War I. The presence or absence of ideals of one sort or another evidently cannot explain the preeminence of the national motif in the labor movement.

The affinity between organized Jewish labor in Palestine and the Zionist movement can be understood, in part, via the calculus of realpolitik.[22] In partnership with organized Zionism, the labor movement elite gained access to material and political resources, the argument runs, that buttressed its authority not only over its mass membership but over its opponents as well. The prestige and the organizational and financial capital that the Histadrut attracted were employed with great effect to suppress or co-opt challengers from both the left and the right. It was this pivotal position between the largest organized section of Jewish civil society and the para-statal bodies of the Zionist movement that gave the Histadrut its extraordinary political potency.

An elite perspective on the Histadrut's attachment to Zionism is not without merit, but it begs an important question: Why were the material and political resources amassed around the Histadrut so compellingly attractive to its members? Perhaps these banal attractions did no more than reinforce their ideological predisposition to internalize Zionist priorities. This predisposition would then constitute the real explanation for labor's actions. I reject this contention. The obstacles facing the economic absorption of Jewish settlers in Palestine were so formidable that they left little freedom for value-based choices. Accordingly, the economic interests of the propertyless newcomers, the self-appointed working class of Jewish Palestine, are indispensable to understanding their motivations.

The Role of Economic Interests

The material position of the proletarian settlers was fraught with difficulties. In the labor market, the unskilled majority were at a pronounced disadvantage relative to indigenous Palestinian labor: They were both less productive and inherently more expensive. Most local labor was semiproletarian, whereas the immigrants depended solely on their earnings from wage labor. The habits and customs of the newcomers made their lifestyle substantially more expensive to sustain than that of the "natives." Unlike other instances of European colonization in which conquest and sovereignty provided the settlers with cheap or free land, in Palestine Jewish individuals or organizations required considerable means to acquire land.[23]

Turn-of-the-century pioneers of the second wave of immigration were spared the full force of these dilemmas because Baron Edmond de Rothschild subsidized the wages of Jews employed in the plantations that he had founded in imitation of French colonization in Algeria. Had the baron continued to support the newcomers in this way, and certainly had he enlarged his support to settle immigrants as independent farmers, the pioneers of the second wave would probably have ended up on the margins of Zionist history, as had their predecessors.

This outcome was forestalled, however, by the withdrawal of Rothschild's patronage in 1900, which obliged the new imigrants to face the full force of their unfavorable competitive position with Arab labor. Their attempts to neutralize the threat are largely consistent with the predictions of the theory of the labor market's "split" between cheap and expensive labor.[24] One response was an attempt to lower costs by imitating Arab manners. Another, its opposite, was the "Hebrew labor" struggle to forcibly prevent Jewish employers from hiring Arabs. It rapidly became clear to the immigrants that as atomized individuals they could achieve nothing. In order to more effectively pursue their struggle for "Hebrew labor," late in 1905 they established two lilliputian parties, one in imitation of the socialist wing of European Zionism and the other a nonsocialist homegrown variety.

During this initial period of experimentation, activists in the emergent labor movement came to two critical realizations. First, Jewish planters would pay the price of hiring coreligionists only if they perceived Arab labor to threaten their personal and collective existence—and Jewish labor, correspondingly, to stand for the defense of the Jewish national interest in Palestine. Second, combining collectivist responses with the subsidy of a new patron, they could offset the cost advantage of Arab labor and even amass sufficient political power to neutralize the planters. The patron that appeared on the scene was the Palestine office of the WZO (World Zionist Organization), established in 1908.

The Mutual Interests of Labor and Zionism

The interests of the labor and Zionist movements in Palestine dovetailed almost perfectly, forming the basis for a close and durable alliance between a settlement movement without settlers and a workers' movement without work. An almost immediate result was the first tiny agricultural commune.[25] WZO support also assisted the fledgling labor movement to establish other bulwarks against the debilitating effect of Arab competition, including training farms designed to improve the Jews' productivity, mutual-aid institutions established under the umbrella of regional workers' associations, and a certain amount of direct subsidy to employers willing to hire Jews.

Unlike in the far more substantial immigrations of the 1920s and 1930s, the newcomers in the second and third waves, who included the labor movement's founding fathers and mothers, were almost all self-selected idealists. It was not Zionist zeal alone that led them to seek out an alliance with the WZO. Workers (including labor movements in the Diaspora) had insignificant representation in the institutions of world Zionism. Indeed, the Zionist movement's largely petit-bourgeois rank and file, particularly its elite (composed in part of Jewish magnates and closely tied to them as financiers) were regarded by the socialists as aliens and even class enemies.

The most important basis for collaboration was exchange. The worker-pioneers, unlike most other Diaspora Zionists, were willing to make the move to Palestine. They were ready to actively compete with or help circumscribe Arab labor rather than reinforce the Arabs' presence by employing them. Unlike the farmers, they could be persuaded to develop economic frameworks that would enhance Jewish autonomy and provide the basis for absorbing propertyless Jewish immigrants. Finally, the laborers, out of both inclination and necessity, were willing to take on the most arduous and financially least-rewarding roles in the settlement process. The labor movement's options were similarly confined. By World War I the problem of Arab competition on the plantations had been resolved in the worst possible way—the exclusion of (Jewish) high-cost labor. The alternatives—whether based on wage labor or communitarian rural settlement—were unrealistic without massive aid from world Zionism.

The requirements of the Labor Zionist partnership made an indelible impression on the Histadrut. They go far toward explaining the distinctiveness of the Histadrut's structure (a unitary organization indirectly governed by political parties) and function (the "constructivist" denigration of pure-and-simple trade unionism and a corresponding emphasis on creating and organizing employment). The organizational innovations pioneered by the Histadrut were prerequisites for the receipt of large-scale WZO subsidies.[26] It took on sole responsibility for all of the activities undertaken by all of the existing labor organizations while at the same time removing the direct link between service provision and political rivalry.

The Histadrut leadership exerted considerable efforts to restrain workers' pursuit of their immediate interests in the context of the employment relation. Unlike the class truces that emerged in some European countries in the 1930s, the Histadrut's posture of self-restraint was not rooted in a corporatist transformation of industrial relations. In fulfilling its bargain, the labor elite internalized Zionist priorities, especially in welcoming immigration. Accordingly, it was argued that trade union pressure ought to be directed toward reserving jobs in the Jewish sector for Histadrut members and safeguarding the "Jewish minimum" wage without discouraging investment or harming the country's "absorptive capacity."

The leaders of the Histadrut and the WZO shared the fear that the logic of collective action in the market arena might ally Jewish workers with their Arab counterparts against Jewish employers. The "constructivist" approach offered viable alternatives, such as employment in contracting gangs that built roads for Palestine's newly installed rulers. This work provided wages that Jews could live on because Zionist organizations exerted political pressure on the British and channeled funds to the Histadrut, which used them to purchase tools and tents for the workers thus employed.

Beyond the Formative Era: Jewish and Palestinian Labor

In developing an explanation for the distinctiveness of the Israeli case, I have so far dwelt mainly on the formative era and operated at a rather high level of abstraction. I now move to demonstrate and concretize the Histadrut's close connections to critical turning points in Israel's political economy since the creation of the State of Israel.

As a result of the first Arab-Israeli war, the land base of the State of Israel increased by 20 percent and the Arab population within its new borders fell by 80 percent. By the end of 1948 Israel's armed forces had successfully combated both local resistance and armies of invasion from the surrounding states while thwarting the UN plan for an independent Palestinian state. Some 600,000–750,000 Arabs were driven out or fled; others had lived before 1948 in areas that now came under Jordanian or Egyptian control.

Between 1949 and 1951 as many Jews came to Israel as had been within its borders when sovereignty was proclaimed. Half of the newcomers were European Jews (the majority from Poland and Rumania), many of them refugees whose homes and families had been destroyed during the war. The others originated in North Africa and the Middle East, principally Iraq and the Yemen. This "Oriental" (in Hebrew, Mizrachi) immigration was due in part to the political backlash and upsurge of anti-Semitism in most Arab states following Israel's creation and its military victory. But both of the components of the mass immigration were in addition actively recruited and transferred at Israel's initiative in order "to deepen the nation's military manpower reservoir, to preempt the vulnerable empty places in the land, to garrison the new agricultural colonies, and to create the modernized economy that was indispensable for achieving a Western standard of living."[27]

One of the few aspects of the Histadrut's persona that *did* undergo major transformation in the wake of sovereignty was a shift from exclusion to inclusion of Palestinian labor. The collapse of the campaign for "Hebrew labor" after 1948 constitutes an extraordinary strategic and ideological revolution for the Zionist labor movement. The explanatory framework established so far offers a parsimonious explanation for earlier policies and for the shift away from them.

Simple demographics played a significant role in the development of this constellation: The Arabs in Palestine had been numerous enough to constitute a real threat to Jewish settlers both in the labor market, as cheap competitors, and politically, as an opposing national movement. The problematic element in Palestine (in comparison with the partially analogous cases of Australia and South Africa) was the conjunction of an unfavorable demographic balance with the absence of direct control over the instruments of state power. The Jews could neither swamp their Arabs nor impose their will on the indigenous majority, even if they had wanted to. Labor market conflict therefore could not be resolved in the typical ways that expensive labor uses to eliminate the threat posed by cheaper competitors—either forcible exclusion or construction of a caste system that discriminates against cheap labor while subsidizing the employment of expensive workers in relatively desirable jobs.

"Hebrew labor" was rendered redundant by Israeli sovereignty, not by moral exhaustion, "the end of ideology," or the demise of revolutionary élan.[28] Statehood simply did away with the need for colonization oriented toward the construction of a self-sustaining Jewish enclave. It was no longer necessary that Jews perform their own menial labor. On the contrary, from the Zionist perspective there was good reason to encourage Arabs to depend on working for Jews (so long as this posed no threat to Jewish labor), since this could be expected to discourage any future impulse toward Arab irredentism.[29]

The economic threat posed by Arab labor was by now greatly diminished. First, the scope of the potential threat was dramatically reduced because of the more limited and less permeable boundaries of the new state and because of the flight or deportation of the vast majority of the Arab inhabitants of what became Israel. Second, the geographical separation of Arab from Jewish communities, along with the decision of the new regime to place the Arab minority under military rule, made it feasible for the first time to effectively regulate the employment of Arabs by Jews. Third, with the attainment of Jewish sovereignty came enhanced capacities for the political center to privilege Jewish labor—by means of public employment, capital subsidies to other employers, and social policy (public in-come maintenance, housing, and education).

The mass immigrations of the first few decades of Israeli sovereignty might have severely strained even these protective devices. After a tempo-rary weakening of both the push and pull factors that had prompted the initial immigration wave, in the ten-year period 1955–1964 close to half a million Jews immigrated to Israel. About half originated in North Africa, principally Morocco, and more than a third came from Europe, again mainly Poland and Rumania. By 1965 Israel's population had reached 2.5 million, nearly nine-tenths of it Jewish.[30]

By the late 1950s the exclusion of Arab labor no longer served the inter-ests of either the Histadrut or the state. As the Israeli economy adjusted to the shock of the initial waves of immigration and moved onto a path of rapid growth, institutional obstacles to Arab employment were relaxed. The most important manifestations of this relaxation were the liquidation of Histadrut labor exchanges with the passing of a National Employment Service law and the progressive opening up of the Histadrut to member-ship by the country's Palestinian Arab citizens. With these steps, however, neither the state nor the Histadrut became "color-blind." Quite the re-verse. State labor exchanges, which enjoyed a legal monopoly on the work-seeking process, were not set up in most Arab localities. Arab labor was heavily dependent on jobs in Jewish localities for which local (i.e., Jewish) residents were guaranteed the right of first refusal. As an employer His-tadrut largely retained its traditional Jewish exclusivity. In its capacity as an organ of labor representation, the Histadrut actively recruited Arabs but developed specialized local and national departments for dealing with its Palestinian members that were parallel to and in cooperation with those of the state.

Histadrut functioned as an instrument of political control, employing a wide range of positive and negative incentives to induce Arab citizens to accept the authority of the state and vote for the ruling Labor Party. Its command of health care and other social infrastructures and its ability to co-opt Arab activists into political or bureaucratic careers uniquely al-lowed it to influence Arab communities. This marked a profound change in the content of Histadrut activity, but not the nature of the relationship between the Histadrut and the political center. This remained an alliance rooted fundamentally in "political exchange." Before sovereignty the polit-ical services rendered by the Histadrut were to defend Jewish separatism, but after 1948 they reflected the needs of both party and state for con-trolled integration of the Arab minority.

After Sovereignty: Labor, Capital, and the State

Because its roles in colonization, statebuilding, and political mobilization, and with its nominal function of labor representation overlapped, from the moment of its birth the Histadrut was as much a capitalist employer and entrepreneur and an organ of state (or a state in the making) as it was a labor movement. The end of colonization and statemaking appeared to remove the incentive for the now-sovereign political institutions of the Jewish community to delegate public and communal functions to the Histadrut. It no longer seemed essential for the Histadrut to retain its roles in immigrant absorption, social services, and economic activity. Nor was it inevitable that the Labor Party would continue to rely on the labor organization as its organizing and mobilizing backbone. From Histadrut's viewpoint, however, statehood was a long-awaited opportunity to reinforce its powers and extend its functions by tapping the authority and resources of a sympathetic regime.[31]

The labor movement's longtime leader, David Ben-Gurion, became Israel's first prime minister. He resolutely sought to absorb and unify the statelike functions that had previously been delegated into the institutional framework of the newly founded state. He succeeded in nationalizing the military—a major trauma for both the left and the right—yet largely failed to compel the Histadrut to shed its quasi-state functions.[32] An important reason for Ben-Gurion's failure was the ambiguity characterizing the interests that it was his task to safeguard. The gains to the state in expanding its functions would have been offset by the burdens of mobilizing the necessary fiscal and administrative resources to take over the social services and economic enterprises hitherto operated by the Histadrut.

Wresting functions from the Histadrut would also have engaged the government in a politically costly battle with a powerful ally. Because the leaders of both institutions were from the same political party, the issue ultimately depended on the costs and benefits to the party. Ben-Gurion advocated building the party's political base around the state, but this strategy could hardly compete with the potential for a state-strengthened Histadrut to deliver votes. Moreover, as I have already suggested in the context of Arab labor, statehood ushered in new horizons for political exchange. Legitimation of economic policy and of the state's role in wage regulation were the most obvious new quid pro quos that the Histadrut could offer. The others ranged as far afield as services provided altogether outside of the domestic arena, such as the Histadrut's conduct of Israel's foreign policy with Third World states that refused open diplomatic relations.

Under the unwritten social contract governing relations between the government and the Histadrut after statehood, its role in labor relations for the first time caught up with its corporatist potential. Before sovereignty the structure and interests of both capital and the state prevented the labor organization from acquiring a monopoly of representation and centralized authority to negotiate wage agreements.[33] When the state apparatus became a servant of Jewish interests generally and the Labor Party specifically, sovereign authority was now readily applied to buttress the institutional, economic, and political strength of the Histadrut and encourage it to take on corporatist responsibilities for restraining worker demands. Even without the partisan political benefits, economic steering provided good reasons for the state to share Histadrut's interest. Israel's early years were rent with acute macroeconomic difficulties. Under pressure from the government the Histadrut agreed to cooperate with its austerity program by limiting national wage increases to compensation for increases in the cost of living while permitting payments to individuals under productivity-boosting incentive schemes. Despite widespread (if uneven) wage "drift," average real wages declined. The Histadrut contributed by ignoring the government's blatant manipulation of the official price index and by permitting the employment of new immigrants at below union rates.

During the decade of relative labor peace that followed sovereignty, corporatism functioned within a broader array of state-managed restraints on labor militancy. These included labor market dualism, state subsidy, and institutional and political discipline. The Histadrut leadership exploited the organization's newly strengthened position to insulate itself from the militancy of industrial workers. Instead of implementing recommendations that party control of trade unionism be phased out or acting on a long-standing commitment to establish a single national union for industrial workers, the Histadrut created an all-powerful Industrial Workers' Section staffed by party appointees inside its Trade Union Department, which fixed wages in cooperation with leaders of the Manufacturing Association and the government's economic ministries.

These organizational changes were complemented by the exercise of coercion. A measure of control over unauthorized strikes was achieved by the open or implicit threat of cutting off medical services to wildcatters. In several dramatic test cases where rebels were not deterred by such sanctions, the authority of the Histadrut center was asserted more aggressively. Mapai also launched a vigorous counterattack on the opposition parties' substantial foothold in union affairs at the workplace and enterprise level.

Left-wing militants were ousted from their leadership of a substantial minority of the workers' committees of the veteran working class, and in new-immigrant workforces Mapai bosses were implanted as tutelary committee heads. In office, party delegates used the spoils controlled by the committees—such as dispensation of loans and the power to give or withhold recommendations for promotion—to perpetuate their influence.

Institutional and political restraints on labor militancy were complemented by a third regulatory mechanism, labor market dualism. In principle, the Histadrut might have used its organizational power solidaristically in the interests of the relatively powerless workers in the secondary segment of the market. It might also have left the field completely open to uncoordinated activity by unions and workers' committees. Instead, despite a programmatic commitment to solidarism, the Histadrut's policies and practices contributed to labor market segmentation. Dualist tendencies were further encouraged by strong biases in how the state managed economic activities. Those who were ethnically, temporally (in terms of arrival), and politically closest to the labor movement elite enjoyed definite advantages.

That privileges accrued to the veteran working class that led the state-building effort and that the Palestinian-Arab citizenry suffered disadvantages are not all that surprising. There was also an enduring split within the postsovereignty mass migration along ethnic lines, between Ashkenazi and Oriental Jews. This arose because a larger proportion of the European newcomers enjoyed independent means or cultural, familial, and organizational ties with the prestatehood Jewish population. They also were not handicapped by the perception that they were "primitive" and culturally alien. Without the protection of severance pay or reliable and adequate citizen entitlements to income replacement, and given their poverty and disorganization on arrival in Israel, the Orientals were especially vulnerable to both employers and the state. Their labor market marginality was often tied up with and reinforced by spatial marginality, especially the case for those many who ended up in "development towns" planted in outlying areas. For their part, members of the veteran working class and the more advantaged elements (primarily also Ashkenazim) among the new immigrants were offered privileged routes of entry into the Israeli economy. These included mobility into skilled and supervisory jobs in the business sector, the opening up of managerial and professional positions in expanding public bureaucracies, and a strengthening of the petite bourgeoisie and the bourgeoisie in response to consumer and state demand.

The Contradictions of Full Employment

The synergy between the two massive inflows—of dependent immigrants and of financial gifts—resulted in rapid economic growth. The result was that labor demand rapidly caught up with supply, and by the early 1960s unemployment had fallen dramatically to only 3–4 percent of the civilian labor force. However "full employment," nominally one of the Histadrut's most cherished objectives, increased the risk of union leaders being challenged from below. Rank-and-file workers were unwilling to accept the burden of restraint in the face of labor market conditions favorable to their bargaining power. Under these circumstances, politically and organizationally mediated limits on labor militancy might well cohabit with the discipline of the market—that is, renewed unemployment. There were thus some institutional pressures on the Histadrut leadership to welcome unemployment.

In theory employers stood to lose most from full employment, but they were handsomely compensated by protected markets, access to cheap credit and machinery, and a variety of other forms of state subsidy. The occupants of entrepreneurial, managerial, and other well-remunerated positions were thereby freed of the obligation to convert their profits and incomes into the savings normally necessary to capital formation. The state also made available subsidies to private consumption, to the benefit of the Jewish working class. New immigrants were provided (often with political strings attached) the basic means of existence, which helped persuade many of them to accept marginal locations in the spatial, economic, and political systems—thus protecting vital interests of the state and the ruling party and their veteran supporters.

The state thus simultaneously created stratificational disparities and eased distributional conflicts. Yet full employment was primarily a problem for the state because the more that labor was protected from market forces and employer discipline, the greater was the cost of subsidizing business and the dependence on outside support to finance this generosity. The more that workers were allowed to become independent of labor market dictates, the harder it was to sustain both their material dependence on the ruling party and the territorial and economic roles assigned to them in statebuilding strategies.

In the 1950s and early 1960s, the state's role as an engine of economic expansion had been threefold: It was the source of tremendous direct and indirect demand, the provider of diffuse subsidies that promoted a favorable environment for business generally, and the author of selective incentives designed to stimulate the production of exports and import substitutes and the flow of private (especially foreign) investment. For the state to sustain the massive scale of these activities as consumer, investor, and subsidizer, it needed both the special policy problems of the 1950s (population expansion) and a hard-currency income sufficient to cover the bill. In the early 1960s these exogenous prerequisites began to evaporate. Immigration fell sharply in 1964 and 1965, and there was little prospect of more in the foreseeable future. Meanwhile, unilateral transfers and long-term loans— on which the state relied for cheap capital—had reached a plateau. By far the most attractive source of foreign currency, the reparations paid by the German government to Israel as the legatee of the European Jewish communities destroyed during World War II, was scheduled to dry up altogether.

These trends provided the backdrop to the Mitun, or "moderation," of the mid-1960s, a deep recession that was supported (if not induced) by the policies of Israel's Labor government and endorsed by the Histadrut. A slowdown was well-nigh inevitable at about this time because the running down of immigration and capital inflow were both beyond state control. The evidence is unambiguous that in response to these trends the state, with the aid of the Histadrut, actively sought a recession when unemployment was already rising. In part, this can be understood as what the Polish economist Michal Kalecki called a "political business cycle"—a deliberate withdrawal of the policy supports on which sustained full employment depends in a Keynesian economy.[34]Leading official spokesmen made no attempt to conceal their intentions. It was stated publicly that labor militancy was a (if not the) fundamental cause of Israel's economic malaise and that a dose of unemployment would be the most effective cure. In July 1966, when 40,000 work-seekers were already registered at the labor exchanges, the minister of finance was reported as stating that his economic program would require 95,000 unemployed. Moreover, the authorities continued to delay, for roughly a year, the adoption of countercyclical policies oriented toward easing unemployment. When the recession was ended by the Six Day War (June 1967), unemployment had already passed an astounding quarterly peak, 12.5 percent of the civilian labor force.

In Kalecki's scenario, the state played the role of understudy for capital. Governments would be obliged either to repair the damage full employment had caused to "business confidence" or else to see a collapse of output and employment in the wake of declining private investment. In Israel most business investment had hitherto been directly or indirectly financed by the public sector. The state now found it necessary not only to raise profits by disciplining labor but also to encourage the captains of industry to accept capitalist responsibilities for driving economic performance.

In itself, unemployment could be expected to help employers halt the growth of wages, gain access to a larger pool of labor, and reestablish managerial authority over layoffs and work practices. Capital was also expected to make sacrifices. Vigorous domestic demand—which under Israel's high tariff walls had hitherto shielded most producers from the export imperative—was deliberately run down or simply not revived. There was much talk of exposing industry to the whip of international competition, and insistence that the state's benevolent assistance not go to lame ducks. In practice, these incentives were largely unsuccessful, and state subsidy of capital was resumed substantially before policy softened toward labor.

The strategic logic behind the Mitun was to shift the crisis out of the state's jurisdiction and into the domains of labor and capital. Israel's military victory and occupation in 1967 rendered such a strategy obsolete. These dramatic geopolitical shifts justified and facilitated a reexpansion of the role of the state and provided a new formula for economic growth based on Palestinian workers and consumers, military expansion and industrialization, and greatly enlarged U.S. aid.

During the recession the Histadrut, and even more so private employers, had succeeded in regaining the initiative in labor relations. Labor discipline was sufficiently tightened to decrease the number of wildcat strikes and increase the share of profits in income. After the Mitun, workers' readiness to struggle against the ongoing redistribution of income from labor to capital was dulled by fresh memories of mass unemployment and assisted by the euphoria of military victory and then the hardships caused by the "war of attrition" on the Suez Canal. None of these restraining influences could outlast the conditions that brought them into being. Moreover, the workers' experience of a disciplinary recession hardened their hearts toward its sponsors. In the midst of the Mitun, workers weakened by the labor market crisis discovered that the Histadrut was unwilling and unable to defend them. They turned their anger against the labor organization and subsequently the government as well.

Finding other channels blocked, the stronger of the workers' committees cooperated on a regional and even national basis to launch extra-parliamentary protest actions. Although the potential of these challenges to radically transform the status quo in labor relations turned out to be short-lived, many workers drew the conclusion that self-reliance was their most effective weapon. Under conditions of renewed economic expansion between the late 1960s and the Yom Kippur War (October 1973), Israel experienced its own variant of the rank-and-file revolt that overtook labor relations in all of the advanced capitalist societies. In parallel, the disadvantaged (primarily Oriental Jews, but in part also Arab citizens) embraced a new politics of protest at the ballot box and, in the Jewish sector, in the streets. Their actions presented a grave challenge to the political authority that the Histadrut and the Labor Party had hoped to restore by the whip of labor market discipline. The combination of partial withdrawal of Oriental and Arab support and defections by disenchanted middle-class Ashkenazim administered the fatal blow to Labor Party hegemony in Israel's May 1977 elections, after which leadership of the government was transferred to the populist-nationalist Likud Party.

The Decline of the Labor Movement

Mainstream interpretations explain the decline of the Histadrut's authority and the Labor Party's electoral standing during the 1970s through a combination of trends internal and external to the labor movement. Internal decomposition included a loss of ideological vigor and coherence, bureaucratization, and corruption. External challenges were posed by the policy conundrums that followed the 1967 occupation and by the growing independence and dissent of Oriental Jewish voters. My analysis of the Mitun suggests that the decline of the labor movement can also be interpreted from a political-economic perspective as a consequence of changes in the relations between the Histadrut, the state, and the working class. The punitive strategy adopted by the state and the ruling party in the wake of the political and economic challenges that surfaced during the 1960s left wounds that festered after the post-1967 economic recovery. Workers' disenchantment was further aggravated by the Yom Kippur War, which shook public confidence in Labor Party stewardship and put an abrupt end to economic growth.

The political-economic roots of Labor's political decline were institutional as well as conjunctural. Especially important in this connection was the weakening efficacy of the Histadrut both as a vehicle for mobilizing voters and as a resource for the political management of the economy on which Labor hegemony was predicated. Caught between its political obligations to party and state and the militancy of both entrenched and subaltern sections of the workforce, the Histadrut was unable and often even unwilling to brake wage demands and support the government's economic policy. At the same time, the growing independence of Histadrut economic enterprises from political direction and their burgeoning ties with big business in the private and government sectors made it increasingly difficult for the state to avoid bearing the brunt of the political and fiscal costs of managing a stagflationary economy. It was the decline of state autonomy brought about by these trends that I believe accounted for Israel's twin crises of the late 1970s and early 1980s: the dethroning of the Labor Party, and severe economic disorder (hyperinflation and fiscal crisis).[35]

Israel's political economy reached a critical turning point in 1984–1985, and once again the Histadrut was deeply implicated.[36] Following the 1984 elections the Labor Party joined the Likud in a "national unity" government. The Likud expected its rival to deal more effectively with the Histadrut. For its part Labor was anxious to regain leverage over policy, at least partly to protect the Histadrut, its political ally, from growing threats to the viability of its economic and social-policy functions. Indeed, in return for political and institutional compensations, in summer 1985 the Histadrut's leadership consented to a radical economic stabilization plan that quickly put an end to inflationary chaos in the economy. More important, the enactment of the stabilization plan marked the onset of a new liberalizing phase in which the state successfully regained some of its lost autonomy by slimming down its role in economic ownership and steering.

The Labor Party's success in resolving the economic crisis and also in extricating the Israeli army from a costly and prolonged engagement in Lebanon raised its political stock but failed to alter its political fortunes at the next (1988) elections. Many in the party pointed an accusing finger at the Histadrut, which had largely lost its capacities to get out the vote and instead appeared to be damaging the party's prestige and confining its policy options. Consequently, at the beginning of the 1990s—in a replay of an internal crisis that paralyzed and then split the party in the 1960s—the Histadrut came under attack from disgruntled Labor politicians, particularly those who had risen outside the framework of the Histadrut and the party machine. The Histadrut's critics openly argued that it was a political burden more than an asset and demanded that the party cut its umbilical cord with the labor organization and transfer its nonunion functions to the orbits of the state or the private sector.

The contemporary problems of the Histadrut are real enough. In the labor market, Israel has participated in the global trend toward individual employment contracts, labor contracting, and other changes in employment relations that undermine both the objective and subjective attachment of workers to unions. Because affiliation with the Histadrut ensured health care, this trend did not directly harm the membership rate, but it did aggravate the already severe problem of legitimacy. The disorganization of the labor market, the evident ability of privileged sectors of the organized workforce to make gains on their own, and the lack of any concerted effort on behalf of the disadvantaged all brought the Histadrut's prestige to a new low. Meanwhile, the mainstay of its ability to attract and retain members—the conservative and inefficient Sick Fund—was ill equipped to face rising competition in the health-care field, especially given the high costs of serving its large body of elderly insurees. Consequently, in the 1990s, for the first time since statehood the Histadrut found itself losing members and having great difficulty recruiting new ones. Aggravating the crisis, the labor organization's leadership evidently had no intention of carrying out internal reforms that might have restored its credibility. No less important, the economic enterprises associated with the Histadrut were still in the grips of a decade-long crisis. This presented a serious political problem to the Labor Party not only because of the negative image (outdated institutions that were bleeding the public purse) but because the labor movement economy's desperate need for state support severely limited the party's freedom of maneuver.

Two Critical Elections

As the 1992 general elections approached, the presence of an anti-Histadrut lobby inside the Labor Party was expressed and reinforced by two radical reforms. One was the party's transition from backroom decision-making, dominated by the machine, to primary elections as the main vehicle of candidate selection. The other was the decision to make a public commitment to nationalize health care in a way that would definitively cut the sixty-year tie between membership in the Histadrut and the receipt of health services from its associated Sick Fund. Thus it came to be that Yitzhak Rabin led the Labor Party to the national elections in June 1992 in a way that denied the very core of what had once made the labor movement so powerful—and had later rendered it so vulnerable.

This denial by itself cannot account for Rabin's success in reversing the fortunes of the two leading parties. Among the other factors involved, three are especially noteworthy. Likud's policies regarding peace and territories had led Israel into an economic cul-de-sac that included U.S. denial of enlarged economic aid. Yitzhak Rabin's personal prestige and his image as being tough on Arabs acted as an antidote to the party's dovish image among voters with mildly hawkish tendencies. Disgruntled groups such as

Palestinian Arab citizens, newcomers from the former Soviet Union, and some of the Mizrachim voted Labor. For this political moment, each of these groups had reason to question the efficacy of the parties it found programmatically desirable, and each was attracted by Labor's promise to divert government expenditure from the West Bank occupation to domestic ends.

Had the Labor Party brought the reforms favored by Rabin and his Young Turk associates to fruition, then the Histadrut would have been transformed beyond recognition. This was particularly true for healthcare reform. Experience in other countries has shown that in the absence of nonunion functions (typically unemployment insurance), unions fail to retain members in the unfavorable climate of the mid-1990s.[37] Combined with the trend toward greater independence between the labor organization and the party, such a transformation would have been the end of the distinctive character of political exchange between labor and the state in Israel: its exceptionally diffuse (generalized) character and its complex but undeniable responsiveness to changes in government.

Instead, this scenario was postponed as those who had the most to lose from reform fought an effective rearguard action. Chaim Ramon—a skilled and popular young politician and a close associate of Rabin, who led the internal party opposition to the Histadrut—was twice defeated, first as health minister (his reform plan was rejected) and then as a contender for the party's nomination to head its slate in the Histadrut elections of May 1994 (he was denied the candidacy). As it turned out though, the political masters of the Histadrut achieved only a Pyrrhic victory. Ramon formed a renegade list that (to his good fortune) was ejected from the party, and he used his aggressive critique of what was portrayed as the corrupt regime of the past to claim a landslide victory. For the first time in the Histadrut's history, it was not controlled by Labor (or the parties to which it is heir), which had to settle for the role of junior coalition partner.

In the short time that has passed since the Histadrut elections, the labor organization's functions, staff, and assets have been significantly pruned. However, the process is by no means complete, and it is still a possibility (albeit an unlikely one) that the momentum of reform will be stalled. Nationalization of the Histadrut pension funds and privatization of the Histadrut economy are as yet only in the planning stage. The Histadrut has thus not yet turned into first, foremost, and primarily a roof organization of trade unions. It has not abandoned its system of governance by political parties or its unitary structure based on direct membership in the "federation." Indeed, the new leadership has engaged in intense bargaining with the government in order to preserve this structure with a legally sanctioned checkoff system for dues collection, buttressed by mandatory quasi dues for free-riding nonmembers.

I interpret these developments as signs of the Histadrut's long-postponed adjustment to the transition from a settlement movement to a sovereign state. All of the labor organization's distinctive features were the product of the era of prestate colonization with its peculiar challenge of gaining control of land and employment in the face of Palestinian hostility without being in control of a state apparatus. Sovereignty failed to instantly eliminate the preceding institutional order because it continued to offer political advantages to the ruling party and the new state. The distinctive problems and conflicts of a settler society continued to arise in the new context. For some of these problems, including the political and economic "absorption" of dependent and disorganized immigrants and the management of relations with the remaining Arab population, the Histadrut continued to offer valuable solutions.

Why was the currently ongoing process of "normalizing" the Histadrut delayed for so long? One potentially attractive explanation comes from the sphere of ideology—the delayed entry of Israeli social and political discourse into what has been described as the "post-Zionist" era.[38] Two specific shifts are especially noteworthy. One is the ascendance of a bourgeois worldview that champions the pursuit of personal gain and casts aspersions on the efficacy and desirability of collectivism and state intervention. The other is a sea change in public opinion concerning the national conflict, the fact that since the Palestinian Intifada at least some Israelis sympathetic to the project of a greater Israel have reluctantly accepted the imperative of territorial compromise.

In keeping with my argument regarding the origins of the labor movement, I believe that it would be mistaken to interpret these changing values and attitudes as the source of the contemporary transformation of the Histadrut, although they have certainly reinforced it. For one thing, the new geopolitical and political-economic discourses coexist with opposing "texts." Notwithstanding the prominence of neoliberalism among Israeli elites, there remains a surprisingly robust collectivist consensus in the mass public, which sees the state as broadly responsible for the well-being of its citizens.[39]

In keeping with my interpretation of earlier periods, I think developments in the political economy itself offer crucial clues to understanding why the transformation of the Histadrut was so long deferred. In the Mitun episode, Histadrut was deeply implicated in a struggle by the state to regain autonomy from both capital and labor. In the background to that struggle were changes in economic parameters that threatened the state's ability to manage the public purse and the wider macroeconomy but also gave it the tools to fight back. Since the mid-1980s Israel has again experienced the same dynamic. The state's fiscal standing and policy options are severely constrained by both big business and strong labor groups, and it faces a loss of maneuverability as its foreign earnings from discretionary gift capital become military aid. The state has attempted to turn the threatened exposure to the world economy and to neoliberal ideology into levers for establishing a safer haven for itself in a restructured political economy.[40] In contrast to the mid-1960s, in the 1980s when the state was confronted by economic crisis its interest in regaining autonomy and the interest of the governing party in buttressing its political ally, the Histadrut, no longer converged. Through the Mitun, Israel's political elite had pursued two aspirations: restructuring state-economy relations to conform with the eclipse of conditions for state-led and state-subsidized growth and exploiting the disciplinary effects of recession to restore the labor movement's political authority over the working class. In contrast, the political stewards—whether Likud or Labor—of the partial dismantling of the state's protective role in the economy and civil society since 1985 have been opposed to or at best ambivalent toward the Histadrut.

Finally, it may not be accidental that the liberalizing thrust of recent economic policy in Israel has occurred in chronological proximity to the state's attempt to rid itself of counterproductive burdens in the geopolitical arena by negotiating a settlement with the PLO that by the mid-1990s has at least partially ended the occupation. In any case, the opening of a (however faltering) process of decolonization, just like the trends toward Israel's increased integration with the world economy and the slimming down of government ownership and control, makes plainer than ever the anachronistic character of the Histadrut model of labor organization. Even if the political will of the current leaders of the Histadrut and the Labor Party to reform the Histadrut should falter, the structural momentum of reform now appears to be irresistible.

Notes

I would like to register a special debt of gratitude to the editor of this volume, whose help and guidance went truly above and beyond the call of duty.

1. Shapira's doctoral dissertation, which was her first book, is a partial exception. Yet it is the only one of her books that has not been translated into English. See Anita Shapira, *Futile Struggle: Hebrew Labor, 1929–1939*, in Hebrew (Tel Aviv:

Tel Aviv University and Kibbutz Meuhad, 1977). For a noteworthy exception to the institutional and ideological myopia of social history in Israel, see David De Vries, "Proletarianization and National Segregation: Haifa in the 1920s," *Middle Eastern Studies* 30, 4 (October 1994):860–882.

2. Many of my observations in this chapter are founded on my recent book *Labour and the Political Economy in Israel* (Oxford: Oxford University Press, 1992). This book offers a more detailed analysis and documentation of issues discussed here, up to the mid-1980s.

3. A series of innovations early in 1995 have modified some of the traits noted in this paragraph. The government began to implement a National Health Insurance Law that leaves the general Sick Fund in the hands of the Histadrut but eliminates the link between membership in the labor organization and entitlement to the services of its health provider. In addition, the first convention since the unseating of the Labor Party in the May 1994 Histadrut elections agreed, after an acrimonious debate, to add the prefix New to the Histadrut's official title. For a catalog of official data concerning the Histadrut prior to the crisis years of the 1990s, see Gavriel Bartal, *The Histadrut: Structure and Activities*, 10th ed., in Hebrew (Tel Aviv: Histadrut, 1989).

4. For examples of traditional histories of the labor movement see Zvi Even-Shoshan, *History of the Workers' Movement in Eretz Israel*, in Hebrew (Tel Aviv: Am Oved, 1963); and Walter Preuss, *The Labour Movement in Israel: Past and Present*, in English (Jerusalem: Rubin Mass, 1965).

5. The literature on the labor movement in Israel is extensively surveyed in my book. Two important exceptions to the generalization of scholarly inattention to the Histadrut are Arie Shirom and Lev Grinberg. For example, see Shirom's *Introduction to Labor Relations in Israel*, in Hebrew (Tel-Aviv: Am Oved, 1983); and Grinberg's *Split Corporatism in Israel* (Albany: State University of New York Press, 1991).

6. Beverly Silver, "The Contradictions of Semiperipheral 'Success': The Case of Israel," in William G. Martin (ed.), *Semiperipheral States in the World-Economy* (New York: Greenwood Press, 1990), 161–181.

7. Gershon Shafir, *Land, Labor and the Origins of the Israeli-Palestinian Conflict 1882–1914* (Cambridge: Cambridge University Press, 1989).

8. Joel Beinin, *Was the Red Flag Flying There? Marxist Politics and the Arab-Israeli Conflict in Egypt and Israel, 1948–1965* (Berkeley: University of California Press, 1990).

9. Colin Crouch, *The Politics of Industrial Relations*, 2d ed. (London: Fontana, 1982); Gerhard Lehmbruch and Philippe C. Schmitter (eds.), *Patterns of Corporatist Policy Making* (London and Beverly Hills: Sage, 1982).

10. For details regarding the scope of Histadrut membership and the nature of member attachment see Shalev, *Labour and the Political Economy*, 31, notes 3 and 4.

11. Everett M. Kassalow, *Trade Unions and Industrial Relations: An International Comparison* (New York: Random House, 1969).

12. Yonathan Shapiro, *The Formative Years of the Israeli Labour Party* (London and Beverly Hills: Sage, 1976).

13. Traditionally associated with radical critics of Zionism such as Maxime Rodinson in *Israel, A Colonial Settler State?* (trans. David Thorstad [New York: Monad Press, 1973]), it was also articulated by one of the labor movement's most astute thinkers, Chaim Arlosoroff, in a scathing contemporary attack on what he viewed as the naive pretensions of the orthodox Jewish left. See "The Class War in the Reality of Palestine," Arlosoroff's address to the 1926 Hapoel Hatsair Convention, in Hebrew, in Reuven Cahane (ed.), *The Social Structure of Israel* (Jerusalem: Akademon, 1969), 66–74.

14. This position is common to a number of my contemporaries, specifically Gershon Shafir and Lev Grinberg; and also to some heterodox scholars of an earlier generation, notably Yonathan Shapiro and Zvi Sussman. See the citations to works by the first three authors in earlier notes, and Sussman's "The Policy of the Histadrut with Regard to Wage Differentials: A Study of the Impact of Egalitarian Ideology and Arab Labour on Jewish Wages in Palestine," Ph.D. dissertation, Hebrew University, 1969.

15. Arlosoroff (see note 13) was one of the leading Labor Zionist theoreticians between World War I and the Great Depression and among the few to have any academic training in economics and sociology. He was murdered in 1933 in circumstances that remain obscure. A convenient English source is Shlomo Avineri, *Arlosoroff* (London: Weidenfeld and Nicolson, 1989).

16. Examples are Mitchell Cohen, *Zion and State: Nation, Class and the Shaping of Modern Israel* (Oxford: Basil Blackwell, 1987); and Amir Ben-Porat, *Between Class and Nation: The Formation of the Jewish Working Class in the Period Before Israel's Statehood* (New York: Greenwood Press, 1986).

17. Shulamit Carmi and Henry Rosenfeld, "The Emergence of Militaristic Nationalism in Israel," *International Journal of Politics, Culture and Society* 3, 1 (1989):5–49.

18. Shmuel N. Eisenstadt, *The Transformation of Israeli Society: An Essay in Interpretation* (Boulder: Westview Press, 1985).

19. Sternhell is a major contributor to the study of European fascist ideologies. See his *Neither Right Nor Left: Fascist Ideology in France,* trans. David Maisel (Berkeley: University of California, 1986); and *The Birth of Fascist Ideology,* trans. David Maisel (Princeton: Princeton University Press, 1994).

20. Sternhell's ideas are the subject of a book in progress. The discussion here is based on a lengthy article published in the daily newspaper *Ha'aretz* on May 31, 1991.

21. In this respect Sternhell's thesis bears a remarkable, albeit unacknowledged, resemblance to the far more sympathetic perspective offered by historian Anita

Shapira. Shapira also treats the historical role of socialism in the labor movement instrumentally, as a means to the end of nationalist realization. But whereas Sternhell implies that the founding fathers were insincere and even cynical in their use of socialist metaphors and "figleaves," Shapira views the packaging of laborist nationalism in socialist rhetoric as evidence of the originality and creativity of the Zionist labor movement prior to sovereignty. Anita Shapira, "Socialist Means and Nationalist Aims," *Jerusalem Quarterly* 38 (1986):14–27.

22. This is a thesis that has been most convincingly advocated by Yonathan Shapiro, *The Formative Years of the Israeli Labour Party*, and is indirectly endorsed by Sternhell as well.

23. For fuller discussion of these issues see Baruch Kimmerling, *Zionism and Economy* (Cambridge: Schenkman, 1983); Sussman, "The Policy of the Histadrut"; and Shafir, *Land, Labor and the Origins*. The summary account here relies especially heavily on chapters 3 and 5 of Shafir's volume.

24. Edna Bonacich, "Advanced Capitalism and Black/White Race Relations in the United States: A Split Labor Market Interpretation," *American Sociological Review* 41, 1 (1976):34–51.

25. On the fascinating story of the catalytic role of the WZO in the founding of what became the kibbutzim, see chapter 7 of Shafir's *Land, Labor and the Origins*.

26. This emerges clearly from the timing of the WZO's release of the founding capital of the Workers' Bank. See Yitzhak Greenberg, "From Workers' Society to Workers' Economy: Evolution of the Idea of Hevrat Ovdim in the Years 1920–1929," in Hebrew, Ph.D. dissertation, Tel-Aviv University, 1983, 39–41.

27. Howard M. Sachar, *A History of Israel* (New York: Alfred A. Knopf, 1979), 395.

28. Eisenstadt, *The Transformation of Israeli Society;* Dan Horowitz and Moshe Lissak, *Trouble in Utopia: The Overburdened Polity of Israel* (Albany: State University of New York Press, 1989).

29. See Ian Lustick's conceptualization and illustrations of "dependence as a component of control" of Arabs by Jews in his *Arabs in the Jewish State: Israel's Control of a National Minority* (Austin and London: University of Texas Press, 1980).

30. After the middle of the 1960s immigration fell to comparatively insignificant levels. However, nearly 150,000 Soviet Jews entered Israel during the 1970s, and they were joined by many more in the 1990s.

31. For a sampling of interpretations of the dilemmas facing Histadrut and the Labor Party following statehood, see Peter Y. Medding, *Mapai in Israel: Political Organisation and Government in a New Society* (Cambridge: Cambridge University Press, 1972); Henry Rosenfeld and Shulamit Carmi, "The Privatization of Public Means, the State-Made Middle Class, and the Realization of Family Value in Israel," in J. G. Peristiany (ed.), *Kinship and Modernization in Mediterranean Society* (Rome: Center for Mediterranean Studies, 1969), 131–159; and Gadi Yatziv,

"The Class Basis of Party Affiliation," in Hebrew, Ph.D. dissertation, Hebrew University of Jerusalem, 1974.

32. The "workers' trend" in education and the labor exchanges—both connected in varying degrees to the Histadrut—were disbanded. On the political calculus underlying Ben-Gurion's successes and failures in the nationalization of Histadrut functions, see Asher Arian, "Political and Administrative Aspects of Welfare Policy in Israel," research report submitted to the Israel trustees of the Ford Foundation, Tel Aviv University, 1978.

33. For a detailed analysis of the failure of corporatist industrial relations to develop prior to sovereignty, see Shalev, *Labour and the Political Economy*, ch 4.

34. See Michal Kalecki, "Political Aspects of Full Employment," in Jersey Osiatinski (ed.), Chester Adam Kisiel (trans.), *Collected Works: Business Cycles and Full Employment*, vol. 1 (Oxford: Clarendon Press, 1990), 347–356.

35. Shalev, *Labour and the Political Economy*, ch. 7.

36. See Michael Shalev and Lev Grinberg, "Histadrut-Government Relations and the Transition from a Likud to a National Unity Government: Continuity and Change in Israel's Economic Crisis," discussion paper 19–89, Pinhas Sapir Center for Development, Tel Aviv University, October 1989; and Grinberg, *Split Corporatism in Israel*.

37. Jelle Visser, "The Strength of Union Movements in Advanced Capitalist Democracies: Social and Organizational Variations," in Marino Regini (ed.), *Labour Movements Towards the Year 2000* (London: Sage, 1992), 17–52.

38. Professor Erik Cohen of the Hebrew University has explicitly conceptualized the contemporary era as "post-Zionist" in several conference presentations and as yet unpublished papers.

39. For evidence of the shifts and continuities in Israeli public opinion discussed here, see inter alia Ephraim Yuchtman-Yaar, "The Israeli Public and the Intifadah: Attitude Change or Retrenchment?" in Ehud Sprinzak and Larry Diamond (eds.), *Israeli Democracy Under Stress* (Boulder: Lynne Rienner, 1993), 235–251; and Yochanan Peres and Ephraim Yuchtman-Yaar, *Trends in Israeli Democracy: The Public's View* (Boulder: Lynne Rienner), 1992.

40. Shalev, *Labour and the Political Economy*, chs. 6 and 7.

7

Reading from Left to Right: The Social History of Egyptian Labor

Ellis Goldberg

Arabic, like Hebrew and Persian, is written from right to left, the opposite of European scripts. A survey of Egyptian labor history must begin by recognizing that most of the accounts have been written from the left. Writing labor history in general and Egyptian labor history in particular has been so closely tied to self-proclaimed progressive projects that the moral and political content of the work is easily overlooked. This is certainly true of the English-language writing of Egyptian labor history, which has, since the late 1970s, been profoundly influenced by the discourse of Arab intellectuals and by the political commitments of those active in the field.

Until the late 1960s Egyptian history was primarily a narration of high politics in the conflict waged between colonial officials and nationalist leaders during the preceding eighty years.[1] Emerging Egyptian labor history, like the political conflicts it narrates, has been used to buttress the claims of insurgent nationalism, populism, and radicalism. Arguments about the extent of nationalist, communist, and Islamist influence have grown increasingly sharp in recent years and figure quite prominently in contemporary political struggles.

Since the mid-1980s there have been some exceptionally fine studies of Egyptian workers, their unions, their politics, and of lower-class families, spanning the last century. A peculiarity of the recent concentration on labor and social history, however, is that we lose the sense of how elite and mass social history fit together. Because we lack accounts of capitalists and their organizations at the same level of detail that we now possess on labor and the left, we have a poor idea, for example, of how labor and capital pursued sectoral advantage within the economy.[2] The absence of such accounts is partly the product of the theoretical orientation to conflict between labor and capital as factors of production, which so dominates the existing social and political historiography.

In the following pages I present a narrative of the history of Egyptian labor as we now generally agree on it and a running critique of several of the most important works in English and Arabic from which that narrative may be extracted. In the process I also address three other issues that any social history of labor in our century must consider. First, what do we know of the relationship of institutions that represented the interests of laboring men and women to projects of economic development and growth? Second, what do we know of the relationship of political projects influenced by Marxist analyses to projects influenced by concepts of ethnicity, nationality, and religion? Third, what do we know of the ways in which the social, emotional, and intellectual life of laboring men and women fit into larger patterns of social, emotional, and intellectual life in Egypt as a whole? Egyptian authors—activists and scholars—published research on the labor movement in Arabic and French in the 1960s when the Egyptian government called itself socialist. There have been debates about women, slaves, artisans, and urban life in more general terms, which any detailed picture of labor history ought to address but to which I can only allude.

Urban Labor Before Colonial Rule

Discussion of labor and social history in modern Egypt must begin with André Raymond's *Artisans et commerçants au Caire au XVIIIe siècle.*[3] Raymond addresses the themes around which this chapter is framed. Techniques, social structures, and institutions of artisanal production and small-scale marketing were the foundations of the classical Islamic society. They continue to be important. Whether these techniques, structures, and institutions necessarily retard the creation of a developed capitalist economy and whether they provide a reservoir for political reaction in the guise of Islam or nationalism remain politically potent questions.

Raymond's two-volume work is an exceptionally detailed account of Cairo's artisans and merchants in a long eighteenth century that stretches from 1670 to 1790. It sets a standard for writing social history that has remained unmatched for any other period of Egyptian history. Raymond established the use of Islamic court records as important source documents, and more authors since have mined these rich archives.

Raymond's painstaking work in the archival sources suggests that there was often significant upward mobility among artisans and, especially, merchants. Some of the merchants, especially those engaged in international commerce, became immensely wealthy. Raymond's work on inheritance documents suggests that textile producers were, in general, richer than others, followed by tanners with food producers running last.

Raymond's *Artisans* provides a benchmark of Cairene labor processes and social institutions at the boundary of a critical (but ultimately conceptual) juncture. Eighteenth-century Egypt had a population of about 4 million people, and Cairo was inhabited by some 250,000. Egypt was formally subject to Ottoman rule, although in 1805 an Albanian soldier, Muhammad Ali, initiated a process of dynastic statebuilding. Pre-nineteenth-century Cairo—its urban production, its markets, and its laboring population—are presumed to be in some sense "pure," uncontaminated by the presence of European capitalism and colonialism. It is further presumed that after Napoléon's 1798 invasion, the Egyptian economy entered a new phase governed by the conflict of the new or the foreign with the old and the native. Almost invariably Raymond's work is cited by later authors to ground arguments about how much has changed since the days when Cairo's production was in the hands of craftspeople who divided markets and production processes into a remarkably large number of small niches. Raymond's work is thus taken to provide an insight into an exemplary and static world of small commodity production that was overtaken in the succeeding century by the efficiency and political power of foreign capital acting to create large industrial plants.

Raymond depicts a world with remarkably high levels of specialization and thus of a very great division of labor despite the relatively slight use even of animal power, let alone mechanical power. This account disabuses us of the romantic notion of premodern artisans who work raw inputs into a complex, whole product by means of pure craftsmanship. Raymond's workers specialize, and they do so with remarkably different results. In some fields workers become renowned for their skill, and in others they become equally well known for their shoddy products. Raymond's Cairene artisans exhibited fairly strong localization, clustering in particular neighborhoods. Most of the city's economically active population was engaged in such production, and there was usually some regulation of the labor and product markets by artisanal associations, called *tawa'if* in Arabic. A reading of Raymond in this vein is congruent with explicitly Marxist analyses, which strongly differentiate precapitalist from capitalist modes of production.

Few of the social historians working on nineteenth-century Egypt (or on twentieth-century Egypt, for that matter) appear to be familiar with neoclassical economics, although the problems of voluntary cooperation by merchants who specialize and form monopolies are within its ambit.[4] Nor have many of the historians addressing Egyptian history been very concerned with sociological effects such as population growth and city size. Did the social intimacy of Raymond's Cairo arise from a traditional and Islamic society or simply from smallness? It is as hard to know if the problems of contemporary Cairo arise from the incongruities of modernization or simply from the scale of a city that now contains four of André Raymond's Egypts. Were recent authors to write from the perspective of the problems of voluntary cooperation in small communities or the problems of specialization and monopoly, Raymond's city might appear less distant from the present.[5]

Craft associations or guilds are usually taken to represent an outdated form of association, just as artisanal production is often said to be inefficient. Because production in small shops of limited quantities of goods remains an important part of the Egyptian economy today, the relative merits of small and large enterprises are still contested. At the turn of the century observers debated whether small-scale production was in decline and what might be the causes and consequences of the transformation already evident in the Egyptian economy. Most of the writing about labor process in the nineteenth and twentieth centuries simply assumes the economic irrationality of all artisanal and small-scale production. The survival of such processes has often, then, been linked to the growth of retrograde political currents by the argument that the petite bourgeoisie supports such politically reactionary Islamic or nationalist movements. How historians understand the nature of productive enterprise and collective action by labor has usually been a function of the belief that industrial firms necessarily supplant workshops in all sectors of the economy.

In a major study, *Egyptian Guilds in Modern Times*, Gabriel Baer argued that the guilds existed primarily to serve the state.[6] Their strengths derived from the Ottoman state. As the colonial state pursued a liberal policy toward the economy, the guilds and the artisanal production they organized necessarily declined in influence. Baer may have accepted colonial observations about the Egyptian economy too quickly.[7] Citing Lord Cromer, the most powerful British official, Baer wrongly believed that not only the guilds but artisanal production had largely collapsed by the turn of the century. We may attribute Baer's (and Cromer's) perceptions to Orientalism or faulty statistical technique. Yet Baer's work is an intellectual tour de force. An Israeli historian, Baer could not do archival research in Egypt but meticulously employed printed sources and available European archives. Frequently revisited and revised, Baer ensures that we do not forget that all organizations of those who work at least need to win the acquiescence, if not the support, of the government.

Three younger historians, Ehud Toledano, Judith Tucker, and Juan Cole have provided a much deeper vision of how the urban laboring classes in Cairo near the middle of the nineteenth century organized themselves. Their works give at least a somewhat clearer picture of a laboring world that comprised artisans, vendors, servants, compelled workers, and slaves.

Ehud Toledano's *State and Society in Mid-Nineteenth Century Egypt* is a lively if sometimes dispiriting picture of how employers and laborers alike resolved problems of trust: through a resolute insistence on hiring the known, the vouched-for, and the guaranteed as much as possible with occasionally tragic results for the alien, the unknown, or the excluded.[8] Toledano's major analytic premise is that Egypt was divided into a Turco-Circassian elite (with the Khedive or Ottoman viceroy at its head) and the mass of the Egyptian lower strata, but the book itself teems with accounts of how difficult it was for the lower classes to resolve conflicts among themselves, let alone with their social and political superiors. For Toledano, Egyptian social history is to be written in the key of Robert Darnton and Clifford Geertz: the search for meaning. Toledano's narrative more frequently details the absence of trust than of shared meaning. If trust rather than meaning is the key of social history, then Ernest Gellner and Roy Mottahedeh might be better guides to late-nineteenth-century Egypt than Clifford Geertz.[9] Toledano also often reveals the world of slavery to us in unexpected and powerful ways. We know little of how relations between slaves and masters were regulated in Cairo then, although the slave population was less prominent than in the New World and yet far more prominent than in postmedieval Europe. Toledano's suggestion that slaves had rights that they could hope to enforce is tantalizing.[10]

Judith Tucker's rich and insightful study *Women in Nineteenth Century Egypt* employs sources similar to those used by Raymond.[11] Tucker also reviews much of the material in Raymond, and her book gives English readers a convenient and thoughtful exposition of the themes involved as well as an original account of women. Tucker alerts us that the crafts were not wholly the domain of men. Women appear to have worked widely in the factories established by Muhammad Ali and to have played an especially prominent role in textile-related industries.[12] Women were also a disproportionately large share of the slave population because slaves seem to have been mainly household servants.[13] Women were also employed in the amusement of men, whether as prostitutes, dancers, singers, or other entertainers. We do not know how large these sectors of the urban workforce were, but by the 1920s and 1930s it was widely believed that prostitution was increasing in scale.[14]

In *Colonialism and Revolution in the Middle East*, Juan Cole addresses the world of urban artisans and merchants just as Egypt's political subordination to Europe became formalized. The dominant organizations of skilled and unskilled laborers in the nineteenth century were still the guilds, or *tawa'if*, which by regulating entry into professions, attempted to set wages. Cole describes in considerable detail the way guilds used income-sharing practices to maintain monopolies. Such communal institutions in the premodern period resolved collective-action problems but turned out to be extremely fragile when the state withdrew its support or when private individuals contracted directly for the services provided. The growing role of European officials in the Egyptian state in the last third of the nineteenth century and the growth of European private business interests set both processes in motion. Consequently, after the British occupied Egypt in 1882, solidary communal institutions were under constant pressure. In response to this pressure, guild members petitioned the state and changed their leaders through elections.

These elections and petitions to bureaucrats allow us to look more deeply into mid-nineteenth-century urban social life than ever before. Formal voting procedures were instituted by official decisions in 1865, but some form of consultative canvassing was already common.[15] Elections became a widespread form for choosing leaders of associations in which many eligible members participated and may have had some socialization effect in terms of what urban craftsmen and merchants thought about how the national government should work.[16] These elections were not regularly recurring processes. Although members could elect their leaders, they could not easily depose them or elect new leaders, and thus journeymen continued to appeal to the government for aid against their masters.

The Occupation of Egypt

Cairo had become a city of a third of a million people when British troops put down a revolt led by Ahmad Urabi in 1882. The early years of the occupation accelerated the processes of domestic liberalization and international free trade, the latter of which had already begun to erode artisanal structures of marketing and production. At its new size, problems of anonymity and trust became more acute in Cairo, especially because many of the new residents were in-migrants from the countryside and were without the social networks providing the webs of trust and credit through which workers found work and housing.

Everyone agrees that the British occupation changed social and political life in Egypt. For two decades, the Egyptian economy enjoyed an era of expansion. At least part of the price was the direct administrative influence of British officials at all levels of the Egyptian government and the gradual loss of jurisdiction by Egyptian courts over the economy to the foreign-dominated Mixed Courts. By the early years of the twentieth century, however, both the economy and the ecology had suffered dramatically under British domination. During World War I, Britain's need for food at home and manpower support in the Syrian campaign profoundly affected Egypt's population and caused widespread hunger and anger over conscription. The massive revolt of March 1919 was put down with force but led to the creation of an almost independent kingdom in 1922. The new state had its own constitution, a weak parliament, and the old ruling elite. Britain retained the political and military capacity to dominate Egypt even after nominal independence was gained.

British domination is conventionally taken to have ended in 1954, when Gamal Abdel Nasser negotiated the withdrawal of the last British troops from Egyptian soil. The most massive study of Egyptian labor for this period is *Workers on the Nile* by Joel Beinin and Zachary Lockman. Beinin and Lockman write clearly from within a late-Marxist perspective. For them Egyptian labor history between 1882 and 1954 is the story of Egypt's integration into large-scale patterns of commercial exchange, the world capitalist market, and the creation of new social groups. The Great Depression provides them with a rather neat boundary between two distinct phases in this process, which correspond to what are two quite distinct books. The first half, originally a dissertation by Lockman, recounts the integration of Egypt into a world market and examines the economic sectors most affected: the artisanal industries (such as cigarette making), which declined, and the transportation industries, which expanded. The second half, based on a separate dissertation by Beinin, is a discussion of early attempts at import-substitution industrialization, especially in the domestic textile sector.

Classes for Beinin and Lockman are quite literally phenomenological: they are manifestations of economic and cultural processes rather than entities in themselves. Specifically, Beinin and Lockman argue that classes

are the effects of "struggles which are structured by the totality of economic, political and ideological-cultural relations [and] should therefore
not be regarded as entities which exist independently of political and ideological practice."[17]

Egyptian backwardness in their view is largely the result of the origins
of investment funds: European business interests were either hostile or indifferent to Egypt's developing along the normal, that is, European, capitalist trajectory. Beinin and Lockman reject the Marxist notion that ownership of the means of production uniquely creates interests but they are
far more sympathetic to the idea that political parties can both define and
represent interests and classes. Thus the Liberal Constitutionalist Party
represented the agrarian bourgeoisie, the Wafd represented the urban and
rural middle classes, and the communists were champions of the interests
of the industrial working class in the textile industry, which began to develop in the 1930s.

We lack good studies of how parliamentary or administrative authorities
made law regulating social interests in the period. Although we know the
social composition of the partisan leaderships, there is no reason to believe
that in the Egyptian elite any more than in the lower classes the relationship to the means of production uniquely determines consciousness.

Beinin and Lockman succinctly propose a framework for analyzing the
growth of trade unions and their likely political orientation. Over time,
the growth of capital invested in industry attracts workers into the cities
from the countryside; these workers create unions as a form of collective
action in regard to owners and as a form of interest representation in regard to the state.

In the colonial era, "economic and social grievances are directed against
a foreign-run state apparatus as well as a foreign dominated economy
[and create] the basis for close links between indigenous workers and the
emerging nationalist movement."[18] These links appear to be both instrumentally calculated alliances and more diffuse ideological ties that induce
workers to view their world in a nationalist perspective. The narrative dis-
plays nationalist ideology as playing an independent role in transforming
the expected trajectory of class politics and, insofar as it is successful, as following the leftist currents in nationalist historiography in Arabic. The critical moment at which a new pattern of labor politics emerged in Egypt was
the 1919 revolt against the British occupation. In Beinin and Lockman's
framework, physical deprivation aggravated by monetary inflation provides the economic backdrop for worker militancy, which is primarily defensive in nature. The success of unions appears closely related to their

ability to take advantage of political instability whose primary locus is the demand for political independence. As political independence nears, however, political leaders no longer privilege their working class followers, and some workers pursue a learning curve that takes them out of the nationalist field. At the further end of this process of social learning, workers create stable organizations; these reflect a growing sense of shared political and economic interests, and their leadership is drawn largely from the workers' own ranks.

This is an attractive and concise thesis, but as Beinin later suggested, it led to a book that focused on a rather formal institutional approach.[19] The study of institutions themselves, however, need not dwell only on a schematic, descriptive approach. The so-called new institutionalism is premised on the importance of explaining why people create some institutions rather than others.

The data to which *Workers* lends itself most easily are a broad institutional history of unions that is an extremely valuable contribution to Egyptian history and labor studies. Data, of course, exist for other sorts of studies, probably inimical to the Marxist tradition, that assert the historical importance of the formation of the working class. Beinin and Lockman make plausible claims about historical (but not cross-sectional) patterns of strike activity, and they make some interesting asides (which both authors have expanded in later work) on the language and culture of labor.

The book opens with a coalheavers' strike, which places Egypt in the historical perspective of imperial expansion and places *Workers* in the context of arguments about proletarianization. Coalheavers were the unskilled laborers who carried coal down narrow and unstable walkways from ships laden with it and then back to other ships needing fuel in the days before bunker fuel was widely used. For Beinin and Lockman the strike is not—as Gabriel Baer described it—of guild members against their masters but of peasant laborers resisting foreign capital in a long process of acculturation, proletarianization, and ethnic conflict. More recently Juan Cole, following Zayn al-Abidin Najm, has suggested that Baer's story may be correct after all and that the strike proves that guilds not only survived but remained vital until late in the nineteenth century.[20]

Coalheavers aside, new sectors of the economy and new groups of workers have continuously been formed throughout the twentieth century. Foreign capital provided the impetus to expand cigarette production by employing skilled labor and utilizing market recognition. In most accounts of labor unions, the long-term conflict over income shares forces investors to seek ever greater exploitation of labor, usually through deskilling mechanization. Cigarette production in Egypt provided a counterpoint to the coalheavers, for it was just at the junction of skilled and artisanal work, and these highly skilled artisans of mass production provided the core of trade union movements in many countries and played a prominent role in early Egyptian union history. Their social cohesion often arose from the highly interdependent nature of the work process and from ethnic homogeneity. Cigarette rollers were done in by machines and coalheavers by fuel oil because capitalism is relentless.

Toward Independence and Beyond

Industrial production was still an extremely small portion of the Egyptian economy before World War I and consequently the wage-labor force engaged in industry, transport, or commerce was relatively small. Of a labor force of about 9.5 million, about 280,000 were in manufacturing with about another 200,000 equally divided between construction and transportation. Such figures can provide an erroneous impression of the size of the workforce in mechanized industries, since a large fraction of these workers were in small workshops, labored in small gangs, or drove animals. One of the strongest trade union organizations was the Manual Trades Workers' Union, which had about 3,000 members on the verge of World War I and which was closely connected to the nationalist party led by Muhammad Farid, the Watani Party.

Much of what we know about artisanal production in the early years of the twentieth century we owe to the research of two French scholars, Jean Vallet and Germain Martin. In 1910, Martin arrived at the Egyptian University to give a series of lectures on political economy. He had already made a considerable reputation for himself as a student of French industrial development and labor organization, and his prize-winning work in France dealt precisely with how large industrial undertakings provide crucial economic support for modern states. These themes were consonant with growing elite interest in industrialization. Martin was well acquainted with Marxian and liberal economics. He was especially interested in the size and efficiency of markets and undertook a short study of Cairo's local markets—the bazaars—which remains an important source. Martin did not set out to write ethnography but to address an important issue of economic analysis: Were Egyptian markets efficient? Martin appears to have concluded, as we might expect, that Egypt's urban markets were least efficient in the countryside and that the bazaar economy did a reasonably good job of bringing buyer and seller together at a common price. When Martin compared merchants and craftsmen in the bazaar with urban and rural markets in France, he saw sectoral technological backwardness but did not necessarily see economic inefficiency.[21] The organizations of urban craftsmen and tradesmen did not necessarily serve to stunt Egyptian economic growth. A close look at the work of Martin and Vallet places them in the context of a longer tradition of writing about workers in France, which has been extensively discussed by William Reddy and William Sewell.[22] Sewell and Reddy argue that mid-nineteenth-century French scholars had a ready-made discourse through which to present their own working classes as physically miserable, economically marginal, and morally suspect.[23] These same themes recur in the work of Martin and Vallet and Egyptian commentators down to the present when they merge with left, Islamist, and liberal discourses about the immorality of workers. Whether the Egyptian workers were badly off in quite the ways suggested ever since must be open to question.

Most of what passed for industrial production in Egypt until well after the turn of the century was somewhere on the boundary between highly skilled work in mass production and extensive artisanal production. Among the few places where a recognizable industrial proletariat composed of semiskilled wage earners could be found was in transportation, mainly on the tramways and in the Egyptian State Railways. Turn-of-the-century rail transportation required relatively large capital investments, high levels of mechanical skills, and frequent social interactions among those who worked in it. In Egypt rail transport provided a key link in capitalist development because the agricultural sector required an advanced transport system to move cotton to international markets.

Tramway workers ceased to be the leading sector of the working class after 1942, when the textile workers, especially in the medium-size factories in Cairo and its suburbs, emerged and provided the base for left-led unionism. The textile workers provided this leadership again in part because of the conjunction of capital investment, mechanical skills, and the social solidarity of the employees and because they were on the cusp of the transition of Egypt in the direction of import-substitution strategies, which provided a progressive next step in the development of capitalism.

Metaphors of weight, solidity, attraction, and explosion dominate *Workers on the Nile.* Capital concentrations effect concentrations of labor, which in turn create centers of gravity (or leading sectors).[24] Workers in these sectors experience discrimination, mistreatment, or exploitation, and in response they "melt," "explode," and "burst."[25] These metaphors abound because Beinin and Lockman—despite their phenomenology—retained a Marxian argument that the class-producing structures of a liberal economy necessarily tend to create revolutionary conflict.[26]

Labor Historiography Takes a Turn

Why a Marxist approach to writing social history emerged in Middle East studies just as it was fading elsewhere is an intriguing question. One perennial answer is that studies of the Middle East are in some way as underdeveloped as the region itself.[27] Peter Gran has obliquely suggested that the turn to Marxism was due to the socialization of researchers outside universities.[28] P. J. Vatikiotis has suggested that the endogenous structure of university recruitment and tenuring processes forced Marxism on aspiring professors.[29] Marxism, however, had some cognitive content: a theory of imperialism that claimed to delve more deeply than any other into processes of how ordinary people lived through a period of dramatic economic and political change.[30] Marxism also fits rather easily into the evolution of a critical interpretive approach that demands linguistic and literary skills rather than, for example, quantitative ones.

Students of Egyptian labor history, like other labor historians, have made the discursive turn. The concept of discourse appears, in labor history at any rate, to have three primary kinds of reference; these touch on but are somewhat different from the older Weberian and Hintzian concepts of *verstehensoziologie*. For Gareth Stedman Jones, discourse implies a research strategy focused on shared meanings and cultural context in which what people say about their own problems and likely solutions must be taken seriously. If nineteenth-century English workers said they wanted universal manhood suffrage and frequent parliaments (the Charter, as it was known), then we ought to take that seriously as a way of understanding working-class protest between 1820 and 1840 rather than ignoring it.[31] Another meaning of discourse appears to be the constitution of popular and elite conceptions about the state of the world. The world may be constituted differently from those conceptions, but, the argument goes, people act on the conceptions. Language is an available stock of ideas that, in the last instance, structure the social field. Finally, discourse can refer to the ways in which scholars reconstitute either of these two prior meanings of discourse: that is, a rational reconstruction of events begins shortly after they occur.

Each of these concepts of discourse has been deployed in accounts of Egyptian labor history, although they have not been differentiated from each other. Discourse as reconstruction of history may explain why nationalism looms as something to be explained. For leftists writing labor history, it is difficult to understand why their preferred political outcomes, presumably embedded in history itself, did not provide political direction to real institutions. Discourse as an instance of the constitution of reality by communities of workers is no doubt worth deeper study. Unfortunately, what requires explanation in such a case is not why the left failed but why it succeeded. Where the discursive field was dominated by Islamic and nationalist conceptions, it is not so easy to understand why Marxists should find a significant following.

My own book *Tinker, Tailor and Textile Worker*[32] began in what Peter Gran calls a neo-Marxist framework, but no reviewer other than Gran appears to have seen the book as Marxist. It has more widely been seen as a neo-Weberian or rational-choice approach, but my primary motivation was to explain the distribution of political ideologies across specific environments of production. The book covers ground similar to that of Beinin and Lockman, but in the writing of the book it became apparent that neither the Marxist nor the Weberian paradigm made much sense of the empirical material that my research had uncovered.

The theme of the search for advantage coupled with ideologies as bearers of cognitive content was a plausible way to understand trade unions and their politics. Such is the basic theme of *Tinker*. From outside the Marxist perspective there was no reason to believe any group of workers were likely to become Marxists (or anything else for that matter). What does seem clear is that already by the 1930s there were significant sectors of the labor movement whose conditions and wages were far more likely to be affected by government intervention of one kind or another than by cooperation or conflict with employers. The government set wages in the public sector, which included the heavy industrial settings of the railroads and the arsenal as well as officials, bureaucrats, and low-level employees. The government also set the terms under which many multinational firms operated by either its taxing, concessionary, or tariff-making power, and in these areas politicians could have considerable influence over the wages of their political supporters. Especially in monopoly or quasi-monopoly settings such as crude oil production and refining and cigarette production (which from the 1930s on was an important source of revenue for the state), owners were willing to share a portion of the rents with the workers.

From Depression to Revolution

Labor success in the mid-1930s was similar to the pattern of 1919. During the first years of the Great Depression, Ismail Sidki, an authoritarian politician who had headed the Egyptian Federation of Industry, ruled with the support of the king. The middle years of the decade saw a renaissance of the nationalist movement in which the Wafd returned to power after a stormy period of demonstrations and protests. The labor movement, concerned about unemployment and falling wages, showed renewed militancy and was part of the nationalist coalition that returned the Wafd to power and helped to write a new Anglo-Egyptian agreement in 1936, which restored more (but far from all) Egyptian independence. A similar pattern appears to have held in the years following World War II, when high inflation and the dramatic collapse of military demand again stimulated defensive trade union militancy.

The story that we have often appears exceptionally good at linking labor militancy with the general political atmosphere. There is much more about the relationship between politically prominent actors and the labor movement than either my book or the Beinin-Lockman volume could address because of the absence of data.[33] Still, the data at our disposal *would* have allowed a sharper focus on Coptic-Muslim relationships in Egypt during the 1920s and 1930s, something that eluded us as we thought of Egyptian labor history. Far more research would be needed to develop a clear picture, but such an approach would draw together our present stories in a very different way. Both books present, for example, the Democratic Party as a small, leftish, secular party led by Aziz Mirhum, himself a paternalist Wafdist leader of labor. In Beinin and Lockman's account another influential labor leader, Raghib Iskandar, appears as a would-be paternalist adviser to the workers. Iskandar and Mirhum were both Copts and were both on the executive board of the party, and both left it over the issue of the Adli-Curzon negotiations in 1921.[34]

It is possible to construct an alternative narrative in which radical non-communist elite Copts played an important role in developing a secular labor movement. Rather than seeing Muslim-Coptic unity as surging up from the society in an unproblematic way, historians might be more accurate (and their analyses perhaps more fruitful) if they considered the Egyptian labor movement as a field in which members of the Coptic elite—such as the prominent labor attorney and head of the Egyptian bar Makram Ubayd—worked with Muslim counterparts to structure a new political culture and new political institutions. Such an approach might also make more sense of the recurring theme of the threat from Christian proselytization, which was prominent in the 1930s and which remains so prominent in the Arabic historiography of the period but not in accounts in English (with the exception of Nadav Safran).[35] We know far more about the role of Jews in the communist movement (although their presence among industrial workers themselves was negligible) than we do about other religious minorities.[36]

A great many labor activists published their own memoirs between 1980 and 1990. These range from those of leaders, such as Fathi Kamil, whose careers were more fully in union organization, to Taha Sa'd Uthman, whose career in the Shubra al-Khaima textile mills spanned a decade, to memoirs by Fikri al-Khuli, which provide rich details of life in the giant textile center of Mehallah al-Kubra.

The period just before and after World War II marks another era in Egyptian labor history. State officials as well as Egyptian-domiciled business interests had determined that the textile industry would provide a strategic nexus for economic development.[37] Egypt was an important producer of cotton for the world market, especially long-staple cotton, most of which was exported to England. A small, highly protected textile industry had existed since the turn of the century outside Alexandria, but in the 1930s there was a dramatic expansion of capital invested in textiles. Much of this investment and the bulk of the consequent employment was in Mahallah al-Kubra in the middle of the Delta, where some 35,000 workers were employed in a truly gigantic operation. Egyptian and English investors built a fine spinning and weaving plant at Kafr al-Dawwar outside Alexandria, however, and the neighborhoods to the north of Cairo, especially Shubra al-Khaima, were also the site of a relatively large number of small- and medium-sized firms in which tens of thousands were employed.

World War II was a period of especially dramatic gains for the labor movement. In 1942 the British, alarmed at the complacent attitude of the palace about Rommel's advance toward Egypt, brought their old antagonist, the Wafd, to power. Ironically, this nationalist party, which had been created to demand complete independence from Britain in 1919, was the only party in 1942 on which the British could rely to keep Egypt secure. Trade unions until 1942 were, strictly speaking, neither legal nor illegal. The Wafd legalized the unions, thereby increasing their power, but it did so by having them register with the Ministry of Social Affairs. The government reserved to itself the right to cancel the registration and dissolve the unions. Within a year and a half there were more than 300 registered unions with some 120,000 members; most of the unions had fewer than 200 members, but most of the members were in very large unions.[38]

The war years saw a dramatic boom in the demand for textiles woven in Egypt, and fortunes were made selling textiles legally and on the black market (to circumvent price ceilings). An unusual group of labor activists in the Shubra area emerged, some of whom were initially members of the Muslim Brothers and others of whom were socialists of Christian and Muslim background. Several of these trade unionists entered the orbit of an Egyptian communist intellectual and attorney Yusuf Darwish. The most successful attempt to create an independent and radical trade union movement in Egypt emerged in the northern Cairene suburbs, although the union itself (the General Union of Mechanized Textile Workers of Cairo and Its Suburbs) was disbanded by a non-Wafdist government in 1946. These suburbs were filled with new workers who were frequently laid off; housing was often poor and conditions were raw. They thus remained contentious sites through 1952, when the Free Officers came to power, and it was not uncommon for contemporary observers to see them almost as revolutionary zones.

Mahallah had been chosen for massive investment by the Misr investment group largely in the hope that it would be distant enough from the bright lights and agitators of the city to remain without labor strife. Turnover was terrifically high, the bulk of the workforce was poorly skilled, and discipline was often physical force.[39] There was a major strike at Mahallah in 1947, and it appeared a revolutionary tide was about to sweep the country. At the most generous estimate, however, only about a million were employed in manufacturing, construction, and transport out of a labor force estimated at more than 16 million people; as in the earlier period, a large number of these workers were not in modern industrial settings. The country was in ferment because of the winding down of the wartime boom and the loss of the Palestine War of 1948 and because the postwar era also saw the waxing of full Egyptian sovereignty after almost sixty years of occupation.

Between 1942 and 1952 labor became the object of a significant legislative effort. The legalization of labor unions and increased legal recourse for workers not only crossed political boundaries in the ancien régime but was continued into the new dispensation as well. The continuities between the old and new have been little studied. It is apparent, however, that state officials increasingly saw labor legislation as an instrument to gain allies among the wage-earning population and as a tool with which to extend the control of the state into larger sectors of the economy. Prior to 1942 what little labor law there was in Egypt primarily regulated the employment of women and children and highly dangerous occupations. The motivational forces behind this legislation were diverse. Some were due to international pressure, and some were the result of large businesses attempting to stifle competition from smaller ones. By 1944, the Wafd had initiated the transformation of the factory into an arena for public as well as private control by legalizing unions, creating conciliation and arbitration commissions to deal with labor disputes, and passing laws directing foreign-owned firms to hire Egyptians. In 1948 the promulgation of a unified civil code replacing older Islamic law (shari'ah) and the defunct Mixed Courts expressly expanded the area of positive law affecting the firing of workers and their discipline on the job. A common theme among workers at the time (and now) was a profound sense of grievance about physical coercion as well as fiscal discipline in the factories.[40]

We have a far better sense of the history of the communist movements in this period than we do of the laboring communities that the communists wished to lead.[41] The roughly 4,000 militants associated in one way or another with the various communist groups in the country were in no position to lead an insurrectionary movement. There was an attempt to create a new trade union federation in late 1951, which collapsed in the confusing and repressive atmosphere after the burning of downtown Cairo on January 27, 1952.

A New Beginning Under the Free Officers

Six months after the burning of Cairo, in June, the Free Officers came to power in a coup. Two weeks after the coup, police moved to end a sit-in and protest at the Misr Spinning and Weaving plant in Kafr al-Dawwar. An exchange of gunfire caused seven deaths among workers, police, and soldiers. Two workers were executed, and it appeared to sections of the left and even some foreign business interests that the regime was poised to repress the labor movement in order to attract external investment. The regime also moved rapidly to confiscate the property of the royal family and its closest allies and to institute land reform.

In December 1952 the new regime issued more extensive labor legislation, although how much it helped workers has been a matter for debate. There is no doubt that after 1952 the state was far more deeply concerned both with managing the economy and with the texture of discipline and power within factories and workshops than had ever before been the case in Egypt.[42]

The role of the state in decisions ranging from investment to discipline was consequential. The general trajectory of the first decade of the regime was corporatist. In March 1954 sections of the trade union movement played a key role in helping Gamal Abdel Nasser defeat opponents within the junta and oust the nominal president, General Muhammad Nagib. Whether intentionally or not, the unions exchanged political support for limited economic benefits. Union independence, especially on the political level, was curtailed, as was the right to strike. Union density was increased more or less by fiat, preparations were made for a trade union confederation, workers were encouraged to undertake court actions against employers, and firing workers was made more difficult. In 1956 in response to the refusal of the World Bank to fund the building of a new dam at Aswan, Nasser nationalized the Suez Canal. In the following years the other foreign-owned property was nationalized and by 1960 Egypt had a large socialist sector. Egypt's population in 1960 was almost 26 million, of whom perhaps 750,000 worked in industries of various sizes.

The organized union movement came to comprise primarily workers in medium and large industrial enterprises of the public sector. The founding of a national federation of trade unions had originally been set for October 30, 1956, but was postponed when the Israeli invasion began on October 29. The Egyptian Trade Union Federation was founded on January 30, 1957, by a meeting of 101 union leaders who affirmed Anwar Salama, the regime's choice, as president. As Amin Izz al-Din points out, Salama's federation had little independence of the government from the very beginning, and it had to engage in bureaucratic battles with the government as well as with employers, administrators, and insurgent workers.[43] The federation had nearly 1,300 local unions in twenty-eight industrial subfederations with over 310,000 members in 1957.

A decade of nationalizations, sequestrations, and direct investment by the state increased the size of publicly owned enterprises, and it appears that labor activism declined for a decade or more in this part of the economy. By 1964 almost 1.1 million workers were nominally members of trade unions affiliated with the national federation. As the union movement grew, its subordination to the state grew as well, and the official union movement (and perhaps the workers as well) became increasingly passive.

Marsha Posusney has documented this passivity and argues that it occurred as a function of the regime's attack on political opposition (including the left), the entry of more peasants into the workforce, and company unionism.[44] Another view of how corporatism and passivity in the labor movement occurs is founded in an argument about rationality. In "The Foundations of the State-Labor Relations in Contemporary Egypt," I argued that we can conceptualize corporatism in Egypt as a large-scale agreement between workers and the state to exchange job security and state-regulated benefits for economic and political quiescence.[45] Three conceptual advantages emerge from taking this perspective. First, it is possible to appreciate the instrumental and thus temporal limits of the corporatist compromise. Second, it is possible to evaluate the corporatist exchange as a preferential claim of the organized sector of the workforce in the public sector that left behind unorganized workers in far less protected labor markets where they received lower wages for more intense work. Last, it is easier to understand the importance of closing the local markets to international competition as well as the intertemporal degradation of the economy that results. Among the shortcomings of the rational-choice approach is that it is hard to believe that any such compromise was fully and intentionally envisaged by the partners from the outset. The outcome may represent an explicable equilibrium, but it is doubtful that the parties reached the equilibrium other than by trial and error.

A large portion of the urban workforce remained in the so-called informal sector through the 1970s and 1980s. Recent studies of Egyptian interest-group politics that include analyses of labor politics have tended to focus on the concerns of the top union leadership without showing an understanding of what was happening at the base or even of the statistical information available from the government. An excellent case in point is Robert Bianchi's *Unruly Corporatism,* which more or less willfully misreads changes in the sectoral composition of the Egyptian workforce by ignoring the role of those who work in firms with fewer than ten employees.[46] Employees in these firms have not generally been counted for statistical purposes, but their number remains quite high. It is amusing to read an account of the Egyptian political economy in which tailors and handwashers appear to be of minuscule importance when their presence in Cairo is ubiquitous. If we take establishment size as the criterion for defining the "informal" sector, it appears that even in 1976 the informal private sector had 2.5 million employes.[47] More manufacturing workers were probably employed in the informal, or small-establishment, sector than in the entire public sector.[48] If previous Egyptian history is a guide, working conditions were likely far worse in the private sector. Labor organization and politicized class conflict were probably far less common in these workshops than in the large public-sector factories.

Labor has long had an important symbolic and practical role for Egyptian governments. By law, 50 percent of parliamentary deputies were required to be workers or peasants, ostensibly to enhance democracy. Because government officials chose these representatives, they actually enhanced the power of the central state and thus also served to make the liberal professions far less prominent in political life than had been the case in the old regime or in capitalist democracies. A new electoral law in 1983 mandated proportional representation instead of the previous practice of single-member constituencies. Article 87 of the constitution, which mandates that 50 percent of the legislative seats be filled by workers and peasants, allows the government to limit the translation of candidate lists into parliamentary seats.[49]

The relative closure of Egypt to the international market economy from 1956 to 1973 and the years of war had a negative effect on the Egyptian economy. Real wages certainly ceased growing by 1968, although in any given industry the peak may have been before or after the war. Overtime and bonuses allowed workers to compensate for declining wage rates, but incomes began to stagnate as well. The collapse of the regime's legitimacy as well as its growing inability to keep its economic bargain appears to have prompted some reemergence of labor protest after 1968. A hiatus occurred after 1968 and continued until the death of Gamal Abdel Nasser in 1971.

Back to the Future?

To the surprise of many, Anwar Sadat, Nasser's vice president, was able to consolidate power in 1972 and began to open Egypt once again to the world capitalist market, a policy known as the *infitah*. It was not until the years following the 1973 war between Egypt, Syria, and Israel that widespread strikes and protest riots occurred. These culminated in the January 1977 uprising, in which the government lost control of the capital during two days of spontaneous mass protest. Any policy of linking Egypt once more to the capitalist world implied the privatization of state industries and a concomitant pressure to reduce wages, the number of employees, and the quality of working conditions in the pursuit of efficiency. In general both workers and trade union leaders opposed privatization, although the union leaders were subject to significant pressure from the state and the ruling National Democratic Party, with which they were tightly linked.[50] No matter how dominant the state, it is far from immune to pressure from the urban laboring poor. Ibrahim Karawan argued in 1993 that Anwar Sadat's decision to go to Jerusalem in November 1977 in search of peace with Israel arose directly from his perceptions of the costs of increasing domestic conflict in Egypt centered in the urban working class.[51]

Posusney's accounts of the rising number of protests in the mid-1970s through the 1980s are striking, and in a real sense Marxism seems descriptively accurate. Workers and state managers were locked in combat over how to divide a static, if not shrinking, economy, and none of the union members or leaders had any clear idea about how to enlarge the Egyptian economy. To the degree that labor regulations were codified, that workers in one area knew the outcome of conflicts elsewhere, and that there was a growing demand for Egyptian labor in the Arabian peninsular countries—which translated into labor shortages at home—nominal wages in the unionized public sector ratcheted upward. There were important strikes, but the largest section of the workforce remained outside the modern industrial sector. These families depended on subsidized basic commodities, and when the International Monetary Fund attempted to enforce an austerity budget on the country in 1977, two days of riots broke out.

Posusney elaborates her argument about Egyptian workers in "Irrational Workers: The Moral Economy of Labor Protest in Egypt," where she argues that the older English labor historiography works well for contemporary Egypt.[52] In essence, Posusney's argument is that in repressive authoritarian regimes, such as that of Egypt after 1952, protest by workers necessarily requires a heroic willingness to risk further repression. This heroism is usually precipitated, she argues, by workers' attempts to sustain what they perceive as a community rather than an economic exchange, that is, they desire a moral economy.

Posusney reminds us of how conflictual a relationship labor had with the state in the period after nationalizations. By the late 1960s, no doubt many workers in mass-production industries believed that government officials in the public sector and in the ministries were out to feather their nests at the expense of ordinary workers.[53] The moral-economy paradigm was developed more to explain differences between patterns of artisanal and industrial protest than variations of industrial protest. Posusney implicitly, therefore, carries forward the argument that Egyptian industrial workers retain worldviews similar to those motivating artisans in the nineteenth century. She also details the willingness of the state to use threats, arrests, and physical intimidation to keep the increasingly buoyant trade union movement of the 1980s in line. Posusney's data do not allow

us to draw any conclusions about strike frequencies in more conventional
ways that would track economic changes. Recent conventional studies
about labor and innovation in advanced capitalist countries suggest we
look at resistance in more nuanced ways.[54]

What is especially unfortunate in this regard is that it is almost impossible to distinguish whether the improved conditions for Egyptian workers
resulted from their protests or simply because—in the period after the
1973 war—so many workers left the country, thus leaving more opportunities for those who stayed. The role of migration grew through the 1970s
and into the 1980s. Egypt had been a country with little emigration, but
this changed after the October 1973 war. It has been estimated that from
1970 to 1988, as many as 3.5 million Egyptians, mainly men, emigrated for
brief periods or permanently in search of work. The focus of migration in
the 1970s was toward Libya and the Arabian peninsula. Sadat's assassination in 1981 brought Husni Mubarak to power, and Mubarak has cautiously pursued elements of democratization without, however, being
willing to transfer power away from the government. The years since 1980
have also seen continuous growth of the Islamic movements, partly because Sadat favored their growth among students in the early 1970s and
partly because of socialization experiences of migrants in the Gulf.

According to Ministry of Planning estimates, in 1986 industry accounted for about 14 percent of the workforce at home, and agricultural
employment continued to decline. Although large industry directly supports only a fraction of Egypt's 53 million people, urban and industrial life
is the norm in 1990s Egypt. Husni Mubarak has made considerably more
progress than Anwar Sadat in attracting foreign investors to Egypt, in pri-
vatizing sections of the economy, and in forcing productive firms (but not
government offices) to become more efficient.[55] Labor at both the leadership and popular level has generally viewed such changes as threatening
because both employment and wage levels are in jeopardy. After 1984 several large-scale strikes occurred, and there was a renewal of social conflict
in several important cities in the Delta.[56] There were extensive strikes, sit-
downs, and shop occupations by workers throughout the 1980s. These included strikes among textile workers at Kafr al-Dawwar, strikes at the
Egyptian State Railways, and (in 1989) a strike over bonuses and union
representation on the board at the iron and steel plant at Helwan.

Rising social tensions in Egypt have not translated into increased support for unions or the political left, and in the 1986 election the leftist
Tagamu Party, whose leadership is historically associated with labor militancy, won only about 2 percent of the vote.[57] The Labor Party did win
slightly more than 16 percent of the vote, but only because it was in al-

liance with the Muslim Brothers. Although the government won almost two-thirds of the vote, there is little reason to believe that it had quite such strong support, because there were high levels of abstention and ballot manipulation.

The rise of Islamist movements has been reflected dramatically in working-class neighborhoods, which themselves have undergone significant change since 1952. The Imbaba area in the northern part of Giza across the Nile from Cairo, where government troops engaged in an armed search for Islamist militants, is a case in point. Today Imbaba is a slum and surrounded by wealthier districts to the west and north. Forty years ago it was an impoverished but isolated working-class neighborhood with model workers' barracks. Similar changes have occurred in the Shubra area, for example, as well as in popular neighborhoods in Alexandria. These conflicts were exacerbated by the decline of oil prices, which limited government income and also ended years of increasing demand for Egyptian labor in the peninsular countries. Some 300,000 Egyptians who returned before the second Gulf War required employment, although Egyptians employed outside the country still send home billions of dollars a year in remittances that provide private and public demand for hard currency.

Problems of Social History

We still know more about politics and workers in Egypt than about workers and the society as a whole. Unni Wikan's work on the relations of poor neighborhoods in Cairo broke ground as a study of urban women, although her work has been criticized as a relentlessly negative image of life among the poor. Evelyn Early has more recently focused on the women of a Cairene neighborhood, and her account is broader than Wikan's.[58] Mona Hammam's accounts of women factory workers has provided some brief illumination of what life is like for the small segment of the industrial workforce that is female, a segment that may well grow dramatically in years to come.[59] Nadia Hijab has written broadly of the problems of working women and women of the working class in the Arab world.[60] According to official statistics, only 8.1 percent of the Egyptian female population was economically active in 1983 (as against roughly 30 percent of the population as a whole), but it is widely understood that figures such as these critically misstate Egyptian reality.[61] As Hijab points out, "the small number of women in the labor force in official statistics does not mean that few Arab women work or even that few earn money."[62] In both urban and rural society, women make substantial contributions to family income from work that is not paid for by wages, and there also appears to be significant underreporting of women's work. Women do participate in factory work at quite low levels. Their participation in labor union protest including strikes and factory occupations is weak because of larger cultural constraints against, for example, women spending unsupervised time with men to whom they are not married.[63]

The best urban ethnography of the contemporary Egyptian working class is *Avenues of Participation* by Diane Singerman, which covers life in the Cairene lower-class neighborhood of Gamaliyyah.[64] In Singerman's account of urban life, class disappears as a useful conceptual tool. Singerman's urban poor do not think of themselves as proletarians, and in the classical sense, they are not. Much of their time is consumed in strategies for gaining privileged access to the government and in the kind of dense interaction that characterized urban life a century ago.

There is room for considerably more study on the truly social aspects of working-class life in Egypt (and elsewhere one might add—including nineteenth-century Europe) as opposed to either the institutional or discursive approaches that have dominated labor studies in recent years. Not much familiarity with the demographic literature on Egypt is required to grasp that truly profound changes are under way that affect working-class social life as well as that of the middle class. We are almost wholly ignorant of how these transformations are occurring in individual lives. Family sizes across Egypt have been dropping steadily since the 1950s, and in Cairo and Alexandria the decline has been almost 50 percent.[65]

The left was especially prominent in the labor movement in the 1940s and it has had some limited periods of influence since. For generations born since 1952, the left has "apparently been unable to articulate an alternative vision of society that workers find realistic and worthy of struggle."[66] Students of Egyptian communism have suggested that Marxists have been incapable of providing such a vision for Egyptian workers because Marxism is an alien language created primarily in Europe to address European problems. With the collapse of Marxist parties in most of the world as well as of states premised on Marxism, it might be more apt to say that this failure has less to do with Egypt than with Marxism as either a utopian vision or a political analysis. Islamic movements are likely to step into the breach left by the decline of Marxism.

It is impossible to know whether the Islamist movements will capture leadership roles in the urban working class as important as the ones they have managed to obtain among students and the professional associations. Historically the political elites in the Islamist movements (such as the Muslim Brothers in the suburban textile-industry neighborhoods of Cairo) have been unwilling to recognize the existence of structural conflicts between employers and owners. However, trade union leaders associated with such groups (such as Anwar Salama) made careers in the 1940s and 1950s within sections of the working class just because they could give practical leadership to struggles to increase workers' share of income. A more likely strategy by Islamic groups to gain a social base in the large working-class suburbs surrounding Cairo and Alexandria today is the direct provision of social services. These movements made a profound impression on local populations after the 1992 earthquake, when they were able to mobilize relief more quickly and effectively than the state. The Muslim Brothers are clearly the majoritarian political force in Egypt today in the mid-1990s. If they were to govern, they would have the power to affect the conditions and levels of employment and thus could gain the acquiescence (if not the allegiance) of significant sections of the organized workforce and of broader groups of the working poor, for whom the state will remain a crucial source of economic benefits for the foreseeable future.

Notes

1. See, for example, P. J. Vatikiotis, *The History of Egypt* (New York: Praeger, 1969) and subsequent editions to the 4th in 1991; Afaf Lutfi al-Sayyid-Marsot, *Egypt and Cromer: A Study in Anglo-Egyptian Relations* (New York: Praeger, 1969); Robert Tignor, *Modernization and British Colonial Rule in Egypt, 1882–1914* (Princeton: Princeton University Press, 1966); or Farhat Ziadeh, *Lawyers, the Rule of Law and Liberalism in Modern Egypt* (Stanford: Stanford University Press, 1968).

2. The literature on communist and socialist parties in Egypt and their relationships to each other and to trade union activities or general politics is quite large. See, for example, Selma Botman, *The Rise of Egyptian Communism* (Syracuse: Syracuse University Press, 1988); and Rifaat Said and Tareq Ismail *The Egyptian Communist Movement* (Syracuse: Syracuse University Press, 1990), as well as the many books in Arabic by Said. A remarkable retrospective vision by a communist labor leader of the period 1935–1950 is Taha Sa'd Uthman, "Thoughts on the Relationship of the Egyptian Working Class to the Second Socialist Movement, 1944–1956," *Qadaya Fikriyya* (July 1992):193–198, and the following piece by Atiyya al-Sayrafi ("Notes on the Role of the Workers in the Egyptian Socialist Movement," 199–205), which express significant discontent with the intellectuals who led the socialist movement for being too concerned with organizational advantage and too loosely related to the problems faced by workers. On capitalists, besides the work of Tignor cited in note 1, are the works of David Landes, *Bankers and Pashas* (Cambridge: Harvard University Press, 1958); Eric Davis, *Challenging*

Colonialism: Bank Misr and Egyptian Industrialization (Princeton: Princeton University Press, 1983); Robert Tignor, *State, Private Enterprise, and Economic Change in Egypt, 1918–1952* (Princeton: Princeton University Press, 1984), *Egyptian Textiles and British Capital* (Cairo: American University in Cairo Press, 1989); and a revisionist account by Robert Vitalis, *When Capitalists Collide* (Berkeley: University of California Press, 1995).

3. André Raymond, *Artisans et commer[alc]ants au Caire au XVIIIe siècle,* 2 vols. (Damascus: Institut Fran[alc]ais du Damas, 1973).

4. Tucker, for example, notes in passing that specialization and enhanced division of labor can help promote monopolies but never develops the idea (*Women in Nineteenth Century Egypt* [Cambridge: Cambridge University Press, 1985], 70).

5. Craig Calhoun argues that the location and density of habitation of urban workers before and during industrialization can play a crucial role in making their collective action easier or more difficult. See Craig Calhoun, *The Question of Class Struggle: Social Foundations of Popular Radicalism During the Industrial Revolution* (Chicago: University of Chicago Press, 1982). For another view of Raymond's work and a brief discussion on the role of urban wage earners and the question of whether they formed a proletariat, see Zachary Lockman, "'Worker' and 'Working Class' in pre-1914 Egypt: A Rereading," in Zachary Lockman (ed.), *Workers and Working Classes in the Middle East: Struggles, Histories, Historiographies* (Albany: State University of New York Press, 1994), 79–80.

6. Gabriel Baer, *Egyptian Guilds in Modern Times* (Jerusalem: Israeli Oriental Society, 1964), 133. Baer's other contributions to the field are *Fellah and Townsman in the Middle East* (London: Frank Cass, 1982), and *Studies in the Social History of Modern Egypt* (Chicago: University of Chicago Press, 1969).

7. Kenneth Cuno has shown that a somewhat parallel argument—that the traditional peasantry was inducted into a monetary economy and private property only after exposure to European ideas and power in the early nineteenth century—is not empirically well founded. See Kenneth M. Cuno, *The Pasha's Peasants* (Cambridge: Cambridge University Press, 1992), 4–5 and 198–199.

8. Ehud R. Toledano, *State and Society in Mid-Nineteenth Century Egypt* (Cambridge: Cambridge University Press, 1990).

9. A finely detailed ethnography of the dilemmas of trust for a merchant are in John Waterbury, *North for the Trade: The Life and Times of a Berber Merchant* (Berkeley: University of California Press, 1972). Mottahedeh's argument that we should examine moral community focuses on the critical realm "between coercion and chance," where social networks beyond family are built. See Roy Mottahedeh, *Loyalty and Leadership in an Early Islamic Society* (Princeton: Princeton University Press, 1980), 5; and Ernest Gellner, "Flux and Reflux in the Faith of Men," in Ernest Gellner, *Muslim Society* (Cambridge: Cambridge University Press, 1985).

10. See Ehud Toledano, "Shemsigul: A Circassian Slave in Mid-Nineteenth Century Cairo," in Edmund Burke III (ed.), *Struggle and Survival in the Modern Middle East* (Berkeley: University of California Press, 1993).

11. Tucker, *Women in Nineteenth Century Egypt,* 201–202.

12. Ibid., 86–89.

13. Ibid., 165–166. Tucker argues that because slaves made up 5 percent of the Cairene population, they were not very important in the Cairene political economy. The point is probably well taken but not necessarily because of the numbers. Beinin and Lockman and I all argue that a much smaller proportion of textile workers in factories were important.

14. Ibid., 150–155. There does not appear to be an Egyptian counterpart to Salah Khalaf, *Prostitution in a Changing Society* (Beirut: Khayats, 1965), or to Alain Corbin, *Le temps, le desir et l'horreur* (Paris: Aubier, 1991).

15. Juan Cole, *Colonialism and Revolution in the Middle East: Social and Cultural Origins of Egypt's Urabi Revolt* (Princeton: Princeton University Press, 1993), 169–170.

16. Ibid., 174.

17. Joel Beinin and Zachary Lockman, *Workers on the Nile* (Princeton: Princeton University Press, 1987), 4.

18. Ibid., 17.

19. Joel Beinin, "Will the Real Working Class Please Stand Up?" in Lockman, *Workers and Working Classes.*

20. Cole, *Colonialism and Revolution.* The underlying reference is to Zayn al-Abdin Shams al-Din Najm, *Port Said: Its History and Development 1859–1882,* in Arabic (Cairo: Egyptian General Book Organization, 1987), 88–90. Using the provincial archival records, Najm was able to trace the growth of the workforce in the 1870s as well as to provide information on conflict within the guild between elected gang leaders and members. Lockman has further comments in "'Worker' and 'Working Class,'" 83–87, in which he discusses identities as "subjectivities constituted by competing (and sometimes contradictory) discourses."

21. If, as O'Brien and Keyder argue, French industrial development in the nineteenth century relative to Great Britain was based on a larger number of small workshops, then Martin might have been far more amenable to looking at variations in efficiency in the bazaar than were English colonial officials. See Patrick O'Brien and Caglar Keyder, *Economic Growth in Britain and France: 1780–1914: Two Paths to the Twentieth Century* (London: G. Allen Unwin, 1978).

22. Reddy's argument parallels Martin's in part by comparing discourses that efficient markets in labor existed with rates that suggest they did not. Reddy's argument is at odds with Timothy Mitchell's claims in *Colonising Egypt* (Cambridge: Cambridge University Press, 1988) that nineteenth-century practices and discourses ran together.

23. Many of these themes are invoked today to explain how misery drives Egyptians into the orbit of Islamist politics. Behind images of miserable Egyptians living "ten to a room" is an image of moral degradation and consequent political extremism. Recognizing that a cliché has been substituted for analysis does not require accepting the anticliché in its place, however.

24. Beinin and Lockman, *Workers on the Nile* 40, 155, 273–274, 449, 450.

25. Ibid., 72, 74, 75, 84, 91, 105, 111, 126, 155, 190, 201, 222, 341, 354, 412.

26. Bent Hansen, *Egypt and Turkey* (New York: Oxford University Press, 1991), 104, acknowledges the problem but tartly suggests that we do not have a very good idea about why the Egyptian economy stagnated.

27. See the assertions in Hisham Sharabi (ed.), *Theory, Politics and the Arab World* (New York: Routledge, 1990), especially by Lisa Anderson ("Policy-Making and Theory Building: American Political Science and the Islamic Middle East," 52), Sarah K. Farsoun and Lisa Hajjar ("The Contemporary Sociology of the Middle East: An Assessment," 160), Judith Tucker ("Taming the West: Trends in the Writing of Modern Arab Social History in Anglophone Academia," 200), and Peter Gran ("Studies of Anglo-American Political Economy: Democracy, Orientalism, and the Left," 228). It would help if someone would define theoretical underdevelopment in explicit terms.

28. Gran, in "Anglo-American Political Economy" (240–241), refers to the authors in this field as political economists working within the East Coast school.

29. See P. J. Vatikiotis, "The New Western Historiography of Modern Egypt," *Middle Eastern Studies* 27, 2 (April 1991):323.

30. See Tucker, "Taming the West," citing Charles Tilly, "Retrieving European Lives," in Oliver Zunz (ed.), *Reliving the Past: The Worlds of Social History* (Chapel Hill: University of North Carolina Press, 1985), 198.

31. Gareth Stedman Jones, *Languages of Class: Studies in English Working Class History 1832–1982* (Cambridge: Cambridge University Press, 1983).

32. Ellis Goldberg, *Tinker, Tailor and Textile Worker: Class and Politics in Egypt 1930–1952* (Berkeley: University of California Press, 1986).

33. Beinin and Lockman note among such lacunae "the role of women . . . the composition and structure of workers' neighborhoods, popular culture and religion." *Workers on the Nile*, 21.

34. See B. L. Carter, *The Copts in Egypt* (London: Croom Helm, 1986), fn. 47 at 82–83.

35. Nadav Safran, *Egypt in Search of Political Community* (Cambridge: Harvard University Press, 1961).

36. Joel Beinin has devoted much of his later work to this topic. See *Was the Red Flag Flying There?* (Berkeley: University of California Press, 1991).

37. For more on coalitions of investors see Vitalis, *When Capitalists Collide*. For a fine-grained picture of one particular coalition see Tignor, *Egyptian Textiles*.

38. Beinin and Lockman, *Workers on the Nile,* Table 8 at 294.

39. An American research team was asked to do a survey of worker attitudes in Mahallah. "The Mahallah Report" was completed just as the old regime was collapsing (William Morris, "The Mahallah Report," Ford Foundation, Badr al-Sheyn, 1953, mimeo). At least one left-wing worker from the period, Fikri al-Khuli, has also published his memoirs on the period, *Al-Rihla* (Cairo: Al-Ghad, 1987).

40. See my "Workers' Voice and Labor Productivity" in Lockman, *Workers and Working Classes.*

41. Selma Botman has suggested that Beinin and Lockman overestimated the role of communist leadership in just such a way. See Botman's review of *Workers on the Nile* in *Social History* 15, 3:405–407.

42. Beginning in 1944 and accelerating after 1952, the state's claims to the workplace increased, and the legal authority of the owner was consequently diminished. Statutes prescribed, for example, what penalties owners could use to discipline workers and restricted owners from verbally abusing workers or denying them promotions. Even if we grant the theoretical nature of this restriction, it is apparent that the legitimacy and texture of workplace discipline was under challenge.

43. Amin Izz al-Din, *Tarikh al-harakah al-'amilah al-misriyyah* (Cairo: Dar al-Ghad al-Arabi, 1987), 896–897.

44. See Marsha Pripstein Posusney, "Workers Against the State: Wage Protest in Egypt 1952–1987," paper presented at the Middle East Studies Association (MESA) meeting in Los Angeles, 1988.

45. See Ellis Goldberg, "The Foundations of State-Labor Relations in Contemporary Egypt," *Comparative Politics* (January 1992):147–161.

46. Robert Bianchi, *Unruly Corporatism* (Oxford: Oxford University Press, 1989).

47. See Soad Kamel Rizk, "The Structure and Operation of the Informal Sector in Egypt," in Heba Handoussa and Gillian Potter (eds.), *Employment and Structural Adjustment: Egypt in the 1990s* (Cairo: American University in Cairo Press), 172.

48. Two hundred public-sector enterprises employed 645,000 workers in manufacturing in 1976, whereas the informal private sector employed 620,000 according to a government survey. Private-sector employment since has grown, and public-sector employment has declined. Compare Tables 33 and 51 in Handoussa and Potter, *Employment and Structural Adjustment.*

49. An account of how the laws work, including the use of the 50 percent rule to limit partisan opposition to the regime, is in Ahmad Rif'at Taha, "The Legal Organization of the 1986 Elections," in Ahmad Abdallah (ed.), *The Parliamentary Elections in Egypt,* in Arabic (Cairo: Arab Studies Center, 1990), 63. The laws governing the representation of women in parliament appear to work in the same fashion (65).

50. Mustafa Kamel al-Sayyid, "Privatization: The Egyptian Debate," *Cairo Papers in Social Science* 13 (Winter 1990).

51. Ibrahim Karawan, "Foreign Policy Restructuring: Egypt's Disengagement from the Arab-Israeli Conflict Reconsidered," unpublished manuscript, University of Utah, 1994.

52. Marsha Pripstein Posusney, "Irrational Workers: The Moral Economy of Labor Protest in Egypt," *World Politics* 46, 1 (October 1993):83–120.

53. In the words of one study, "Egypt's state-owned enterprises play a dominant role in the economy and probably account for the largest share of GDP and employment among all mixed-economy developing countries." See Heba

Handoussa, "Crisis and Challenge: Prospects for the Future," in Handoussa and Potter, *Employment and Structural Adjustment,* 14.

54. Such data do not appear to exist for Egypt. Paul Willman's case studies on British industrial change in the 1970s and 1980s suggest, first, that plant inefficiency may be due to managerial shortcomings and second, that any workers resist innovation when their own wages or employment are directly affected. The latter case is most likely to occur when industries employ spot contracting, which implies that levels of employment are directly related to often-volatile market conditions. See Paul Willman, *Technological Change, Collective Bargaining and Industrial Efficiency* (Oxford: Oxford University Press, 1986), 248.

55. For a review of how the drive for efficiency has had negative effects on employment and wages see Heba Handoussa, "Reform Policies for Egypt's Manufacturing Sector" in Handoussa and Potter, *Employment and Structural Adjustment.*

56. Posusney, "Workers Against the State," 43–44.

57. By receiving fewer than 8 percent of the votes nationally, Tagamu was awarded no seats even in constituencies in which it might have been majoritarian.

58. Unni Wikan, *Life Among the Poor in Cairo,* trans. Ann Henning (London: Tavistock, 1980); and Evelyn Early, *Baladi Women of Cairo: Playing with an Egg and a Stone* (Boulder: Lynn Rienner, 1993).

59. Mona Hammam, "Women and Industrial Work in Egypt: The Chubra el-Kheima Case," *Arab Studies Quarterly* (Winter 1980):50–69; and "Textile Workers of Chubra el-Kheima," *MERIP Reports* 82:3–12.

60. Nadia Hijab, *Womanpower* (Cambridge: Cambridge University Press, 1988).

61. See Guillaume Prache, "La protection sociale en Egypte," *Bulletin du CEDEJ* (January 1984):99–121.

62. Hijab, *Womanpower,* 72.

63. See Hammam, "Textile Workers," for dissatisfaction of women with the union organization and descriptions of the penalties they would face if they stayed overnight in factories under occupation.

64. Diane Singerman, *Avenues of Participation* (Princeton: Princeton University Press, 1995).

65. Philippe Fargues, "Un siècle de transition démographique en afrique méditerranéen 1885–1985," *Population* 2 (1986):205–232, 225. See also Gad Gilbar, "Population Growth and Family Planning in Egypt, 1985–92," in Ami Ayalon (ed.), *Middle East Contemporary Survey XVI 1992* (Boulder: Westview Press, 1994).

66. Posusney, "Irrational Workers," 120.

8

The History of Labor and the Workers' Movement in North Africa

Claude Liauzu

Progress is a truth which imposes itself on our lives; we see it,
we feel it, but our minds remain closed to it, and therefore we,
Africans, live in two contradictory worlds to the benefit of those
who rule us

Tahar al Haddad
Hawatir, 1933 (published 1974)

The history of labor and North African social movements cannot be considered a coherent body of research. Of the 3,000 dissertations concerning North Africa that were defended in French universities between 1973 and 1987, only 17 dealt with trade unions: seven on Algeria, seven on Tunisia, two on Morocco, and one on Libya. Even with the addition of several recent titles to the list, the study of the workers' movement has hardly attained its maturity.[1] Social conflict as linked to work also has no clearly defined place in the development of the social sciences as constituted at present in the newly independent countries.[2]

This situation can be readily explained. First, there is outside censorship of and self-censorship by researchers, especially in Morocco. There is also the weight of the historic Franco-Algerian debate about colonialism, more ideological than scientific, in which nationalism and communism were the poles. This debate is linked to the nature of the war of liberation and the secondary role of the French Communist Party and Algerian Communist

Party in it. Was "the best conflict" that of the National Liberation Front or of the Communist Party? Were "the wretched of the earth" to be understood as historical actors because they were proletarians or because they were peasants and the urban underclass?[3]

Questions posed in so dichotomous a manner and responses phrased in such contradictory language severely constrained how researchers could understand the object of their study. Those who felt the impact of the conflict and participated in the debate over independence, whether they were in agreement with the communists or in opposition to them, can be called the Algerian generation. This same generation, of course, produced and directed academic studies from the 1960s to the 1970s.

The heady days of the "decolonization" of history and of the history of *social movements* (the name of a scholarly journal to study the workers' movements and colonialism) are over. The decline of such studies follows the curve of third worldism and Marxism in academe; these studies have suffered from the effects of the withdrawal of French research interest in the field. The marginality today of studies of work and workers is confirmed when one recalls that only one volume (1982) of the *Annuaire de l'Afrique du Nord* out of thirty dealt with this theme. No additional volumes are in sight.

Contrary to many expectations, studies focused on the premise of an opposition between nationalism and communism did not help labor studies develop. On the contrary, such endeavors steered the study of a rich social history in the direction of theoretical (or perhaps theological) controversies that were wholly scholastic. What Marx, Stalin, or Thorez said about colonialism or about nationalism became the focus rather than what happened. Does the working class exist for itself or in itself?[4]

In North Africa some works of high quality have been produced, but the universities were formed too recently for a critical scientific mass to exist. The universities are also constrained by prior claims on their existence that work from two main directions: developmentalism and the cult of nationalism. Social sciences exist in the shadow of the future. An epistemological gap exists in which sociology is reduced to explaining the political economy of development and developing a nationalist historiography. Its job is primarily pointing out obstacles in the way of following the path of universal progress.[5] The strong nationalist approach is largely responsible as well for the relative absence of comparative studies. They do not occur at the level of North Africa. They also do not occur for the Arab world as a whole or even in the research done by those trained in the French and English university perspectives.

The intellectual landscape of the 1960s and 1970s has recently been convulsed by a complete transformation of interest to the emergence of Islamism. Religious figures who formerly constituted only a background for the social sciences now overshadow the study of the national and labor movements. The cultural expels the social as a field of inquiry. The present overabundance of work concerning Islamism contrasts sharply with the rarity of good work on labor conflicts and urban movements.[6]

The uncertain status of the field of labor movement studies means that we do not have a narrative framework, well-refined methods, research agendas, and arguments between opposing schools. We do not have, in short, what makes up a critical mass for scientific research. I present here, therefore, a provisional balance sheet of what we do know under three chronological and thematic rubrics: first, the origins of the trade union movement in the colonial era; second, relations between trade unions and the national movement; and third, trade union development since independence.

Origins of Wage Labor and the Workers' Movement Under Colonialism

I begin with the idea of the colonial situation as developed by Georges Balandier, which allows us to understand the workers' movement as a part of a set of relationships. These relationships are between the capitalist economy and a colonized society in which social relations are linked to ethnicity.

The relationship between the capitalist economy and the colonized society is basic to understanding the origin of wage labor. The indigenous community of artisans underwent a crisis when it encountered competition from industrial production and the traditional corporate or guildlike structures were destroyed. The years of the Great Depression were decisive here. In Tunisia, for example, the export value of chechias (wool skullcaps)—as well as silk work, rugs, blankets, and cottonstuffs—equaled only 10 percent of the value of imports. In the eighteenth and nineteenth centuries, Tunisian trade in these articles was far more important. By 1935, however, the value of these exports was only 3 percent of the value of cotton imports. The booths in the marketplaces of Algiers and Fez became mills of Maître Cornille, and one report by the International Labor Organization called the situation of the artisan "worse than that of the agricultural laborer."[7]

The collapse of this universe entailed more than economic consequences and affected all aspects of the life of the old city, or medina. These artisans, for example, would play an important role in the trade union and nationalist movements and even more so at the intersection of them. This was possible because they already had an urban outlook and a higher level of schooling than the mass of manual laborers. Their protest movements thus tended to develop less between owners and workers than between medina and colonialism.

It would be wrong, however, to believe that wage labor was created rapidly by the disappearance of the old mode of production. Rural society, in which the vast majority of the population lived, resisted proletarianization for a long time even where it was most profoundly affected by expropriation and the shock of colonialism in Algeria. Temporary emigration was one move in the strategy of survival of the peasantry, as shown in the turnover of the Algerian workforce in France. An observer as attentive as the geographer Augustin Bernard remarked that the *zobrai* returning to the port of Algiers threw their caps into the sea. He was not simply repeating an Orientalist tale. The Moroccan phosphate mines were also the scene of an impressive turnover of laborers until independence.

This instability of the workforce, moving back and forth between the countryside and the capitalist enterprise, was not due only to peasant strategies. The employment strategy of the colonial owners paradoxically coincided with that of the colonized workers. A case in point is the Societé Sfax Gafsa, a financial empire that centered on the port of Sfax, the railroad line, and the mining region that employed 20,000 workers in the 1920s. The Societé maximized its profits by utilizing the rural labor force in a vast "migratory basin" that extended from Tripolitania in Libya to Morocco. In this basin there was a huge and incessant coming and going of exploited rural miners. Low salaries compensated for the absence of a stable and skilled workforce. In 1937 an International Labor Organization inquiry, the first of its kind in North Africa, demonstrated this absence. Because the report showed that the incomes of the miners were insufficient to sustain families, it implied that the countryside was contributing to the maintenance of the wage-labor force. The proletariat that refused to come into being was also a proletariat refused. Conditions such as these determined the constitution of the labor movement.[8]

In a more general way the characteristics of the working class were a function of colonial capitalism. The statistics show masses of workers in the mines, transport, public works projects, and ports. There was also a sprinkling of enterprises in food preparation, mechanical construction, and the building trades. Such a configuration can be explained because the colonial society was a market for produce from the center, a provider of primary materials, and a source of superprofits for capital investment. In such a setting the world of labor was not the site of a working class comparable to those of the industrial societies. Rather, groups of workers came together in a variety of complex intermediary and transitional ways that make it easier to understand the emergence of a complex and contradictory political consciousness.

Such a situation became even more complex because of the way in which the question of class identity intersected that of ethnicity. A million and a half French and other European citizens lived in the North African states before they became independent; a million of these were in Algeria. They composed between 6 and 10 percent of the overall population of the three countries. Locally they could constitute majorities, as in Tunis at the turn of the century or in Oran, Algeria, in the 1950s.

How these colonies came to be rooted in North Africa requires some explanation. Contrary to the nationalist (and colonialist) discourse, there was no systematic French policy of populating these lands in order to rule them. Even in Algeria the myth that a "new French race" had taken root and that a new peasantry had been set in place was far more important in imagination than in reality. Farmers who obtained land for colonization barely made a go of it. Napoléon III, Jules Ferry, Marshal Lyautey, and other French officials were often hostile to the creation of a population of poor whites who were likely to become privileged, demanding, and spiteful tyrants.

After all, France, which was a country of immigration as early as the middle of the nineteenth century, hardly possessed the demographic capacity to undertake a project of large-scale colonial population. The French were a majority of the labor force only among government officials and in certain sectors that constituted a security concern for the state. The bulk of the Algerian French population resulted from the naturalization of the Jews (by the Crémieux decree of 1870) and the application of French nationality law to other Europeans. The so-called jus soli applied to "foreigners" after the second generation.

These foreigners were primarily from the Italian Mezzogiorno (south) and Spain. Two reasons account for the flow of these workers. First, Mediterranean Europe was experiencing a more general period of emigration after the 1870s. Second was the rather strict limits within which the colonized population entered economic activity. Few women entered the workforce (still the case), demographic expansion was low, and overall mobility was low. The local workforce could not respond easily to the needs of early capital investment in infrastructure. Not until the great crisis of 1929 would the first signs of "demographic explosion" be perceived. Then the word "bidonville" was invented to portray the unsettling of the rural society and its consequent exodus to the urban slums. By then the first phase of the creation of the working class was already complete.

In Tunisia it was Italy that provided numerous skilled workers in food production, Piedmontese masons, Sicilian and Sardinian miners. They also made up a large portion of the unskilled labor force, the *braccianti*, who provided the hands to build large public works projects—roads, ports, and rail networks. In Morocco and the Algerian West, such projects were carried out by Spanish workers.

In such a social structure, class was linked to ethnic membership throughout the colonial period. In 1962 Pierre Bourdieu underlined the degree to which, in colonial Algeria, the poor white was at once the rival of and the model for the poor Arab. Findings such as these retained their validity as long as economic organization contained a double logic, that of class and caste and that of interest and community, to use some approximate formulas. Communal identity won out over common economic interests.

In colonial North Africa there was no legal framework regulating society and labor on the basis of an explicitly racist doctrine, as was the case with the South African color bar. Ethnic privilege was fully present in the setting of wages, however. In the government, the famous "colonial third"—the expatriate bonus—was reserved for the French even if they were born in North Africa. Tunisian functionaries in the 1950s demanded and obtained this bonus, although it was later abolished by the independent state as a costly anomaly. In the rest of the economy, including the private sector, unequal wages were paid in accord with a strict hierarchy distinguishing French, Europeans, and Arabic-speaking inhabitants. It was so in the Tunis Tramway Company and in the mines, with justifications based on the inequality of skills or needs of the various populations or on political necessities linked to the colonial order.

The colonial situation especially allowed the owners to avoid the costs of the social insurance legislation in place in the metropolitan country. Accident insurance was not in place in Tunisia until 1924. Formerly the victim had to prove employer negligence to collect an indemnity. In Algeria only the French gained the benefits of the welfare state.

It is therefore easy to understand why economic interests doggedly resisted the extension of social benefits under the Popular Front government. The exercise of trade union rights provoked even more social conflict than the provision of social benefits. In principle, Algeria enjoyed the

French laws of 1864 (the right to strike) and of 1884 (trade union free-dom), but Muslims were subjects rather than citizens. They were therefore subject to a series of legal measures called, in the manner of the time, the native law, which prevented the free enjoyment of these as well as political rights. Despite the formal integration of Algeria into France, the right to travel between the two required government authorization until 1947. Not until 1955, after the failure of an attempt to create working-class associa-tions, or *jamaat,* was freedom of association recognized in Morocco. Under the supervision of colonial officials, these councils, borrowed from a model in rural society, became very limited institutions for arbitration that was controlled by company administrators. In Tunis, where the trade union movement developed early, the French law of 1884 was in force in 1932. In an ironic twist, however, it excluded foreigners from the leader-ship of unions—in accord with the letter of the law—and thus excluded Tunisians.

There is not much point in focusing on labor legislation because labor relations followed the larger relations of power, which in turn largely fa-vored the owners. The few exceptions were the fortuitous periods in which politics favored mass protests: in 1904, 1920–1924, 1936–1938, 1945–1947, and during the period of decolonization. Trade unionism made progress by steps that were usually linked to waves of strikes.

An immigrant labor aristocracy—masons, cabinetmakers, printers—brought with them their own traditions of association such as friendly so-cieties, insurance cooperatives, and craft unions. These were of little quan-titative importance and drew into their orbit few of the colonized subjects, the more so as the "poor white phenomenon" gave birth to racist attitudes.

The Algiers Commune of 1871, for example, had very little in common with the Paris Commune of the same year. The civilian antimilitarist ide-ology at home arose in the context of the Arab policy of Napoléon III and was perceived as a brake on the desires of the *colons.* Shortly thereafter the Dreyfus affair instigated an anti-Jewish impulse in which the French of Al-geria saw themselves well represented. Even someone such as Jean Jaurès, the leader of the Socialist Party, claimed to be able to see in the anti-Dreyfus movement the elements of social protest, distorted but clearly there.[9] The confusion between populism and socialism would not last long. On May 8, 1898, the election of Édouard-Adolphe Drumont, an anti-Semitic leader, to the Chamber of Deputies from Algiers and the pop-ular acclaim he received (in which the crowd unharnessed his horses so as to pull his carriage themselves) proclaimed the fascist-leaning attitudes in the *pied noir* population. These attitudes were to remain in the majority from 1930 to independence. *The Blood of Races,* a novel set in Algeria by Louis Bertrand, and the folklore of *Cagayous* express this mentality in which clientelism wins out over class consciousness and ethnic solidarity over that of class.

The first great strike in Tunis, in 1904, was in the line of ethnic rather than class conflict, for it was primarily the work of the *muratori,* Italian masons who marched behind their national flag. Nevertheless, by the breadth of the protest and its date, May 1, it overcame its original limits and drew along the native laborers, at least at the rear of the procession. It is among the Italians as well that we find in Tunisia the first socialist and, especially, anarchist currents. Tunisia had been a refuge for the Italian opposition beginning with Garibaldi, who found asylum there in the mid-nineteenth century. He was followed by liberals as well as by Mezzogiorno peasant militants threatened by the Mafia. Socialists did not organize in the French colony until the beginning of the new century. The media that expressed what we now call public opinion also came into existence, but their audience was limited and they were banned whenever they passed beyond the strict limits fixed by the colonial authorities.

The institutions of political life also contributed to the partitioning of communities. The Consultative Conference and the Grand Council in Tunis, the General Delegations in Algeria and their equivalents in Morocco, were all sites at which the French and colonized communities were unequally represented. In them, as in the Algerian city councils, the major concerns were fiscal and budgetary problems. Agrarian and entrepreneurial interests dominated these councils. Until World War I, one could hardly talk of a prehistory of the workers' movement.

We can see all of these elements more clearly during the first great protest movement in Tunisia, which occurred in the 1910s. This impulse was brutally repressed, but it is important because it so clearly shows the contradictions that the left had to face in the colonial situation, especially that between internationalism and class solidarity. The conflict began with an attempt by the Tunis municipal authorities to condemn for speculative purposes a portion of the land belonging to the Muslim cemetery in Djellaz. Inhabitants of the older, poorer areas of the city opposed this proposal and confronted the army in the course of violent protests aimed at the European part of the city.

The emotions evoked by the Italian entry into Libya and the French takeover of Morocco contributed to a mobilization without precedent in the history of the regency after 1881. In this situation we can even see the emergence of the *qabada,* a local gang leader and ambiguous hero of the urban lower classes who protected them and maintained their honor. The thin ranks of French democrats interpreted the anti-Italian protest movement as an outbreak of plain fanaticism and barbarity. Islam, which assumed the role of mobilizing myth of the colonized people, was thus perceived as an obstacle to progress.

During this period the Second International enunciated the doctrine of colonial socialism. While criticizing the abuses of colonial capitalism, socialists saw colonialism as a necessary path to civilization. The issue was perceived as the social emancipation of individuals (not nations) and their liberation from the prisons of tradition and religion.[10] This doctrine, which hardly changed over the years, did not, of course, address the concerns of the colonized.

The riots of Djellaz were the same type of confrontation between communities that became more common during the 1930s and 1950s (Constantine 1934, Sétif 1944) in which poor whites and Algerians were on opposite sides. These characteristics were also found in another movement, the 1912 boycott of the Tunis tramways by the Muslim population. The pretext for the boycott was a traffic accident. A deeper reason was the profound unhappiness with the racial hierarchy instituted by the Tramway Company and an attempt by the medina to outface the power and symbolism of the new colonial city. The Tunisian example, coming as early as it did, shows with special clarity the elements of the workers' movement in the colonial setting.

Nationalism and the Workers' Movement: From the 1920s to Decolonization

A third of a century separates the end of World War I from the period in which the North African states became independent. During these years the trade union movement developed by stages occurring roughly between 1920 and 1925, 1936 and 1938, and 1945 and independence. This chronology corresponds to that of the development of popular and anticolonialist movements, which continued to ripen in the colonized society. At the same time, the progressive nationalization of the trade union movements occurred, first as the colonized joined unions and then as the nationalists took control of them.

In this process communists took a hand much earlier than the nationalist parties. The French Communist Party (PCF) was the first French political force to engage in anticolonial activities, albeit episodically. It did so under pressure from the Third International rather than on its own behalf and in accord with strategic decisions made in Moscow. The PCF was most strongly rooted among some groups of French workers, especially those in the railways, naval shipyards, and a few crafts. It also gained a foothold among the indigenous workers in these same fields as well as sectors such as the docks, the mines, and the emigrant community.

The PCF and its branches in Algeria and Tunisia were effective social actors until the period of decolonization; at that time they were ousted by the nationalist parties, which were hegemonic in the popular movements. The problem of the relationship between social and national conflicts and between Marxism and ideologies of identity have been posed most frequently in terms of a confrontation between communism and nationalism. If, however, as Jacques Berque has suggested, the task of the historian is not so much to "predict the past" as to search for multiple possibilities concealed in historical situations, this problem merits reexamination.

For the communist organizations of North Africa, the PCF was initially the organization center. It later became a fraternal party but remained the older brother. Their development was almost wholly dependent on political decisions made in Paris except when the Comintern provided a court of appeal. The issue of colonialism remained secondary in the PCF despite the eighth condition required for the adherence of socialist parties to the Third International. This condition imposed the burden of support for national liberation movements and the creation of a second anti-imperialist front on the communists. It was explicitly rejected from the very beginning by French militants in Sidi Bel Abbes, a small "red" colonial city in Algeria. It was only on the intervention of the Fourth Comintern Congress that this "deviation" was condemned. Stung, the PCF created a colonial commission to determine its next course of action.

The Rif War, in which the Berber population of northern Morocco opposed the French and Spanish armies from 1921 until 1926, provided the occasion for an attempt to mobilize the French working class. The Confédération Générale du Travail Unitaire (CGTU) called a general strike, and the Communist Youth undertook antimilitarist agitation among the troops sent to Morocco. It also agitated against the colonial troops sent to occupy the Ruhr Valley in Germany at the same time. Hoping to heighten the insurrectional waves that then reverberated in the Near East and Egypt, communist parliamentary deputy Jacques Doriot sent a congratulatory telegram to Abd al-Karim and expressed the hopes that the two could find a way to link the struggles of the European left and the anti-imperialist guerrillas of Morocco. (Doriot was expelled from the French

, Communist Party in 1934. During World War II Doriot was associated with the French government based in Vichy that collaborated with the Nazis in World War II.) This effort proved abortive, as did the campaign against the Rif War. The anticolonial struggle in France never touched more than a militant minority of either intellectuals or workers. The only exceptions were France's military involvement in Vietnam (due to the importance of the Vietnamese Communist Party) and the end of the Algerian War of Independence.

Only with difficulty was the CGTU able to attempt to organize North African workers in France, partly because of their high turnover and partly because of the prejudices of the French members. In 1924, for the first (and last) time in its history the PCF nominated colonial subjects in legislative elections, and they won nearly as many votes as French candidates. They were ineligible to serve, of course, because of their colonial status.

In the final analysis, communism was more effective among political activists. The colonial commission of the PCF played an important role in organizing colonial residents in France. It supported a pioneer organization, the Union Intercoloniale, whose members included militants from Senegal and the Antilles, Algerians such as Messali Hadj and the young Vietnamese Nguyen Ai Quoc (later known as Ho Chi Minh). Besides students and workers, individuals such as Messali who had made a break with the colonial world emigrated to France.

Members of the Union Intercoloniale undertook initiatives of great import. Its magazine, Le Paria (1924–1927), undertook a debate about colonialism and the relationship between communism and nationalism. The Union Intercoloniale had a brief life, but it was the origin of the communist and nationalist organizations of Vietnamese in France and influenced the négritude movement and the North African Star.[11] Among Asian immigrants in France, communism tended to replace nationalism. However, relations between the PCF and the North African Star rapidly deteriorated during the 1930s.[12] After a brief period in which the colonial order appeared to stabilize and the national movements to decline, the 1930s were years of decisive progress for the nationalist movements in North Africa. The colonized society began to break up during the depression, and the colonial governments were unable to develop a strategy to neutralize the resulting tensions.

The very extent of the economic crisis of the 1930s transformed the mass of subproletarians into a reserve army of radical movements. It also made violence, uprisings, and communal confrontations part of the new political landscape. The PCF was no longer in a position to provide leadership for such a mobilization. After 1934 the French communists were involved in an antifascist strategy that gave priority to European problems, and the PCF reentered the French political system. During the long period surrounding World War II, the PCF distanced itself from its initial revolutionary enthusiasm and its role as a popular tribune. It entered an alliance with the socialists (the Popular Front period of 1936–1938), engaged in trade union unification, and played the parliamentary game. It then helped animate the resistance to the German occupation of France and again briefly entered the government after the war. Communist political strategies during the Popular Front period and after the liberation of France made the issue of colonialism of marginal importance. In 1936 the PCF condemned nationalism as an ally of fascism (an argument that in certain cases is not without foundation). In 1944, priority went to national reconstruction, a task also incumbent on the colonies. After 1947 the Cold War and support for the Soviet Union structured the relationship between the PCF and the North African nationalists. Slowly, then, the PCF allowed the Neo-Destour Party (in Tunisia after 1934) and the Algerian People's Party (after 1937) to monopolize the demand for independence and thus popular legitimacy. In 1939, Maurice Thorez asserted that an Algerian nation did not yet exist: It was only coming to be based on the fusion of multiple peoples present in Algeria—Berbers, Arabs, Jews, and Europeans. He was not saying anything either new or provocative in regard to the canons of the French left, which had always refused to recognize an identity based on Islam and Arabism. Whether such a vision of nationality arising out of multiple ethnicities had ever been plausible, I do not know. Any possibility of realizing it vanished even as the communists made it their "line."

The nationalists at that time were a handful of leaders such as Habib Bourguiba, Messali Hadj, the "historic leaders" of the Algerian uprising in 1954, and an activist core that surrounded them. They utilized the only resources they had: the mass movements. They employed the mobilizational authority of Islam, which included the conservative and irrational elements of the popular "culture of poverty." Communism and nationalism, as Maxime Rodinson has argued, provided powerful conceptual tools. Nationalism had the added advantage of reanimating the deepest myths inscribed in the Arab-Islamic collective imagination. In 1924, Muhammad Ali (one of the founders of Tunisian trade unions) spoke to miners in the south. Their ranks had been formed out of a diverse population at once tied to and sundered by the ties of communities from which they had come. He was best understood by his listeners when he began with a verse from the Qur'an: "You are the best community that the earth has ever known . . . "

Amar Ouzegane, who left the Algerian Communist Party to join the Algerian national movement, never let an opportunity pass to underline the "crass ignorance" of atheist communism in regard to popular religion. Convincing as Ouzegane's critique may be, it nevertheless leaves a question posed by Rodinson unanswered: Islam may well serve to create an identity of resistance, but can it serve all purposes? Can we, for example, ask within its confines a question such as Did the Prophet's horse Buraq really exist (and did he ascend to the heavens on her)? By extension, when "atheist Muslims" employ Islam in a wholly instrumental fashion, do they not reinforce the antidemocratic elements in the popular consciousness?

This is a debate that retains its relevance. Those elements of working-class culture that entered North African life through the trade union movement and the social reforms of 1936 and 1945 could develop further among the colonized masses only by being made to conform to nationalist sentiments. The content of these elements of working-class culture were submerged by formally similar features in the communal culture. For a sharper look at this phenomenon, I turn my attention to the Tunisian trade union movement.

The character of Tunisian trade unionism owes much to its early appearance. It was formed apart from (and indeed before) the Destour Party, and its leaders, especially Ferhat Abbas, played independent local and international roles. As a consequence, the Neo-Destour Party was able to control the Tunisian trade unions only in a limited way and late in its development.

The Confédération Générale des Travailleurs Tunisiens (CGTT) was founded in 1924. There was nothing like it in the French colonial empire or in the Arab world, with the possible exception of the Wafd-dominated federation that existed briefly in Egypt at the same time. The fact that a truly Tunisian trade union organization was formed even though a branch of the French trade union organization (Confédération Générale du Travail, or CGT), which was primarily European, already existed in Tunisia is due to several factors. First was the existence of a small group of Tunisian and French militants. Although nationalist historiography has long ignored or belittled the contribution of the latter, their influemce was considerable and began in the 1920s, when Tunisia was the home of one of these militants, Robert Louzon; he is also one of the great figures of revolutionary syndicalism. Louzon had, along the lines of the prewar politics of the CGT, opposed the Union Sacrée of World War I.[13] For a while

Louzon was able to win the Section Française de l'Internationale Communiste (SFIC) to this position. He then moved toward Trotskyism and later founded Proletarian Revolution. Between 1920 and 1925, when he was expelled from Tunisia, he was the organizer of a communist group to which trade unionists gravitated.

The role of these activists recalls that of ethnic minorities—Egyptian Jewish militants and North Africans—in the mingled histories of the working-class movement, socialism, and communism in Africa. As working-class members of the communist movements, they were social half-castes analogous to the half-caste ethnicity that characterized similar activists in Egypt and elsewhere. As early as 1921, in an atempt to attract North African Arab readers, the French *L'Avenir Social* had headlines in Arabic. It was proscribed, then reappeared under a different name and was finally suppressed when the law caught up with this subterfuge.

This small group also created a program that attempted to link internationalism, the workers' movement, and the specifics of Tunisian life around the demand for independence. All of this has been rapidly forgotten, even erased, from the memory of succeeding generations of communists and Tunisian union militants. Certainly we have here one of those silences through which history often speaks eloquently. This small group attracted attentive young nationalists who already followed the self-proclaimed innovations of Soviet Central Asia, Iran, and Turkey. Tawfiq al-Madani, future leader of the Algerian ulama, was a participant for a while. In the light of the radicalization prompted by this group, the Destour Party, which was led by notables of local families and did not have much popular support, appears as a rather anemic organization.

The significance of this small group—at most 200 members—lay primarily in its having seized the opportunity of an important popular mobilization in connection both with the Rif War and with a general movement for social demands. The Destour leaders were hesitant in regard to this rural war and eager to avoid a direct confrontation with the colonial authorities. By contrast, Tunisian townsmen made Abd al-Karim their champion and a truly epic character.

The second factor leading to the formation of a Tunisian trade union was a strike by stevedores in 1924. This event provided the founding moment for Tunisian trade unionism. The docks of Tunis, like all the colonial docks and indeed those of all the great ports of the day, were the site of unbridled conflict among those seeking jobs. A succession of poor harvests had added a new group of laborers to compete with the already too numerous workers and had also increased the cost of living. This occurrence betrays the influence of agricultural life on the urban world of work. The precarious balance was broken and could be reestablished only by imposing working-class solidarity—through violence if necessary—over the competition for employment. The 1924 docker strike, like the miners' strike of 1936 and the strikes of agricultural labor, took on the character of collective bargaining by riot. It was this struggle that established a balance of power that forced the owners to recognize the workers as a collective agent and to accept some regulation of labor relations. During the strike the *bouchkara* ("the man with the sack," derived from the jute fragment with which dockers covered their heads) came to be seen as a positive figure whose importance went far beyond the port. As it turned out, the stoppage of the export of grain caused the price to decline, which made the strike quite popular. There was an additional impact of the strike in the suburbs. There the stevedores, dock workers, drivers, and clerks of southern extraction (mostly Gabès) lived with neighbors from the same original communities that were drawn into the conflict. Professional and communal memberships converged in this instance.

This southern milieu has provided quite a few trade union, communist (Ali Djrad), and nationalist militants and intellectuals. Two individuals from this background are of particular interest. As a child, Muhammad Ali, leader of the CGTT, had carried the baskets of colonial ladies in the Tunis marketplace. A voluntary exile in Germany and Turkey and perhaps Soviet Central Asia as well, Ali made his living as a driver. Self-educated, he was truly a graduate of the school of hard knocks. In this regard he is similar to the Algerian militant Messali Hadj, who fled the repression of the colony for France. There he discovered the red flag and mass struggle in his contact with the French labor movement. Muhammad Ali himself had only a brief moment in Tunisian history. In 1925 he was exiled from Tunisia thanks to an edict of the precolonial Muslim crown that allowed the French consul to expel its subjects—an example of how the colonial government used arcane laws to control its subjects. He died several years later in a highway accident, but popular memory made him a more potent symbol by retaining the notion that he had tried to join Abd al-Karim and the Rif warriors. True or not, this story illustrates very well the symbiotic nature of trade unionism and popular nationalism.

Muhammad Ali may have been the soul of the CGTT, but its intellectual leader was Tahar al-Haddad, also born in Gabès. Al-Haddad was a remarkable figure in many ways, not least because he was a student at the Grand Mosque (Zaytuna in Tunis) and thus had a thoroughly legal, theological, and Arabic education. He is an example of what might be called a

proletaroid intelligentsia, excluded both from a career in colonial government or enterprise and from status in the traditional city of Tunis because
of his family's poverty. A minority of the students at the mosque contested
the Zaytunian order as that of the notables, demanded modernization of
the education, and became increasingly radical due to their participation
in popular movements. The Zaytunian majority, however, locked itself
into a dispirited traditionalism and a suicidal rivalry with the new intellectual class, graduates of the Sadiki College who had both an Arabic and a
French education. It was from this group that Bourguiba and the leaders
of the rising Neo-Destour Party came.

Tahar al-Haddad remains relevant for the effort that he undertook to
develop a reform program for his society. He wrote a history of the CGTT
that at the time was still a unique example of the labor-studies genre. In a
second work, *Imra'tuna* (Our Woman, 1932), he argued for the liberation
of women through education and entry into the labor force. The innovative character of this work is all the greater when it is recalled that only
4 percent of Algerian women were in salaried employment in the mid-
1990s.[14] This work criticizing the temptation in Muslim society to exclude
women from public life created a scandal. The ulama condemned the
book and demanded that Haddad's diplomas be annulled. He found no
support even among the secular leaders of the Neo-Destour, who were
more concerned to attract mass support. Tahar al-Haddad was, in effect,
placed on the index by his own society.

Whence came these reformist ideas and whence also his knowledge, surprisingly great for a student whose education was exclusively in Arabic, of
the history of the European labor movement and the Russian Revolution?
Part must have been from the Egyptian press, but no doubt much came
from the militant culture developing among trade unionists and communists in the souks. The premature disappearance of Tahar al-Haddad, who
died of tuberculosis in his thirties, was not only a personal disaster. Along
with him went a generation of angry intellectuals, the "bare heads," which
included also the poet Shabbi. This was a doubly radical generation. Its
roots went far more deeply into its own society than did those of the new
elites, and its break with the archaisms of Arab-Islamic society was so
thorough that it left almost no historical trace. The Neo-Destour Party
took the reins. With it a completely different group of intellectuals came to
the fore who were almost exclusively graduates of the French university
system and who arose from the northern coastal middle classes. The still-
born project of Tahar al-Haddad is worth reconsidering today in the light
of the blind alleys into which Tunisian modernity has led and the emergence of contemporary popular but fundamentalist Islamist currents.

Thoughts (*Hawatir*), which Tahar al-Haddad wrote at the end of his life, was an uncompromising reflection on the double vice that grips North African society: dependency on Europe and Islamic archaism. It was not published until half a century after his death.

When we look at the formative period of 1920–1924, it is also imperative to recall the extraordinary speed with which groups of militants were worn out and cast away. This may have been due to colonial repression or exclusions within the communist and nationalist movements themselves.

The situation and men of the mobilization of the years 1936–1938 are quite different from the earlier period. This period saw a struggle in which two sides, the French and the nationalists, struggled to assume control of the labor movement. The development and avatars of the dockworkers' unions provide an exemplary case. This group, in order be a professional union, closed entry to competitors whose members were the unemployed. Alongside the characteristic of corporate closure we can also see the role of primary solidarities of birth and the importance of the port for political parties. Partisan support ensured that the dockers received the needed external aid, but it also caught them up in the toils of clientelism.

In a more general way, the Popular Front period allowed North African trade unions to benefit in a partial way from the advances obtained by workers in the metropolis. By that very fact it tended to dissociate them from other popular movements. The reunification of the communist and socialist trade unions allowed a rearrangement of forces in the movement itself. Communists maintained control of the organizations representing manual laborers—miners' and public works unions and even a newly created agricultural trade union movement—whereas the socialists were more influential among the white-collar workers and the labor aristocracy. Ferhat Hached himself became more prominent in this period in the Tunisian branch of the CGT.

Borne along by the legislative program of the Blum government, which sought to codify labor relations, the trade union movement was in ever greater need of cadres who could master judicial problems and undertake organizational functions. The entry of this staff was at the expense of the old agitators and strike leaders. One important result was that for the first time the trade union movement itself was more fully staffed by North African than by French unionists, at least in Algeria and Tunisia.

Aware of the growing importance of trade union power, the Neo-Destour turned its attention toward countering the influence of the CGT. This attempt, which neither Moroccan nationalists nor the Algerian People's Party (APP) was able to imitate, failed except in certain limited sectors. The structures of labor relations were still largely the province of the CGT and the Popular Front reforms rather than the nationalist project of the Neo-Destour, which had no specific social content. Limitation of the workweek, minimum pay scales, institution of fiscal councils (les Prud'hommes) were all the work of the French left and the socialist government. These reforms were the consequence of a socialist dream of neo-colonialism in which local elites, including wage earners, would remain associated with France. The reforms reached their highest expression when the Blum-Violette Bill was presented to the Chamber of Deputies in 1936 to give full French citizenship to about 20,000 Muslims. This bill foundered on the opposition of the French population in North Africa, and with its defeat, the politics of assimilation was no longer viable in Algeria. The death of the hopes of the Popular Front brought the structural reality back to that of communal conflict. It was henceforth the left that had to assume responsibility for the antinationalist repression of 1938 and of the state of siege utilized to end the violence and opposition of the Neo-Destour and the APP.

It was in this period that the trade union model clearly took hold in a portion of the North African proletariat. It found its own cadres in certain categories of wage labor, the labor aristocracy, and state employees; all of these were French at first but with time, more and more of them were North African. The trade union leadership was already quite distinct in its origins from the bulk of the membership. Most members came from the service sector and the ranks of officials. These officials—teachers, above all—were less members of the working class than of the middle class. Their future was blocked by the colonial reality, and they helped to organize the legions of labor and formed the natural bridge to the nationalist movement.

In the period after 1945 the most important problem was that of decolonization and the politicization of the masses. This led to a new inflow of North African members of the unions even as the European membership dropped. Although there was real economic growth in the postwar period, the colonial majority experienced primarily impoverishment and descent into the underclass. It was among these workers rather than among the already organized section of the working class that the nationalist movement found its mass appeal. The only political force that might have emerged as a rival to the nationalists was the communists. The communists, however, were torn apart by the contradictions between national realities and international (or even Soviet) strategies as well as between the European and Muslim communities. The tragedy of Sétif, whose population fell victim to repression that turned into a massacre by the colonial militia, created a break that could not be healed.

It is plain that during the period of decolonization, legitimacy rested with the nationalists. This was the underlying factor in the nationalization of the trade union movement. This occurred in Tunisia in 1946 when the General Union of Tunisian Workers (UGTT; it replaced the French-linked CGTT) was created under the pressure of Ferhat Hached. Yet if he was able to supplant the CGT, it was thanks also to the support of Force Ouvrière and of the International Confederation of Free Trade Unions. They were engaged in a Cold War conflict with communist-led unions and seeking to find allies in the Third World. It is not irrelevant that Tunisian trade union leader Ferhat Hached himself was quite able to maneuver between submission to the colonial order and the dangers of direct confrontation while finding support in the international arena. The UGTT rapidly became a queen on the chessboard of Tunisian politics, itself able, even more than the Neo-Destour Party, to direct popular movements and to orient the nationalist project toward more socioeconomic concerns. The assassination of Ferhat Hached by the Red Hand, a terrorist group that prefigured the Secret Army Organization of Algeria, deprived the North African trade union movement of its dominant leader. His death provoked demonstrations in Morocco, a testimony to the progress of the idea of North African working-class solidarity.

There was, however, no equivalent to Tunisian trade unionism in Algeria, where the General Union of Algerian Workers (UGTA) was only created in 1956, or Morocco, where the Moroccan Labor Union (UMT) was formed in 1955. In these cases the union movement appears more as a creation from above than from below. It served far more to orchestrate the bureaucratic control of labor than as the dynamic expression of its own interests. Here we enter into the postcolonial period, when trade union organizations took part in the rivalry for power and were rapidly subordinated to the nationalist bureaucratic order.

Trade Unionism and the Nation-State

The process of decolonization differed significantly from place to place across North Africa. It was relatively peaceful in Tunisia and Morocco, where the Neo-Destour and the sultan, respectively, were negotiators recognized by France. It was especially violent in Algeria, where a seven-year war preceded independence. Nevertheless, the trade union situation in each of the three countries had some common characteristics.

The UGTT played a decisive role in the confrontations between the two wings of the Neo-Destour Party by supporting Habib Bourguiba against Salah Ben Youssef. Ben Youssef adopted a maximalist position by opposing any compromise with France and by refusing a staged transition offered by the Mendès-France government from internal autonomy to independence. In so doing he played the card of Arab nationalism and solidarity with Gamal Abdel Nasser and the National Liberation Front (FLN) of Algeria. The content of the "Youssefist" program had little more substance than this. The coalition behind him was made up of disparate elements. It comprised Zaytunians (from the ordinary student to the aristocracy of the ulama) united primarily against the Sadikis, the palace entourage, and the notables and old landed gentry. It also included regional interests centered in Sfax and the south concerned with the predominance of Bourguiba's northern coastal supporters. Bourguiba himself was able to constitute what Antonio Gramsci called a "historic bloc" around a modernization program in the orbit of the West. He accomplished this by assembling the middle classes who had been touched by French culture together with the organized working class and was actively supported by the French government.

It was, then, the leaders of the UGTT who neutralized the *fellagha* (guerrillas) in the central part of the country as well as the miners in the south. These latter had launched what amounted to an insurrectionary strike movement in sympathy with neighboring Algeria. It was these same leaders who were able to limit the breadth of a gigantic wave of protest that had a special claim on the rural world. The protestors sought redress from the large Tunisian landowners as well as the Europeans by raising the issue of agrarian relations. That they did so in a confused way did not detract from the breadth of their movement. This gamble on moderation paid off despite the risks it ran in regard to pan-Arab sentiment and Nasser's prestige among popular circles. It was not only an instrumental choice. It corresponded to a modernizing project, a sort of enlightened despotism. It employed the structures of the state, the party, the unions, and the schools to gain the consent of the nation to transform the consciousness of the society. In so doing, Bourguiba created a myth of the tutelary state analogous to that of the French Third Republic. Agreement with the project was facilitated by the great social mobility that resulted from the exodus of the European *colons* and the extension of the state bureaucracies. Trade unions, engaged in furthering independence, were willing to carry out anything in order to have something to show for it. This was also the case for Ahmad Ben Salah, who became prime minister, and for other leaders as well.

In Algeria the military balance of forces was the principal factor deciding who came to power. The National Liberation Army under the command of Colonel Houari Boumedienne arrived to install Ben Bella in power shortly after July 1, 1962, when the referendum on independence gained 97 percent of the vote.[15] The erratic attempts of the UGTA to play on divisions within the FLN were rapidly broken. In the name of the Algerian people, Ben Bella was able to toss out the leadership with his goons. The first congress was to a largely empty room in 1963. FLN ideology stigmatized trade union particularism, which it accused of cultivating privileges inherited from the colonial social legislation on behalf of a labor aristocracy in an impoverished country. The unions, moreover, appeared to be lukewarm in their nationalist zeal. The prevailing discourse was nationalist and populist and it exalted the myth of the peasant revolution. The peasants, however, had supplied only the manpower for the revolution, not its policies.

The hegemony of the FLN left even less place for trade union independence when the PCA was forced to dissolve into it. The PCA had lost its credibility due to the gyrations of the PCF and to the weakness of the anticolonialist movement in France. The French branch of the FLN was also put aside when it appeared to be in danger of becoming a progressive opposition. Emigrant students and workers had adopted positions considerably more democratic and secular than those of Algiers. The shriveling of the French population of Algeria, its allegiance to the Organisation de l'Armée Secrète (OAS)—a terrorist settler group that hoped to forestall independence—at the end contributed to unleashing an intercommunal violence that submerged any other identification in terms of class or ethnicity. The exodus of the *pied noirs* opened up the perspective of a spoils system on a far larger scale than had occurred in Tunisia. Its balance sheet is as yet not fully known, but its corrosive effects have long been evident. The Algerian working class was relatively weak. There were some 300,000 workers and employees in the industrial and service sectors along with 50,000 state officials and 150,000 officially unemployed workers, which made about a quarter of a million people in an economically active population of 2.5 million. The underclass overwhelmed the working class. Not until 1975 would strikes reappear in an independent Algeria. The taboo of national union and the weight of unemployment and underemployment bore heavily on the creation of any movement for social demands and trade union independence.

Morocco presents a different case. The existence of multiple parties allowed the UMT to escape the exclusive domination of one, and the Istiqlal

(Independence) Party could not control the trade unionists, as had the fol-lowers of Messali Hadj, the FLN, and the Neo-Destour. By 1958 the secre-tary of the UMT had left the leadership of the Istiqlal, thereby affirming his independence. The UMT had its own bases of support in the new industrial zones created by colonialism, such as the mines of Kouribgha and the city of Casablanca. There, the bourgeoisie, which was centered in Fez, had no support. Above all, the monarchy was the key player in the political game. It was able to maintain control over the Moroccan depths, the old urban cen-ters and the countryside, which limited the grasp of the parties.[16] The sul-tan's legitimacy was heightened by the process of decolonization, in which he had held so critical a role as both negotiator with France and symbol of the nation. The independence of the North African countries in very differ-ent conditions was largely marked by the neutralization or tutelage of the trade union movement as well as of any wider protest movement.

The state of the entire people or the state of the masses, whether in Tunisia or still more in Algeria, posed as the guarantor of development, social progress, and national identity. There was therefore very little room left for an autonomous civil society. No clear alternative was visible, how-ever. The only opponents to populism were self-proclaimed Marxist or third-worldist movements that represented intellectuals, had little real in-fluence, and impersonated Asian and Latin American revolutionary movements. The primary characteristic of the two decades that followed independence lay in the adherence of the labor movements to state poli-cies. This subordination had objective causes in the structure of the work-force and of society in general. The weakness of the bourgeoisie and the absence of any group of entrepreneurs made the state the managing part-ner in an international division of labor and responsible for changes in so-cial structure. In much of the Third World, and especially in the Arab world, the state does not express the interests of a class as much as it is it-self the very condition under which classes exist. Classes cannot organize themselves on a purely economic basis.

This can be seen most clearly in Algeria, where gas and oil rents provide a fiscal surplus that can be redistributed by providing jobs in the public sector and the bureaucracy as well as by controlling prices. The strategy of investment here since independence has been more toward protecting a social base for the regime than toward economic development per se. What is called socialism—under Ben Bella and Boumedienne or in the Tunisia of Ben Salah—is a state-centered system of social control. The government itself is bound to respect a duty to protect society and engage in its tutelage. This can be seen variously as a trait of Muslim political culture, a strategy of clientelism, or a constraint of underdevelopment. Most analyses of the incomes of the lower classes do not have any difficulty showing that a market economy could not integrate the bulk of society into the economy. The level at which the worker and urban inhabitants live depends on price controls of primary goods, a policy whose costs are usually borne by the peasantry. Those groups with the greatest potential political capital receive a kind of structural rent.

A look at the bottom line of independent Algeria in 1977 is sobering. The number of workers drawing wages was 1.7 million, about 72 percent of the economically active population. This appears to mark a considerable advance on the earlier period in terms of social transformation, but it is far less encouraging at the level of productive labor. The industrial workforce was only 400,000, but Algeria had some 550,000 people officially looking for work. Underemployment explains the constant pressure of emigration between 1962 and the closure of the European frontier in 1974. By that time there were 727,000 North Africans working in Europe, of whom 425,000 were Algerians. There were, thus, more Algerians working in Europe than employed in industry at home, and these immigrants composed 20 percent of the total number of wage workers. This situation was the result of a complex history. Since the beginning of the century, Algerian workers had crossed the Mediterranean. During World War I, hundreds of thousands of colonial subjects were forced to serve in uniform or in factories on the French mainland. Thus a movement of migration began and continued to grow: There were 100,000 North Africans in France between the two world wars, half a million in the 1960s, and 2.5 million in 1994, according to the French Census.

The importance of this migration transcends statistics, for it has deeply affected politics, as the previous account of the North African Star shows. The Star was formed in France by Messali and the French Communist Party; it was France that formed a second pole for the Algerian working class whether in populist, communist, or postindependence oppositional politics. It is not possible to study North African working-class history and leave aside this fraction of the workforce. Nevertheless, the emigrant society has not found a role in North African politics but has been attracted to integration in European society. For the generations of North Africans born north of the Mediterranean, returning to the Maghreb appears highly improbable.

Several factors converge and help to explain the relative social peace of North Africa for the first two decades of independence. After independence, strikes disappeared almost totally from North Africa except for Morocco.

The decline of protest movements was accompanied, as in the larger society, by a bureaucratization of institutions. Institutions were engaged in the dirigiste and technocratic economic policy of a state bourgeoisie that controlled how the social surplus was taken and distributed. By 1969 in Tunisia and after the death of Boumedienne (in 1978) in Algeria the system entered a period of profound double crisis. On the one hand the slowdown in the world economy decreased the income drawn from exports and limited the foreign capital available for investment. On the other, the state-run economy proved increasingly incapable of integrating the unemployed masses into the economy. The transformations of economic policies (including liberalization and openings to the West undertaken first by Tunisia and then by Algeria) created a new set of conditions.

Each North African country has its own rhythm and its peculiar features, but it is also possible to distinguish common features. The world of work has deeply changed quantitatively and qualitatively. The new generation of workers has schooling, and their culture is no longer that of the Maghreb of their fathers or that of the fathers of the Maghreb. The nationalist ideologies are used up, and the prestige of the historic parties and political leaders has evaporated. The death in December 1978 of Boumedienne, whose funeral was the object of an immense spontaneous demonstration of mourning and anxiety, and the ouster of Habib Bourguiba in 1986 represent two critical turning points.

Social contradictions have conferred on labor a new status. The stakes have been heightened with the rise of a business class, the privatization of the economy, and the bet on subcontracting, which is not likely to keep its promises regarding employment opportunities. The appeal for foreign investments presupposes an incomes policy that will work only if consumer prices can be kept low. Controlling the prices of basic consumer goods in a situation of declining relative food production requires an enormous fiscal effort. The terms of trade, the absence of international credits, and the pressure of the International Monetary Fund make such control nearly impossible. Especially in acceding to IMF pressure to reduce external debts, the governments risk inflaming the lower class and creating one of those "uprisings of pain" that are landmarks in the Arab world from Morocco to Egypt.

Beginning in 1975 the curve of strikes began to move upward again in many sectors, including the public service, an infallible sign of the degradation of the image of the state. Most remarkable, textile and clothing workers participated as well. The streets of Tunis saw long lines of demonstrators and the UGTT leadership co-opted at least one militant. Under the guidance of Habib Achour, a veteran of the Ferhat Hached period, the

UGTT affirmed its independence. In January 1978 the attempt by the government to regain control of the UGTT was the origin of the first major social confrontation since 1954. The trade union protest was overtaken by an eruption of anger from the subproletarian masses. Three years later, in 1981, a new outbreak of violence greeted a brutal increase in the level of administered prices and marked a definitive break between the Supreme Warrior (Bourguiba) and his people. It was a set of events similar to what would occur in Algeria in 1988. It cannot be emphasized enough, however, that the violence in Algeria did not arise from a vacuum. It was preceded by a wave of strikes, and in the 1990s trade unionism is again an actor that seeks to confirm its independence.

Conclusion: The Power and Contradictions of Trade Unionism

A false debate burdening labor studies lies in the insistence on a research agenda based on the polarity, especially in Algeria, between Marxism and nationalism. Research has suffered from this highly ideological way of approaching such studies. Researchers on the labor movement usually have in mind a European model implying that labor issues are central to society. They are seen primarily through the scheme of class struggle based on a principal contradiction between labor and capital.[17]

It is true that the numerical growth of the wage-labor force is real. It is equally true that this group remains a minority dispersed into unconnected sectors and broken up into highly localized or highly protected islands such as construction and public works, petroleum production, and the Algerian steel industry. Economic liberalization and the opening to foreign capital have evoked a limited development in only a few sectors; these are in financially precarious positions and thus are highly unstable in terms of employment. A profound status difference exists between that portion of the workforce incorporated into the state apparatus and the public enterprises and workers in the private sector. The primary reality for the majority remains unemployment. The weight of this reality is going to continue to increase. Most studies predict that it will be impossible to place the majority of those becoming old enough to work into the labor force until after the turn of the twenty-first century. Emigration, the myth of a European Eldorado, has overtaken the myth of national development not only for the underclass but for white-collar employees and service workers as well. This myth has, at the same time, created economic dependence on the European economy and a cultural dependence on the Western model of consumption. As early as the 1960s it was possible to observe the rapid increase in North African consumer demand, which was then based on the model of the poor white. This demand has continued to grow apace.

It is difficult to speak of the working-class consciousness on the model of that created in industrial Europe, which has been nourished by two centuries of conflicts and utopian mobilizations. "Producers, we must rescue ourselves," wrote Eugène Pottier in 1871 in the workers' anthem "The Internationale." The mythology of the worker has lost its meaning in developed societies without ever taking hold in the Maghreb. It is therefore a populist rhetoric rather than a labor one that dominates North African political discourse. The revived UGTT has named its newspaper, which was the most widely read in Tunisia after 1978, *Al-Sha'b* (The People). The language of this paper is essentially that of the dominant discourse when it describes the local elites as speculative rather than exploitational. It also calls on the elites to replace their bad nationalism with a new national union for the good of the people. Insofar as such an appeal directly addresses the question of the role of the state and political conflict, it has the capacity to overturn a highly bureaucratized single-party system.

Conflicts over the organization of trade unions and their role in society has been all the greater in North Africa because this is the only debate that refers to a known historical set of institutions and policies whether bread-and-butter, Social Democrat, or communist unionism. It is also the only public discussion that has occurred in structured organizations with real social support. The importance of the organized trade union movement has also clearly been shown in North Africa and elsewhere to have at least two significant limitations. The first limitation occurs in the context that it is possible for the highest levels of union leaders to make economic or political choices that affect society as a whole. Attempts to create an alliance with the state bureaucracy and exchange wages or employment levels for social peace lead to perennial conflicts and to technocratic and authoritarian isolation. Such attempts make the wage-labor force a privileged sector whose privileges are paid in the coin of political dependence. Economic liberalization has exposed the fragility of this form of rent-seeking behavior. The second limitation becomes apparent at the lower levels of the trade union movement, where workers press for higher wages. It is true that such pressure does not create problems for society as a whole but reveals them. These demands provide a focus for a range of other popular discontents the political impact of which may be antagonistic to the organized labor movements themselves.

The governments know how to play on the contradictions among their opponents with consummate art, and they push the strike movements in the direction of uprisings. The trade union leaderships seek to avoid them and to contain the possibilities of the eruption of the underclass. Nowhere is this more true than in Morocco. They thus seek to join the "civilized" section of society, which is well paced in the dominant system of modernity linked to the West, and remain its captive. Because the North African population is now primarily urban, the cities have become the principal sites in which social conflicts are fought out. The cities in the 1990s are locations of conflict that is cultural as much as, if not more than, simply material.

It is difficult to understand the progress since 1990 of Islamist movements in the huge new cities and their capacity for popular mobilization without understanding that their programs are not based so much on a coherent social and economic program as on the myth of the Prophet's urban society based in Medina. Confronted with such a myth, the nationalist and laborite ideologues have shown their inability to create a vision through which these societies can provide meaning in daily life. The destruction of these alternative points of departure may mean that the North Africa of the mid-1990s is about to undergo a wholesale remaking, a remaking that will take the form of an Islamizing totalitarianism.

Such a possibility may be disturbing. It must also be recognized that the appeal to the larger community, the *umma,* has had a far greater social resonance since the mid-1980s than appeals based on nation or class. This appeal has been able to bridge the gap between the issues of society and identity. The future of the labor movement will depend on the outcome of the duel between forces that seek to follow the project of modernity and those committed to that of the City of Islam. The labor movement itself has so far been unable to create an independent pole of attraction. It has not been able to split the left from the FLN in Algeria or to create a labor party in Tunisia or to make the Union Nationale des Forces Populaires in Morocco a political expression of the trade unions.

Thus far, then, the progressive currents, which are based on a portion of the intellectuals, the middle classes, and the wage laborers, have been unable to develop a political alternative to Islamism. Nothing requires that they be able to do so. But one thing is sure: The elaboration of a democratic political culture cannot be carried out without addressing issues of social conflict.

Notes

1. Works to consult include Albert Ayache, *Le mouvement syndical au Maroc, 1919–1949,* vol. 1 (Paris: l'Harmattan, 1982); Nora Benallegue, "Histoire du syndicalisme algerien à l'époque," (Ph.D. dissertation, University of Paris); Jacques Droz, *Histoire générale du socialisme* (Paris: Presses Universitaires de France, 1972), 3 vols.; René Gallisot, *Mouvement ouvrier, communisme et nationalisme dans le monde arabe* (Paris: Éditions Ouvriers, 1978); Mustapha Kraiem, *Nationalisme et syndicalisme en Tunisie 1918–1928* (Tunis: Imprimerie de l'U.G.T.T., 1976); Claude Liauzu, *Militants, grévistes et syndicats: Etude du mouvement ouvrier maghrébin* (Nice: Centre de la Méditerranée Moderne et Contemporaine, 1979); Abdelatif Memouni, *Le syndicalisme ouvrier au Maroc* (Casablanca: Éditions Maghrébines, no date); Houari Touati, *Dictionnaire biographique du mouvement ouvrier de l'Oranie: Les militants syndicaux* (Oran, Algeria: Centre de Documentation des Sciences Humaines, 1981).

2. IREMAM, *Le monde arabe et musulman au miroir de l'université française* (Paris: Centre National de la Recherche Scientifique [CNRS], 1990).

3. Amar Ouzegane, first secretary of the Algerian Communist Party, was expelled in 1948 because his attachment to Algerian nationalism was considered excessive. He later wrote a book titled *The Best Conflict,* which sharply critized the PCA for its attachment to the European community in Algeria and consequent lack of support for the nationalist movement (*Le Meilleur Combat* [Paris: Juillard, 1962]). Born in Haiti, Frantz Fanon came to Algeria in 1952 to establish a psychiatric practice. An early supporter of the NLF, his accounts of the Algerian revolutionary experience were influential in debates during the 1960s because he argued that urban labor movements in colonial countries were essentially conservative. Revolutionary action could be expected, as implied in the title of one of Fanon's most important works, only from the "wretched of the earth"—impoverished peasants (*The Wretched of the Earth* [New York: Grove Press, 1966]).

4. Maurice Thorez was the general secretary of the French Communist Party in the 1940s and 1950s.

5. Characteristic of this nationalist vision is the refusal by some historians to include French activists of the colonial period in a now discontinued biographical dictionary of the North African labor movement prepared by, among others, Houari Touati. (*Le dictionnaire biographique et le mouvement ouvrier maghrébin* [Oran, Algeria: University of Oran, 1983–]).

6. Claude Liauzu, *Enjeux urbains au Maghrebi crises, pouvoirs et mouvements sociaux* (Paris: l'Harmattan, 1985).

7. R. Plissard, "L'artisanat en Tunisie," *Revue Internationale du Travail* 34 (1936).

8. Claude Liauzu, *Naissance du salariat et du mouvement ouvrier en Tunisie* (Paris: CNRS, 1980).

9. Madeleine Rebèrioux, *Jean Jaurès: Textes choisis contre la guerre et la politique coloniale* (Paris: Éditions Sociales, 1959).

10. See, for example, M. Haupt and Madeleine Rebèrioux, *La deuxième internationale et l'Orient* (Paris: Éditions Cujas, 1967).

11. The nearest contemporary analogy to the Union Intercoloniale was the Tricontinental organization centered in Cuba in the late 1960s and early 1970s. L'Etoile Nord-Africaine, or the North African Star, was an organization of North African immigrants to France founded by Messali Hadj in 1926. In 1937 the North African Star became the Algerian People's Party and after World War II the Movement for the Triumph of Democratic Freedoms (known by the acronym MTLD in French).

12. Claude Liauzu, *Aux origines des tiers mondismes: Colonisés et anticolonialistes en France entre les deux guerres* (Paris: l'Harmattan, 1982).

13. Prior to the war socialists had believed their class interests outweighed any national affiliation. In Europe, however, the working classes and the socialists largely went over to prowar positions, of which the French instance is the Union Sacrée.

14. Philippe Fargues, *Atlas du monde arabe* (Paris: Bordas, 1992).

15. Muhammad Harbi is the best guide to an understanding of the struggle for power and the nature of the National Liberation Front. See Harbi, *Le FLN, mirage et realité* (Paris: Éditions Jeune Afrique, 1980).

16. On the Moroccan system and the place of the monarchy as well as the limits of trade union activity and of the left, the best study remains that of John Waterbury, *Commander of the Faithful* (New York: Columbia University Press, 1970). See also Rémy Leveau, *Le fellah marocain, défenseur du trône* (Paris: Presses de la Fondation Nationale des Sciences Politique [FNSP], 1985).

17. This approach weighs heavily on Algerian research and on the volume edited by Nur al-Din Sraieb, *Le mouvement ouvrier maghrébin* (Paris: CNRS, 1983).

About the Book and Editor

Once considered of little import, the social history of labor in the Middle East emerged in the 1980s as a major area of research, as historians sought to uncover the roots of working-class organizing. This volume, the first in an important new series, presents a broad overview of recent literature on the history of workers in the Middle East since 1800 in a bold effort to bring together new directions in research and to reexamine the relevance of established ones.

Contributors explore the history of labor by situating state-led industrialization within the context of older artisanal social communities. They examine how industrialization enhanced government control over the economy as a whole and analyze the public's reaction to centralized economic authority. They also explain the longevity of social coalitions supporting state industrial monopolies and examine their breakdown, along with the emergence of Islamist and other oppositional movements. Taken together the essays provide a historically grounded context for viewing the shifting relationship between states and the world economy as well as between particular states and classes and form a rich synthesis of current interdisciplinary literature on work and workers in the region.

Ellis Jay Goldberg is director of the Middle East Center and associate professor of political science at the University of Washington. His published work includes *Tinker, Tailor and Textile Worker: Class and Politics in Egypt 1930–1952* (1986) and articles on contemporary Egyptian politics and economics in *Comparative Studies in Society and History, Comparative Politics and the International Journal of Middle East Studies*. To ensure his continued well-being his children decorate as many items of his clothing as possible with the ancient Middle Eastern symbol of handprints known in Arabic as the hand of Fatima and in Hebrew as the homsa.

About the Contributors

Günseli Berik is assistant professor of economics and women's studies at the University of Utah. Her study *Women Carpet Weavers in Rural Turkey* was published in the series Women, Work and Development in 1987 by the International Labor Organization, where she has worked as a consultant. Among her most recent publications is "Industrialization Strategies and Gender Composition of Manufacturing Employment in Turkey" (with Nilufer Cagatay) in N. Folbre et al. (eds), *Issues in Contemporary Economics*, vol. 4 (1994).

Cihan Bilginsoy is assistant professor of economics at the University of Utah. Among his recent publications are "Inflation, Growth and Import Bottlenecks in the Turkish Manufacturing Industry" in the *Journal of Development Economics* 42, 1 (October 1993) and "Quesnay's Tableau Economique: Analytics and Policy Implications" in *Oxford Economic Papers* 46, 3 (July 1994).

Claude Liauzu is professor of history at the University of Paris, VII, where he also directs a research institute for the study of migration and Euro-mediterranean relations. His books include *Militants, grévistes et syndicats: Étude du mouvement ouvrier maghrébin* (1979) and *Aux origines des tiers-mondismes* (1982).

Elisabeth Longuenesse teaches at the University of Lyon II, where she directs the Institut de Recherches sur le Monde Arabe Contemporain (IRMAC). She has been a member of the Near East Committee of the Social Science Research Council and has published extensively on the Syrian economy, working class, and trade union movement. In 1994 she published "Travail et travailleurs dans le secteur public industriel en syrie, une étude de cas" as part of an issue of *Cahiers de Recherche* (no. 3) titled *Travail, Travailleurs et Espace Urbain en Syrie*.

Valentine Moghadam is senior researcher at the World Institute for Development Economics Research at the United Nations University in Helsinki. In addition to numerous articles on Iranian politics and society, she has recently published *Modernizing Women: Gender and Social Change in the Middle East (1993)* and *Gender and National Identity: Women and Politics in Muslim Society* (1994).

Donald Quataert is professor of history at Binghamton University. His extensive publications on Ottoman history include *Social Disintegration and Popular Resistance in the Ottoman Empire, 1882–1908* (1983) and *Ottoman Manufacturing in the Age of the Industrial Revolution* (1993).

Michael Shalev is professor of sociology at Hebrew University. He has written extensively on socialist and social democratic movements in Western Europe including (with Walter Korpi) "Strikes, Industrial Relations and Class Conflict in Capitalist Societies" in the *British Journal of Sociology* 30, 2 (1979), as well as *Labour and the Political Economy in Israel* (1992).

Index